The Evidence of the Senses

The Evidence of the Senses

A Realist Theory of Perception

David Kelley

Louisiana State University Press
Baton Rouge and London

Copyright © 1986 by Louisiana State University Press
Manufactured in the United States of America

Designer: Christopher Wilcox
Typeface: Palatino
Typesetter: Moran Colorgraphic

Library of Congress Cataloging in Publication Data

Kelley, David, 1949–
  The evidence of the senses.

  Includes index.
  1. Perception (Philosophy) 2. Senses and sensation.
3. Knowledge, Theory of.   I. Title.
B828.45.K45 1986   121'.3   85-16610
ISBN 0-8071-1268-2 (cloth)
ISBN 0-8071-1476-6 (paper)

Published with the assistance of a grant from the National Endowment for the Humanities.

Louisiana Paperback Edition, 1988

97 96   5 4 3

The paper in this book meets the guidelines for permanence and durability of the Committee on Production Guidelines for Book Longevity of the Council on Library Resources. ∞

Contents

Acknowledgments

The philosopher who had the greatest influence on my thinking about perception was the late Ayn Rand. She was of course best known for the ethical and political views she expressed in her novels and essays. But her writings also dealt with questions about knowledge, and she developed her views on a range of topics, including perception, in informal lectures and seminars. It is unfortunate that her work has not received more careful attention from other philosophers, for I believe it represents a profound, and profoundly important, alternative to traditional theories in epistemology—an alternative that will be illuminating even to those whom it does not persuade. This book, in any case, has been written in the spirit of her philosophy; my basic assumptions are hers. In applying those assumptions to the detailed problems of perception, however, I have dealt with many issues which (to my knowledge) she did not herself address. The conclusions I have reached about them cannot therefore be taken as a direct expression of her views.

I am also indebted to Leonard Peikoff for his comments on earlier drafts of the manuscript, and for the hours we have spent discussing perception, which helped shape my understanding of many issues (especially perceptual form) at the deepest level. Allan Gotthelf and Fred Miller provided me with detailed written comments

that have improved every chapter. For comments and ideas on individual chapters, I would also like to thank Harry Binswanger and
Aaron Ben Zeev. My friend Roger Donway has been a kind of god-
father to the book, a constant advisor, critic, and supporter from the
moment I conceived it.

I owe a great deal to my teacher and advisor at Princeton, Richard Rorty. My analysis of the idealist strain in contemporary philosophy was inspired by his seminar on the subject, though our
evaluations of idealism differ radically. Several chapters of the book
were presented as colloquiums at Vassar College, and I am indebted to my former colleagues there, especially to Jesse Kalin, Michael McCarthy, and Mitch Miller, for their helpful criticism. In the
Cognitive Science program at Vassar, Janet Krueger Andrews, Carol
Christensen, Ken Livingston, Audrey McKinney, and Marty Ringle
not only discussed parts of the manuscript with me but encouraged
and helped me to pursue my interests across disciplinary bound-
aries.

The two department secretaries I have worked with, Norma
Mausolf and Rosette Uniacke, cheerfully typed more drafts of the
manuscript than any of us cares to remember. Greg Silverman and
Linda Zucchino, my student assistants, were a great help with research and editing. Financial support from the Foundation for the
New Intellectual, during the spring of 1979, allowed me to work full
time on the first draft of Part I. Finally, I want to thank Barbara
O'Neil Phillips, my editor at the Press, for her meticulous work on
my text.

The Evidence of the Senses

Preface

During every waking moment, each of us is party to an amazing transaction. We live our lives bathed in streams of physical energy: sound waves, electromagnetic fields, mechanical forces of every kind. Much of this energy passes us by, leaving behind no discernible trace. But some of it, at every moment, sets off reactions in the cells we call sense receptors, and these in turn set off electrical impulses that reverberate through the physical structure we call the nervous system. Like radios, we are tuned to a portion of the energy that eddies around us. But we are tuned with a sensitivity, and reverberate with a complexity, far beyond anything our engineers have yet dreamed of building. We are high-fidelity receivers of astonishing range.

And there is something more amazing still. Unlike any electronic device, the nervous system gives rise to conscious experience of the world around it. The resonance of my brain to the flow of energy makes it happen that there is a world *for me*, a world I see, hear, touch, taste, and smell; a world I live and move in, following a trajectory no physicist could hope to compute; a world that invites me to understand and to change it, raising a thousand questions, grounding a thousand projects; a world I can know about, and care about. We call this process perception, and it is the crossroads of our commerce with the world.

How does perception work? No one knows the whole story yet. Neurophysiologists understand fairly well how the receptors transform the energy impinging on them into nerve impulses, but have only recently begun to explore the neural circuits that are fed by those impulses. Psychologists have isolated many of the dimensions of sensory experience and have connected some of them, in tentative ways, to neural processes; but they are still struggling to find the proper categories, and the proper methods, for dealing with the full complexity of the phenomena. Philosophers, for their part, have been concerned less with the question of how it happens than with the question of what it is, exactly, that does happen. Philosophers of mind want to know whether the conscious experience is something distinct from the neural events. Epistemologists want to know whether we are aware of objects in the world around us as they really are; and they want to know how we extract knowledge from perceptual experience, and whether all of our knowledge can be derived in that way.

This book deals primarily with the epistemological questions, though I have touched here and there on issues from the philosophy of mind. I have also included a great deal of material from psychology and neuroscience, both to show how inquiry in these areas is often guided by implicit philosophical assumptions, and to show how my own views relate to the empirical findings. Part I is concerned with the nature and validity of perception itself; Part II, with the way we derive conceptual knowledge from perception. I have not presupposed any specific knowledge about the issues or their historical background, and I hope that my argument will therefore be accessible to the general reader. But I do have an argument to make, and it is a new one. I have therefore included detailed discussions of other views of perception so that specialists in the field may see how my position differs from the current as well as the classical alternatives.

The position I defend is a type of realism. I argue that in perception we are directly aware of physical objects and their properties, and that perceptual judgments about those objects and properties can be based directly on perception, without the need for any inference. Realism per se, of course, is not a novel theory. Indeed, for the past few decades it has perhaps been the dominant view in the philosophy of perception, and I have gratefully made use of the work of other realists wherever I could.

As a realist, of course, I reject the classical representationalist view that we directly perceive not physical objects themselves but certain mental entities (images, ideas, sense-data) which represent them. This is the point on which I expect I will have many allies. But I go further than most other realists in rejecting the basic premises of representationalism, particularly in my analysis of illusions, perceptual relativity, and hallucinations (Chapters 3 and 4). Many philosophers, moreover, especially those with an interest in cognitive science, hold that because of the complex neural processes that lie behind even the simplest percept, perception is the product of inference, problem solving, or computation, and is thus indirect. I argue, by contrast, that the integrative processes which produce a percept are automatic and fully compatible with the directness of perceptual awareness (Chapter 2). Finally, perception involves the discrimination of objects from their backgrounds, and the consequent awareness of them as wholes, as entities. Although many philosophers believe that discrimination necessarily involves the use of concepts or categories, I hold that perceptual discrimination is preconceptual (Chapter 5).

The burden of Part I, in other words, is that perception is a preconceptual mode of direct awareness of physical objects. My argument in Part II is that perception supplies adequate evidence or justification for our beliefs about such objects, but that the evidence is nonpropositional. That is, I reject the common assumption that a belief can be justified only by another belief, judgment, or other propositional state; and the principles of justification I present are quite different from those usually discussed in the literature.

In Chapters 1 and 6, I present a highly abstract case for realism. This argument is designed to establish a general thesis—what I call the primacy of existence, or epistemological realism—independently of the specific considerations I offer in support of *perceptual* realism in particular. I expect that the abstract character of the thesis and of my argument for it may seem foreign to many philosophers, especially those in the analytic school. Analytic philosophers are suspicious of global claims and prefer to examine the detailed considerations that weigh for and against positions on specific issues.

If analytic philosophy had a banner, it might carry the device Always Distinguish.

I certainly believe one should attend to all relevant distinctions. But not all distinctions are relevant. There is no privileged level of abstraction at which philosophical discussion must always proceed. Every statement and every argument is abstract to some degree, which means it abstracts from distinctions one could draw, and disregards many features of the instances to which the statement or argument applies. The goal in any particular case must be to find the *right* level of abstraction. And I have found, in analyzing the specific issues surrounding perception, that the arguments philosophers have offered rest on assumptions of a global character; often, indeed, the assumptions lie buried in the very statement of the issue. That should not be surprising. The precision and attention to detail permitted by a narrow focus on a question are purchased at the cost of taking a wider context for granted—a set of background assumptions, a prior conceptualization of the phenomenon, a commitment to a certain methodology, and so forth.

My disagreements with other philosophers of perception do not turn solely on local considerations; they are partly the product of different contexts. I have therefore undertaken to make my own basic assumptions as fully explicit as I can, and to show where I think other theorists are relying on different basic assumptions. The point of Chapters 1 and 6, then, is to lay out those assumptions and to present my reasons for preferring mine. To those who find this procedure too abstract, I can only offer a final, friendly challenge: if you find yourself in agreement with my conclusions about perception and perceptual knowledge, show me how to get there without the argument of those chapters; if you disagree with my conclusions, give me an argument against them that does not in any way rely on the assumptions I criticize in those chapters.

Part I

Perception

1

The Primacy of Existence

Since the Renaissance, there have been three basic positions about the nature of sense perception and its objects. The first, and closest to common sense, is realism. It holds that we directly perceive physical objects existing independently of the mind, that the senses are an open window on a world that is what it seems. Representationalism denies that we can perceive this world directly: the senses, it says, are like television cameras, bringing news of the outer world but subject to all the distortions that medium is prey to. Even further from realism is the phenomenalist or idealist view, which dispenses with the external world altogether. For the idealist, the television screen is all: only the mind and its images exist. "The world that seems to lie before us like a land of dreams" is just that—a dream.

This book is an exposition and defense of realism. In Part I, I will examine perception itself and argue that it is the direct awareness of objects in the physical world, objects which exist and are what they are independently of our awareness of them; in Part II, I will use these results in exploring how we identify perceived objects conceptually and how we justify our beliefs about them. But it would be impossible to enter upon all this without further preamble, as if these were isolated issues. Every theory of perception rests on gen-

eral assumptions about the nature of knowledge and the mind's relation to reality, as well as on observations about perception itself.

As a form of awareness, perception may naturally be approached from various different perspectives. From the outside it is
a physical response to the environment, and one may examine the
way sense organs are stimulated by physical energy, and the way
this stimulation is transmitted and transformed by the nervous system as it ascends the sensory pathways to the brain. Or one may
view it from the inside, as we experience it, describing the features
of objects we can discriminate, the structures and relationships of
which we are directly aware. Along another axis, perception takes
its place in a cognitive hierarchy. It is a more structured and integrated form of awareness than sensation is, but perception is itself
the basis for further integration at the conceptual level. This latter
relationship raises epistemological questions about the way perception can provide evidence for our beliefs, inferences, scientific theories—and with what certainty. Without some general view of
awareness itself, of what cognition is, there is no way to integrate
these perspectives. One cannot decide what relevance the physiological facts have for perception as the awareness of objects, or how
the latter relates to the logical structures of conceptual thought. And
the issues always are decided in this way. The theories of perception of John Locke and Immanuel Kant, of A. J. Ayer and Wilfrid
Sellars, derive as much from general assumptions about the nature
of cognition as from any facts about perception in particular. Nothing less is involved than the relation between consciousness and the
world we are conscious of.

The fundamental question in this respect is whether consciousness is metaphysically active or passive by nature. Is consciousness
creative, constituting its own objects, so that the world known depends on ourselves as knowers; or is it a faculty of response to objects, one whose function is to identify things as they are independently of it? In Ayn Rand's terms, it is a question of the primacy of
consciousness versus the primacy of existence: do the objects of
awareness depend on the subject for their existence or identity, or
do the contents of consciousness depend on external objects?[1] The

1. Ayn Rand, "The Metaphysical Versus the Man-Made," in *Philosophy: Who
Needs It* (New York, 1982), 29.

classical answers to this question define three basic views of knowledge, and the three theories of perception mentioned above are simply their applications to a particular case. Thus epistemological realism affirms the primacy of existence; and epistemological idealism, the primacy of consciousness. A general version of representationalism falls somewhere in between, holding that consciousness creates its own immediate, internal objects, but that these *represent* objects independent of consciousness. A resolution of this issue is indispensable for a theory of perception; my defense of perceptual realism would be incomplete without an account of why I accept the primacy of existence.

Despite the logical priority of this general question, however, it has not always been in the forefront historically. At various times in the history of philosophy, the question has been addressed directly, and positions adopted on general grounds. The invention of the "critical" philosophy by Kant is an example, as is the struggle against idealism by G. E. Moore and Bertrand Russell; in a different form, the question has been raised once again by contemporary philosophers, as we shall see in Chapter 6. More often, however, the different theories are adopted implicitly, in the form of assumptions which determine what questions will be asked about cognitive phenomena, what answers are acceptable, what inferences taken as valid. For example, when Locke uses the physiological facts about perception to infer that we do not perceive external objects directly, the inference is mediated by a representationalist model of awareness and its immediate objects. Or again, some contemporary epistemologists would argue that the questions I address in Part I are largely illegitimate on the grounds that sense perception is not cognitive; their assumption is that all cognition is conceptual, a premise whose origin is the idealist tradition. It is important, therefore, to identify such assumptions as clearly as possible—both my own and those of opposing theories—and that effort will require a kind of philosophical detection, looking behind the theories to the premises that shape them.

The complexity of this task is increased by its historical background. Since René Descartes, realism has run a poor third in terms of popularity among philosophers of perception; and the reason is that most have accepted the primacy of consciousness in some form. It was adopted only in part by Descartes himself, as we shall see.

But the part he did accept led inexorably to its wholesale affirmation by Kant and his idealist successors, and it has rarely been questioned, in a fundamental way, in the two centuries since. The forms this premise now takes, however, are complex, derivative, embedded in the context of specific issues—and employed by philosophers who would reject Cartesianism or Kantianism in their original, systematic forms. As a result, the issues of perception and perceptual knowledge have evolved inside a complicated framework—a framework whose foundation is invisible, but one within which it is impossible to defend perceptual realism. I will identify many aspects of this framework in later chapters, in connection with specific issues; but in order to make clear why I reject it, I must first make visible its foundation. And that means going back to its sources in Descartes and Kant.

Descartes' Representationalism

Although Kant's theory of knowledge is of more direct interest, since he first formulated the idealist principle that the objects of awareness must conform to the subject's mode of cognition, Descartes is the indispensable first step toward that conclusion. Descartes originated, as a fundamental model of consciousness, the view I will call representationalism: consciousness and reality are two separate and autonomous realms, neither dependent on the other, and although the mind is capable of grasping objects outside it, such knowledge is always mediated by a direct awareness of internal objects—ideas—that are its own product.

Descartes was not without predecessors in this. Indeed, he may be seen as a modern exponent of Augustinianism, not only in taking the fact of his own consciousness as the fundamental certainty, but more generally in making the mind a substance radically distinct from the physical world, aware of the latter only through the medium of ideas. Moreover, representationalist theories of perception were common among thinkers of the period. The new physical science seemed to exclude from its conception of physical reality many of the features of perceptual experience, in particular the so-called secondary qualities of color, taste, etc.[2] These qualities were

2. On Descartes' relation to Augustine, see Norman Kemp Smith, *Studies in the Cartesian Philosophy* (London, 1902), Chap. 1; and John Herman Randall, *The Career*

therefore assigned to consciousness, where they were taken as constituting a veil of perception between reality and the perceiving mind. Nevertheless, Descartes is the father of modern representationalism, for he integrated these various premises and trends into a unified, systematic theory of mind and matter.

The mind, for Descartes, is a substance or entity; conscious states such as sensation, thought, and feeling are qualities possessed by this substance; and the mind, with its qualities, is both distinct from and independent of any physical substance whatever. Why distinct and independent? Because the essential attribute of mind is distinct from and independent of the essential attribute of matter. Mind is essentially conscious, matter essentially extended, and consciousness is utterly distinct from extension: either one can be "clearly and distinctly conceived" without reference to the other. Since the various conscious states are modes or determinations of the attribute consciousness, as cubes and spheres are determinations of the attribute extension, no conscious state is inherently or essentially dependent on anything physical. The mind, and everything it has or contains, could exist without any material substance whatever.[3]

This view is normally treated as a statement on the mind-body relation, and dealt with exclusively from the standpoint of metaphysics. But it has epistemological implications as well. To hold that consciousness is an intrinsic attribute of a substance is to deny that consciousness is essentially relational, and thus to deny that it is essentially an awareness *of* an object outside consciousness. Just as a physical entity's extension is an intrinsic, nonrelational feature of the entity itself, so consciousness for Descartes is an intrinsic feature of the mind, the qualitative identity of its states, defining a kind of mental stuff. Thus Descartes implicitly rejects from the outset the realist principle of the primacy of existence. He cannot regard ex-

---

of Philosophy (New York, 1962), Book III, Chap. 2. Locke introduced the terms *primary* and *secondary* to describe this distinction among qualities, but the distinction itself was drawn by the Greeks.

3. This argument is presented by Descartes in *Meditation VI*, and *Principles of Philosophy*, Part I, pars. LI–LX, in G. R. T. Ross and E. S. Haldane (eds.), *The Philosophical Works of Descartes* (2 vols.; Cambridge, England, 1973), I, 190, 239–41. On conscious states as modes of a substance, see also Descartes to Father Mesland, May 2, 1644, in *Philosophical Letters*, trans. and ed. Anthony Kenny (Oxford, 1970), 148.

ternal reality as the indispensable source of the mind's contents, since that would compromise its metaphysical autonomy; its contents are states of consciousness, dependent solely on the mind.[4]

Although Descartes presents this view of mind in the second *Meditation*, after and ostensibly as a consequence of his axiom that he exists and is conscious, the view is already presupposed by the way he validates the axiom. Having used various skeptical arguments to reject all other knowledge as doubtful, Descartes seizes on the fact that he is conscious as the one certainty, indeed as an inescapable certainty, an axiom. He cannot doubt that he is conscious, because the doubt itself would be an act of consciousness. Given the context, the argument of the *cogito* presupposes that consciousness can become the object of awareness, and be identified as consciousness, prior to any awareness of the existence of other things. For this to be true, consciousness would have to *be* something independent of other things: if consciousness were essentially the awareness of objects external to it, one's knowledge that he is conscious could not precede his knowledge of those objects. In affirming the prior certainty of consciousness, as Descartes does in the *cogito*, he is already committed to a view that consciousness does not depend on reality for its contents.[5]

Nevertheless, it is impossible for Descartes to treat consciousness as completely nonrelational; he does not deny that to be conscious is to be conscious *of* something. I will argue later that this is inconsistent, but for the moment the important point is that it forces him to adopt a particular theory about ideas.

"But what then am I?" asks Descartes. "A thing which thinks. What is a thing which thinks? It is a thing which doubts, understands, conceives, affirms, denies, wills, refuses, which also imagines and feels."[6] These various actions are modes of consciousness, species of the general attribute. To individuate the members of each species, however, we must refer to their objects. Conceiving differs from willing because it is a different sort of action; but one concep-

4. *Cf.* Descartes' reply to Gassendi, in Ross and Haldane (eds.), *Philosophical Works*, II, 128.

5. The phrase "prior certainty of consciousness" is from Wilhelm Windelband, *History of Philosophy*, trans. James H. Tufts (New York, 1958), sec. 34.

6. Descartes, *Meditation II*, in Ross and Haldane (eds.), *Philosophical Works*, I, 153.

tion differs from another because it is a conception *of* something different, a conception of the sun, for example, instead of the moon. What, then, is the status of these objects?

The object seems different from the consciousness of it. The identity of ordinary objects of awareness, after all, consists in features such as size, color, and composition that are not characteristics of consciousness. If a determinate mode of consciousness must essentially be identified by reference to such features of its objects, however, then consciousness will not be independent of the world outside it. And Descartes wishes to avoid this. He wants to regard the particular, individual conception as a mode of consciousness, an ultimate determination of the general attribute, as shocking pink is an ultimate determination of the attribute color; the particular conception must then be nonrelational in the same way the general attribute is. His solution lay in the Augustinian concept of an idea. Ideas, for Augustine, were archetypes in God's mind, objects of His awareness, yet contained somehow within His awareness of them, not independent existents. Descartes broadens the term, to apply to the contents of human minds as well, but retains the formal features of Augustine's concept. Ideas are at once the objects of consciousness and states of consciousness.

Ideas thus have a double nature. On the one hand, Descartes describes them as "certain modes of my thoughts," "operations of the intellect," "an act of my understanding."[7] In this sense, the idea is the whole mode of consciousness—for example, the conception of the sun. On the other hand, the idea is that component of the mode which serves as the object of awareness: "I take the term idea to stand for whatever the mind directly perceives." This statement suggests that there are really two elements within the mode of consciousness: the awareness or consciousness proper, and the internal object of which one is aware. Elsewhere, however, Descartes implicitly denies this, distinguishing instead between two aspects of ideas regarded as modes of consciousness. In the third *Meditation*, for example, he distinguishes between ideas "as certain modes of thought" and "as images, one representing one thing and the other another." In technical terms, ideas have a formal nature, as

7. Descartes, *Meditation III, ibid.*, I, 160; *Replies to Objections, IV, ibid.*, II, 105; *Meditations*, Preface, *ibid.*, I, 138.

modes of consciousness, as psychological states; and they have a representational nature—the state has a certain content. The representational nature is not a separate entity, much less an independent entity; it is an aspect of the mode of consciousness: the content is implicit in or an aspect of the awareness of it.[8] These two dimensions of ideas give rise to the two classical Cartesian images of mind. From a formal standpoint, mental phenomena are composed of a certain kind of stuff, they are mental as opposed to physical; from a representational standpoint, the mind is an inner theater, with various scenes appearing before an inner eye.

The theory can perhaps best be captured in terms of an analogy. A determinate mode of consciousness, for Descartes, is like a single frame of movie film being projected on the screen. The projector (the mind) casts a beam of light; light in general, like consciousness, is the essential attribute of the projector, and the different shades and patterns of light are its modes. The light illuminates an image on the screen, it has an object. But the image is not something distinct from the light by which it is seen. The projector is not a searchlight, illuminating objects independent of it. The image is conveyed by the light itself, the image is "in" the light—indeed it *is* the light, seen in cross section. If we wish to identify the particular mode of projection, we can do so formally, with reference to the light itself, noting the specific pattern of wavelengths issuing from the projector; or we can do so representationally, with reference to the image, noting its shapes and colors. In both cases we would be identifying the same thing, only from different perspectives.

Having accepted this theory of ideas, Descartes can regard as completely open the question "whether any of the objects of which I have ideas within me exist outside of me."[9] The representational content of an idea is a feature of the idea as a mode of consciousness. Without the theory of ideas, the question would not make

8. Descartes, *Replies to Objections, III, ibid.*, II, 67–68; *Meditation III, ibid.*, I, 161–62. In regard to sensory ideas, Descartes would differ from twentieth-century sense-data theorists, who held that the sense-datum was distinct from the awareness of it. See, for example, H. H. Price, *Perception* (1932; rpr. London, 1964), 44. For an excellent discussion of this issue in Descartes and his successors, see James Gibson, *Locke's Theory of Knowledge and Its Historical Relations* (Cambridge, England, 1960), 15–18.

9. Descartes, *Meditation III*, in Ross and Haldane (eds.), *Philosophical Works*, I, 161.

sense, for there would be no way to account for the contents of consciousness except by reference to an external world. Thus the skeptical doubts expressed by the question are not presuppositionless.

Consider, for example, the first *Meditation*. Descartes begins by seeking any grounds for doubting the truth of his ideas—*i.e.*, for doubting that they stem from and correspond to reality. The first such grounds he finds—sensory illusions and dreams—are actual occurrences, and in these cases we know that reality is not what it seems. For that reason, however, these occurrences could not raise the general question whether reality exists beyond our ideas; to identify an experience as an illusion, one must have enough knowledge of the objective facts to know that he is misperceiving them. Descartes therefore rests his case for universal doubt on the hypothesis that an evil demon may be deceiving him about everything. But what sort of ground for doubt is this? Illusions and dreams actually occur, but demons do not—the hypothesis is pure invention. As such, it would be completely subjective and could not provide an objective reason for doubting anything. Then why does Descartes suggest the hypothesis? It can only be as a way of concretizing a possibility he has already accepted: that everything we are aware of exists merely as the representational content of our ideas, ideas that do not, because they are modes of consciousness, depend on anything outside consciousness and could therefore be put into our minds by an evil demon even if there *were* nothing outside consciousness. In accepting this possibility, Descartes is clearly presupposing the theory of ideas presented later in the *Meditations*.[10]

In what sense, then, does Descartes introduce the primacy of consciousness into modern philosophy? If realism stands for the primacy of existence, and idealism for the primacy of consciousness, Descartes may be seen as advocating a kind of détente. Neither existence nor consciousness is primary for him; they are separate and autonomous realms, neither dependent on the other. In a deeper sense, however, his representationalism contains a mixture of elements. There is an element of realism insofar as he believes there *is* a reality independent of the mind and insofar as he makes

10. Descartes, *Meditation I, ibid.*, I, 145; *cf.* Bernard Williams, *Descartes* (Harmondsworth, England, 1978), 55–59.

this reality the ultimate object and standard of knowledge. Truth for Descartes consists in the correspondence between the ideas in the mind and the external objects they represent.[11] The immediate object of awareness, however, is contained within consciousness itself, in the representational content of our ideas; and this content does not essentially depend on the external objects to which it may or may not correspond. The ideas that contain it are modes of a self-sufficient substance, which is the immediate source of its own contents. The external world serves only as a possible but dispensable trigger for unleashing this creative side of consciousness.[12] In this respect, Descartes affirms the primacy of consciousness.

But the two opposing principles do not mix; representationalism is an unstable position. Since we are directly aware only of objects internal to our ideas, an external world must be *inferred* as an explanation for our ideas. But since consciousness is epistemologically autonomous, there is no basis for such an inference, no way of showing that any such explanation is required. Thus, in trying to show that his ideas—both innate and acquired—do correspond to an objective reality, Descartes can find nothing in the ideas themselves; he appeals to something wholly outside them. God's veracity provides an external link between ideas and their ultimate objects, as the pineal gland provides an external link between mind and body. Because it is external, however, the link cannot be demonstrated by starting within consciousness as he does—thus the instability of the view. There is no middle ground between the primacy of existence and the primacy of consciousness, only a dividing line of no width, a fence one cannot sit on long without falling to one side or the other. Since the idealist elements in Cartesianism were never challenged, they had to prevail.

Kant's Idealism

Across the Channel, the movement toward idealism began as a revolt in the opposite direction. In his attack on innate ideas, Locke

11. Strictly speaking, for Descartes, only a judgment that an idea corresponds to the object represented can be true or false; but "a certain material falsity" may nevertheless be ascribed to the ideas themselves. Descartes, *Meditation III*, in Ross and Haldane (eds.), *Philosophical Works*, I, 159–60, 164.

12. *Cf.* Descartes, *Notes Against a Programme, ibid.*, I, 442–43, where Descartes argues that because external objects, as material things, can contribute only motion to the senses, all the ideas and the qualities they contain derive from consciousness.

was opposing the kind of autonomy that Descartes ascribed to consciousness. Locke believed that the mind at birth was a tabula rasa, on which reality alone had the power to make inscriptions. Once the mind has acquired a stock of sensory ideas, he claimed, it can combine them in new ways; but it cannot stock itself with those basic ideas.[13] Thus all the materials for knowledge derive ultimately from the external world. This revolt was short-lived, however, for in his analysis of perception and knowledge, Locke reaffirmed Cartesian representationalism, using Descartes' model of consciousness to interpret experience.

As noted earlier, the representationalist theory of perception was a commonplace at the time. Galileo had argued that the secondary qualities—color, warmth, and the like—cannot be intrinsic to physical objects, because they are not quantifiable. They are not, he said, to be located in the external world at all. Secondary qualities are produced by our own sense faculties, responding to the primary qualities of external objects, and are therefore subjective. In arguing thus, Galileo was trying to clear the way for the new mathematical physics, in opposition to the qualitative physics of the scholastics. But his polemic gave fresh impetus to the traditional argument from perceptual relativity. The Greeks had noticed that sensory qualities vary from one perceiver to the next (as in the case of wine tasting sour to a sick man) and from one moment to the next for the same perceiver (as when a body of water feels colder after the hand has adapted to warmth). Many concluded that all sensory qualities are relative to the perceiver. The result of these influences was a common assumption among modern thinkers that our perceptual awareness of a colored, sounding, odorous world is an awareness not of reality but only of the effects of physical reality on our senses.[14]

But where *are* these qualities? What are they qualities *of*? Locke accepts the Galilean view about their subjectivity, but goes a step

13. John Locke, *Essay Concerning Human Understanding*, ed. Alexander Campbell Fraser (1894; rpr. New York, 1959), Book II, Chap. 2, secs. 2–3.
14. Galileo, *The Assayer*, in Stillman Drake (ed.), *Discoveries and Opinions of Galileo* (Garden City, N.Y., 1957), 274–75; see also E. A. Burtt, *The Metaphysical Foundations of Modern Science* (2nd ed.; Garden City, N.Y., 1954), 83–90. The argument from perceptual relativity is stated at length by Descartes' contemporary Pierre Gassendi, in *Exercises Against the Aristotelians*, in *The Selected Works of Pierre Gassendi*, trans. and ed. Craig B. Bush (New York, 1972), Book II, Exercise VI, art. 5.

beyond in providing a home for them. They are the representational contents of sensory ideas. Like Descartes, Locke regards ideas
as the immediate objects of awareness; indeed, he introduces the
term *idea* to "express . . . *whatever it is which the mind can be employed
about in thinking.*" Like Descartes, however, he also regards the idea
as the state of consciousness in which the representational content
is apprehended. Finally, Locke follows Descartes in holding that the
mind is a substance underlying its various operations.[15] Locke's empiricism, therefore, is from the beginning combined with the Cartesian view of consciousness, and it is subject to the same difficulty.

The assault on Locke's theory by George Berkeley and David
Hume is a familiar story, and only a few significant points need be
noted here. The criticism was directed against Locke's confidence
that ideas in the mind have external sources; and the criticism merely
brings to light the instability we noticed earlier in Descartes' theory.
Unlike Descartes, to be sure, Locke asserts that the mind's basic ideas
are not innate but acquired from reality; but in adopting Descartes'
model of ideas, he makes it impossible to support this position.

If the ideas we directly perceive are distinct from external objects, then any claim that the two correspond must explain what sort
of relation exists between them. In the history of representationalism, two basic relations surfaced in answer to this question. The first
was a relation of similarity between the content of the idea and the
qualitative identity of the external object; the second was a causal
relation between the external object and the occurrence of the idea
in consciousness. Given Descartes' distinction between the formal
and the representational nature of an idea, in other words, there
were two alternatives facing the representationalist. He could say
that ideas are related to external objects in virtue of their representational nature, the content of the idea being similar to the object.
Or he could say that the relation holds in virtue of the formal nature
of the idea: as a psychological occurrence, it must have a cause; there
must be something to explain why a given idea occurs at the moment it does.[16] But neither relation proved possible to sustain.

15. Locke, *Essay*, Introduction, sec. 8; *cf.* Gibson, *Locke's Theory of Knowledge*,
18–21; Locke, *Essay*, Book II, Chap. 23, sec. 5.
16. This same distinction reappears in contemporary philosophy and will be
discussed later. Causal theories of perception, knowledge, belief, and reference try
to link a given psychological or linguistic item with its object by means of causality;

The supposed similarity between ideas and objects is a recurrent theme in representationalism: the idea represents the object, as a portrait represents a person, by resembling it. But difficulties arise at once. It was precisely the supposed *lack* of similarity between the content of experience and the real nature of external objects which led to representationalism in the first place. Moreover, both Descartes and Locke expressly deny the similarity in regard to certain types of ideas. Descartes holds that perceptual ideas in general do not resemble their external causes, perception being a confused mode of cognition. Locke claims that although ideas of primary qualities resemble those qualities in external objects, ideas of secondary qualities do not.[17] These cavalier admissions naturally raised the skeptical question, If ideas do not resemble external objects in certain respects, how can we establish that they do resemble them in any respect? Would we not have to step outside our minds in order to compare ideas and objects?

It was Berkeley, however, who pointed out the fundamental problem. How, he asks, can an idea be similar to anything that is not an idea? The similarity is supposed to hold between the external object and the representational content of the idea. Yet this content is not an actually existing thing; it is the content of a state of consciousness, and the latter does not actually have any of the qualities of physical things, primary or secondary. My perceptual idea of a foot-long ruler may represent its length, but it is impossible to explain this representational capacity in terms of a real similarity in length between the ruler and the idea, or anything in the idea. It is nonsense to say that the idea is a foot long in any sense.[18]

That leaves the causal relation; and it is this which Locke sees as the basis of our knowledge of real objects: "For, the having the idea of anything in our mind, no more proves the existence of that thing, than the picture of a man evidences his being in the world,

---

"satisfaction" theories seek the link in the agreement between the object and the intentional (*i.e.*, representational) content of the item. *Cf.* Jaegwon Kim, "Perception and Reference Without Causality," *Journal of Philosophy*, LXXIV (1977), 606–20.

17. See in particular the example of the sun, Descartes, *Meditation III*, in Ross and Haldane (eds.), *Philosophical Works*, I, 161; Locke, *Essay*, Book II, Chap. 8, secs. 7ff.

18. George Berkeley, *A Treatise Concerning the Principles of Human Knowledge*, ed. Colin M. Turbayne (Indianapolis, 1957), secs. 8, 49.

or the visions of a dream make thereby a true history. It is therefore the *actual receiving* of ideas from without that gives us notice of the existence of other things."[19] Epistemologically, that is, the representational content of an idea proves nothing. Even if ideas do resemble external objects in respect of the primary qualities such as length, the bare fact that one is now aware of an idea representing such-and-such a length does not prove the existence, or presence to the senses, of an actual object with that length. The mark of external reality is to be found in the formal nature of the idea—the actual receiving of the idea, its production as a psychological occurrence by external causes.

This causal relation, however, could not withstand the arguments of Berkeley and Hume. Locke's only real criterion for determining whether an idea *is* actually received from without is the passivity of the experience. And Berkeley, like Descartes before him, pointed out that dreams and hallucinations, at the moment we experience them, are equally passive; hence passivity does not prove an external cause. Hume goes further. If we begin with an awareness only of sensory contents, he argues, the only concept of causality we can form is that of a regular succession among these contents. We cannot step back and apply the concept to ideas as occurrences in consciousness, or note patterns of regularity between the imperceptible objects outside and the ideas within consciousness. As we watch the movie screen we may note that whenever the hero's arm swings, the villain rebounds with an expression of pain. But nothing on the screen indicates the existence of the projector or the studio where the film was made. There is therefore no observable correlation between the images we see and either of these supposed causes.[20]

The result of this destructive criticism was the skepticism of Hume. We are reduced, in his view, to the awareness of sensory states of consciousness (though Hume abandoned the thesis that consciousness is an entity underlying its states), with no basis whatever for positing an external cause of those states. The realist element in representationalism has, except in one respect, been

19. Locke, *Essay*, Book IV, Chap. 11, secs. 1–2.
20. Descartes, *Meditation I*, in Ross and Haldane (eds.), *Philosophical Works*, I, 145–46; Berkeley, *Principles*, sec. 18; David Hume, *An Inquiry Concerning Human Understanding*, ed. Charles W. Hendel (Indianapolis, 1955), secs. 4–7, 12.

forced out by the idealist. The exception is that Hume retains the realist standard of truth and objectivity: the principle that ideas must correspond to external objects in order to be valid. This is why Hume is a *skeptic*. Metaphysically, consciousness does not depend on reality, either formally or in respect of its contents; there is consequently no way to show that reality exists or corresponds to our ideas. But such correspondence is taken as the epistemological standard. Hence we cannot show that our ideas measure up to the standard required of them, and so cannot claim any objective knowledge.[21] The obvious next step is to reject this last element of realism and bring the epistemological standards back into line with the metaphysical nature of consciousness. This was precisely the effect of Kant's work.

Kant begins by distinguishing appearance from reality. We are directly aware, he says, only of appearances—or phenomena, as he calls them. These exist only as the representational content of experience and are thus to be contrasted with noumena, or things as they are in themselves, things as they are apart from our experience. In this, Kant follows the representationalist tradition. But his view of the distinction differs from the tradition in two major ways. He regards the noumenal world as unknowable, not merely unprovable but unknowable in principle, by the very nature of consciousness; and he regards the noumenal world—reality—as irrelevant to our epistemological standards of truth and justification. In this respect, Kant is the father of idealism.

Although the representationalists thought the existence of an external world problematic, no one had any doubt about what such a world would be like. It would be as the scientists described it: a world of physical objects, with the properties of extension and bulk, moving and interacting in space. Our perceptual ideas represent extension, and thus the representational contents of ideas form a kind of spatial world within consciousness; but this sensory manifold parallels an actually extended world outside. In Kant's system, however, there is no basis for such speculation. Space and time, for him, are forms imposed on the manifold of sensations by the perceptual faculty itself; space and time are thus as subjective as colors were held to be. There are noumena outside consciousness, and they

21. *Cf.* Kemp Smith, *Studies*, 252.

serve as the trigger for the response of the perceptual faculty, but they do not determine the content of its response. The *only* spatial-temporal world is that which exists within consciousness; we have no idea whatever as to the nature of noumena.

What is the basis for this view? Kant offers various reasons in the *Critique of Pure Reason* and elsewhere for regarding space and time as forms of perception; they derive from the intricacies of an eighteenth-century debate about the nature of space and time. But the fundamental reason for his distinction between noumena and phenomena, and for his claim that the former are unknowable, lies in a premise about the nature of consciousness itself; his theories about space and time are merely the most dramatic applications of this premise. A faculty of awareness, Kant argues, has a specific constitution. It is something definite, it has an identity. And it must function in a specific way, determined by the identity it has. The nature of its response to objects outside it is determined by its own constitution. As a result, he argues, consciousness cannot passively mirror a world outside: its own identity gets in the way, distorting the reflection. The fact that consciousness has an identity prevents it from grasping the identities of things outside it.

From this premise, Kant draws the inevitable conclusion. Any object of which we can become aware, qua object of our awareness, has been shaped by our own faculties of cognition. We can know things only as they appear to us; it is impossible in principle to grasp them as they are in themselves. We can really know only our own manner of cognition:

> What we have meant to say is that all our intuition is nothing but the representation of appearance; that the things which we intuit are not in themselves what we intuit them as being, nor their relations so constituted in themselves as they appear to us, and that if the subject, or even only the subjective constitution of the senses in general, be removed, the whole constitution and all the relations of objects in space and time, nay space and time themselves, would vanish. As appearances, they cannot exist in themselves, but only in us. What objects may be in themselves, and apart from all this receptivity of our sensibility, remains completely unknown to us. *We know nothing but our mode of perceiving them.*[22]

22. Immanuel Kant, *Critique of Pure Reason*, trans. Norman Kemp Smith (1929; rpr. London, 1953), A42 = B59 (emphasis added). The doctrine of space and time is

Kant's premise about the identity of consciousness was implicit in earlier arguments and theories. Indeed, I will show later that it is part of the classical view of consciousness. Consider, for example, the argument from perceptual relativity. It is not difficult to show that the way things appear in perception is partly dependent on our own organs of perception, that sensory qualities are relative to the perceiver. But why should this be taken to imply that those qualities are subjective, or that we cannot really perceive the external object after all? The implicit assumption is that if consciousness has a nature of its own that affects its response to objects, then it can really know only its responses, not the objects. But Kant identifies the principle explicitly, where it had been merely implicit before; and he applies it generally, where before it had been applied selectively.

He applies it, for example, to conceptual as well as perceptual awareness. The Cartesian tradition admitted that sense perception does not reveal objects as they are, but it hoped to circumvent the problem by means of inferences from the nature of experience to the objects outside: the intellect would pierce the veil of perception. Hume had shown that this attempt always failed, but Kant argues that it *must* fail. As a faculty of cognition, the intellect too has a specific identity—it integrates the material of the senses, and it does so by means of a structure inherent in its own constitution. This structure consists fundamentally of a set of a priori concepts, or categories, such as substance and causality; the categories function automatically to organize the flux of individual sensations into a stable world of entities acting according to causal law. As with perception, however, the constitution of the faculty limits us to knowledge of our own creations. The world so organized is the world of appearances; there is no basis for saying that reality apart from us consists of entities, or exhibits causal relations.[23]

---

clearly but an application of this general principle and its implications, and the arguments about space and time are subsidiary to those about consciousness in general. These relationships are clearer in the *Inaugural Dissertation* of 1770. In section 4, Kant makes the general point that "all sensitive apprehension depends upon the special nature of the subject. . . . It is clear, therefore, that things sensitively apprehended are representations of things *as they appear.*" *Kant's Inaugural Dissertation and Early Writings on Space*, trans. John Handyside (Chicago, 1929). Only later (secs. 14ff.) does he discuss space and time as particular features arising from the nature of the subject.

23. Strictly speaking, the organization imposed by the categories creates a sec-

Finally, and most fundamentally at odds with the Cartesian tradition, Kant applies his principle to self-knowledge. Our awareness of consciousness itself, the subject of cognition, is filtered through a faculty of inner cognition that has its own identity and shapes its product. We can therefore know the self only as it appears to this faculty, not as it is in itself. In terms of Descartes' model of ideas, if we can be aware only of the representational content of consciousness, then consciousness itself can be known only as a representational content; the consciousness of which everything is a representational content cannot appear.[24]

Thus by its very nature, by the fact that it has a nature, consciousness is incapable of grasping anything as it is independently of consciousness. As an early follower put it:

> With [Kant] all is phenomenal which is relative, and all is relative which is an object to a conscious subject. The conceptions of the understanding as much depend on the constitution of our thinking faculties, as the perceptions of the senses do on the constitution of our intuitive faculties. Both *might be* different, were our mental constitution changed; both probably *are* different to beings differently constituted. The *real* thus becomes identical with the *absolute*, with the object as it is in itself, out of all relation to a subject; and, as all consciousness is a relation between subject and object, it follows that to attain a knowledge of the real we must go out of consciousness.[25]

Was Kant therefore a skeptic? Like Hume, he believes we cannot know reality; unlike Hume, he believes this does not matter. The epistemological standards of objectivity, truth, and knowledge, he argues, must be redefined in accordance with the metaphysical primacy of consciousness.

---

ond level of "phenomenality." What the categories organize are sensory ideas, which are already appearances. But these appearances, in themselves, are unrelated. Therefore the relations imposed by the categories are really second-order constructs, creating the appearance of order among appearances.

24. This is why Kant distinguishes himself from Berkeley in "Refutations of Idealism" (*Critique*, B274–79). Physical objects are phenomenal, but they do not exist "in the mind" in the only sense Kant allows for that term: they do not exist in the phenomenal mind. They are still, of course, dependent on the real subject of cognition, *i.e.*, the noumenal self; and Kant thus describes himself as a "transcendental idealist." *Cf.* A. C. Ewing, *A Short Commentary on Kant's "Critique of Pure Reason"* (Chicago, 1938), 176–87.

25. Henry Mansel, "On the Philosophy of Kant," in *Letters, Lectures and Reviews* (London, 1873), 171. See also Mansel's *Metaphysics* (Edinburgh, 1866), 299–300.

Kant sees that in the Cartesian model of ideas, which he accepts, the question of objectivity cannot arise in regard to the individual sense content. Consider a sensation of a circular red patch, taken in isolation from other sensations. What could it mean to ask whether it is veridical? What standard could we use to distinguish it from other sensations regarded as nonveridical? The standard cannot be a similarity between the circular patch of red, taken as the representational content of the sensation, and the external object. The fact that the sensation has been produced by our own faculties eliminates any possibility of resemblance. Nor can the standard be a causal relation between the sensation, taken as a psychological occurrence, and its external cause. Causality is a type of organizing principle used by the intellect to integrate sense contents; it could not possibly relate an individual sensation to something in the unknown reality outside.

What, then, could objectivity consist in? Traditionally, it meant a conformity between subject and object of cognition; it meant that consciousness grasps the object as it is. For Kant, however, we cannot be aware of the real object or the real subject of cognition: noumena, including the noumenal self, are unknowable. Our perceptual faculties give us only a welter of contents, existing in a single, undifferentiated manifold. The manifold in fact exists in the subject, as the content of consciousness, but there is nothing in the manifold itself to indicate this fact, nothing to indicate a contrast between what is in the subject and what in the object. We are not aware of the real object outside; nor are we aware of the subject that has these contents. We might of course notice that some of the contents, such as feelings and desires, do not have spatial properties, whereas others, such as colors and textures, do. This gives us Kant's distinction between inner and outer sense. But it is really just a distinction among various contents, based on their various qualities, one of many such distinctions we might draw. It does not indicate a difference in the status of the contents, nor therefore does it yield any distinction between subject and object of cognition. The contents merely exist.[26]

As soon as we introduce the organizing activity of the intellect,

26. Thus sensations in themselves are not really instances of awareness for Kant; they are noncognitive, nonintentional, not related to an object. They just are. "Intuitions without concepts are blind" (*Critique*, A51 = B75). We will encounter this same view later, in a linguistic version, among contemporary philosophers.

however, a distinction does appear, and Kant uses it to define objectivity and truth. When the intellect organizes the manifold of sensations, some of the relations it establishes will reflect its inherent features and will therefore be common to all human subjects, whereas others will be random or idiosyncratic, and not universal. Causality, for example, is a category inherent in the human intellect, and the latter will always function in such a way that the sensations it organizes obey the law of causality. Judgments made in accordance with this law will be universal—anyone experiencing the same sensation would connect it with the same later sensation—but judgments made in disregard of the law will remain idiosyncratic.

There is no real object to which representations may be related—at least, none that is available to us. But representations themselves can be regarded as objects when they have been integrated in accordance with the intellect's inherent nature, because judgments about those representations, when they are made in accordance with the intellect's principles of organization, will be universal: "For when a judgment agrees with an object, all judgments concerning the same object must likewise agree among themselves, and thus the objective validity of the judgment of experience signifies nothing else than its necessary universal validity."[27] Thus the problematic relation to reality has been dismissed as irrelevant, for the standards of objectivity derive from consciousness, not reality. The question of objectivity does not arise in regard to the individual perception; it pertains only to judgments of the intellect. A judgment is to be considered objective when it conforms, not to the real object outside consciousness, but to the internal nature of consciousness itself. The criterion of objectivity is universal agreement among subjects, or intersubjectivity. The locus of objectivity is patterns of coherence among representations, not between representations and what they represent. Consciousness not only creates its own contents but also evaluates them epistemologically by standards internal to itself.

Kant therefore represents the complete triumph of the primacy of consciousness. He has worked out the implications of Descartes' view in such a way that virtually every trace of realism has been

27. Immanuel Kant, *Prolegomena to Any Future Metaphysics*, ed. Lewis White Beck (New York, 1950), sec. 18. See also Kant, *Critique*, A197 = B243.

eliminated, fulfilling the idealist program announced in the preface to the *Critique*: "Hitherto it has been assumed that all our knowledge must conform to objects. . . . We must therefore make trial whether we may not have more success in the tasks of metaphysics, if we suppose that objects must conform to our knowledge."[28]

In this respect, Kant deserves the title of father of idealism. Much in his system was later abandoned, and there have been countless variations on his basic themes. The Idealists of the nineteenth century tried to eliminate the inconsistencies of the system by abandoning the realm of noumena altogether. More important, the forms of perception and the categories, which Kant had thought fixed by the immutable nature of the mind, were relativized and seen instead as products of historical circumstance, pragmatic convenience, linguistic practice. But these are all variations of Kant's essential principles: that the subject of knowledge has a nature through which it constitutes its own object, and that standards of objectivity must be defined by reference to this activity of the subject. From this standpoint, it little matters whether the subject is conceived of as changing or unchanging, individual or social; it little matters whether the forms by which the object is constituted, and objectivity defined, are held to be categories of a noumenal mind, or social practices, conceptual frameworks, rules of language games, and the like. They are so many different ways of asserting the primacy of consciousness. Thus, although I will examine these other, more recent versions of idealism in due course, my defense of the primacy of existence will take Kant as its major foil.

The Primacy of Existence

Realism and idealism, the primacy of existence and the primacy of consciousness, are theories about the relation between subject and object in cognition. Before we turn to the case for realism, it would be well to consider what exactly the issue is concerning that relation.

The issue in its classical form concerns the status of the objects of cognition. Realists claim that the objects exist independently of the subject. Awareness is nonconstitutive, the identification of things that exist and are what they are independently of the awareness of

28. Kant, *Critique*, B xvi.

them. Idealists, on the other hand, claim that the object of cognition does depend on some constitutive activity of the subject—even if, with Kant, they allow that some independent noumenal realm also exists. Corresponding to this basic metaphysical difference is a derivative question concerning the epistemological standards of truth and justification. If the goal of cognition is to identify independent objects, then the measure of success will be truth in the sense of correspondence, and the principles of evidence and justification must be established by reference to that goal. If the objects of knowledge depend on the subject, however, then truth (if one retains that concept at all) must be something other than correspondence, and idealists typically propose some form of coherence.[29] On both of these issues, representationalists side with realists in maintaining the correspondence theory of truth and the independent existence of the ultimate (though not the immediate) objects of knowledge.

As we have seen, however, representationalists were unable to defend these realist elements in their view because of the nonrealist element: the assumption that consciousness is metaphysically autonomous, that it is capable in principle of originating all its own contents, that our mental life *could* go on exactly as it does even if there were no external reality. Here, then, is a third issue, one that divides realists and representationalists. The primacy of existence implies that consciousness is radically noncreative, radically dependent on existence for its contents. However active it may be in processing information, the mind can only work on information derived from its response to objects outside it. Its function is to identify things as they are independently of it. In that respect it can malfunction, it can misidentify them; but it cannot make up its contents *ab initio*.

In regard to any specific type of knowledge, isolating the contribution of the world from the results of cognitive processing will depend on the specific nature of the objects and of the relevant cognitive capacities. Hence there is no specific relation of dependence on reality that can be asserted for knowledge in general. At this level of abstraction, we can only assert a general relation of dependence. The claim here may be understood by analogy with a naturalistic

29. On the connection between the goal of inquiry and the standards of truth, for idealists, see Brand Blanshard, *The Nature of Thought* (2 vols.; New York, 1939), II, 260–66.

view of the mind-brain relation. If consciousness is not an entity but a functional capacity of the brain, then it would be impossible for consciousness to exist without a brain, even if distinct conscious operations and products do not correlate with distinct neural structures in any simple or uniform fashion. In the same way, realism holds that cognition in all its modes is always, in one form or another, dependent on and directed toward external objects, and so could not possibly occur in the absence of an independent world.[30]

Thus realists reject the Cartesian model of ideas, in which an experience or belief is an internal subjective state, with an identity that can be described without reference to the objective world; and in which any relation between the state and the world (such as veridicality or truth) is external, a relation that may obtain but is not essential to the subjective state. If the primacy of existence is true, then consciousness is not in any sense an autonomous realm of inner contents. This raises a fourth issue, concerning our reflective knowledge *about* consciousness. For Descartes, the fact that one is conscious is the primary axiom, known prior to any fact in the external world. For the Cartesian tradition, the ideas which constitute the subjective pole of cognition are known prior to their external objects. Consciousness is the prior certainty. For realism, however, it is not. If awareness is essentially directed toward external objects, then there is simply no way to have knowledge of consciousness before one has knowledge of the world. Of course we *can* have knowledge of consciousness, through introspection, but the object of this introspective knowledge must be some awareness of the world: "A consciousness conscious of nothing but itself is a contradiction in terms: before it could identify itself as consciousness, it had to be conscious of something."[31]

This fourth point is a derivative one, but it has an important implication: if realism is true, there is no way to *prove* realism, to prove that the objects of awareness exist independently of consciousness.

30. This analogy between the subject-object and the mind-body relations is especially fitting, given the link that exists between these issues for Descartes. But I believe it is *merely* an analogy. Many anti-dualists on the one issue are still representationalists on the other, as we shall see. Conversely, a dualist version of realism is at least conceivable.

31. Ayn Rand, *For the New Intellectual* (New York, 1961), 124. See also Jean-Paul Sartre, *Being and Nothingness*, trans. Hazel Barnes (New York, 1966), 23.

A proof requires the use of premises known independently of the conclusion. A proof of the primacy of existence could not begin by premising facts external to consciousness, since that would beg the question. But it could not begin by premising facts about consciousness itself, since the very thesis implies that such facts cannot be known before we have knowledge of the external world. To attempt the latter sort of proof, as some realists have, is implicitly to endorse a Cartesian view that undercuts their case. The primacy of existence is therefore not a conclusion at all. It must serve as an axiomatic foundation for any inquiry into the nature and functioning of our cognitive capacities.

This does not mean, however, that the thesis is an arbitrary postulate or an act of faith. The point is rather that it is self-evident, and its self-evidence can at least be *exhibited*. I will try to do so in three different ways. First, everything I have said about the primacy of existence could also be said about Descartes' *cogito*. It would be impossible for me to prove that I am conscious, since that fact is implicit in the grasp of any premise that might be used to establish it, as it is implicit in *any* knowledge. Yet reflection on the *cogito* reveals that the truth of the proposition "I am conscious" *is* implicit in all knowledge. In the same way, the primacy of existence cannot be established by argument because it is implicit in any instance of awareness, but *that* fact can be revealed by reflection on the thesis. Second, because the truth of the *cogito* is thus inescapable, it cannot coherently be denied, the denial being itself an act of consciousness. Similarly, it can be shown that any attempt to deny the primacy of existence implicitly affirms it. Third, a certain assumption concerning knowledge has traditionally stood in the way of the primacy of existence, by making representationalism and idealism seem the only alternatives to an unacceptably naïve form of realism. It is important to examine this assumption and to show why it should be rejected.

Consider once again Descartes' *cogito*. I know that I am conscious. The fact is self-evident to me; I could not possibly be wrong in believing it, since even a false belief presupposes that I am conscious. But it is equally self-evident that to be conscious is to be conscious *of* something. Awareness is inherently relational. Whenever we see, hear, discover, discriminate, prove, grasp, or know, there is some object of the cognitive state. Even the faintest sensation is a sensation of *something*—a patch of color, a wisp of sound. If we take away all such content, we have taken away consciousness. Since Kant at least, this point has been a phenomenological truism. But the point has normally been expressed in such a way as to make the content a feature of the awareness of it. In his famous statement of the thesis of intentionality, for example, Franz Brentano says that "every mental phenomenon includes something as object within itself," explicitly distinguishing the intentional existence of an object for consciousness and its real or actual existence.[32] It is precisely this contrast that realism denies—as inconsistent with the first-person, phenomenological experience of awareness and as unsupported by any secondary arguments. The object of awareness *is* the object as it actually exists.

A typewriter sits on the desk before me. I see it against the background of desk top and papers, I feel the keys and hear the whirring sound it makes. Do these things exist in my consciousness? Certainly not, not in any way that is available to me from my standpoint as the subject of my perceptual awareness. When I reflect on my awareness of those objects, I am aware of it as something completely uncreative, merely a revelation of what is there. The desk, the typewriter, the keys exist in a world that I am in, not one that is in me. My attention to each object comes and goes, but the onset of attention is not experienced as the coming-to-be of that object. When I turn my head to view the room behind, what comes to be is not the room but my awareness of it; the room is experienced as a permanent existent which I can explore sequentially. Each thing I perceive has an identity, it is something. And it is what *it* is, not what I make it. These things before me are not at all like the objects of imagination, which I can shape to suit myself. And even my awareness is something independent of my reflective awareness of it. As I turn my attention to the fact that I am aware of these objects I experience that awareness as something which had been going on all along.

From this standpoint, the thesis that consciousness is primary is literally unintelligible—unless one drops the context in which we grasp what it is to be aware of an object. Consider Descartes' ques-

32. Franz Brentano, *Psychology from an Empirical Standpoint*, ed. Oskar Kraus, trans. Antos C. Rancurello, D. B. Terrell, and Linda McAlister (New York, 1973), 88.

tion "whether any of the objects of which I have ideas within me exist outside of me." Having an idea of something means being conscious of it, and the *consciousness* of an object may be said, metaphorically, to be "within" me. But Descartes is suggesting that the object I am conscious of might also be within me, *i.e.*, within my consciousness. How could that be? I can isolate my consciousness only by distinguishing it from the objects I am aware of. Those objects (the typewriter, the room, etc.) are the "out there" against which I can isolate my consciousness as the "in here." To suggest that these objects themselves might exist in consciousness is to deny the very condition that makes it possible to understand what consciousness is. So far, then, the idealist claim that the objects of awareness depend on consciousness, or the skeptic's worry that they might so depend, is simply unintelligible.[33]

Could anything make it intelligible? Up to this point we have considered only the perceptual awareness of the immediate environment. At the conceptual level, the matter is more complex, even if we retain the first-person standpoint. At this level, I *am* conscious of initiating conscious processes—of comparing, distinguishing, inferring, imagining, speculating, weighing—that affect the content of my awareness. This means that I can formulate ideas of things which do not exist, facts which do not obtain, and I can do so even knowing that these cognitive contents are not real. Further, when I do arrive at conclusions I can affirm as facts, contents I could count as recognitions or discoveries, the conclusions have been produced by conscious processes. Both these points, however, serve only to confirm our phenomenological sense that consciousness is not creative.

When I imagine a unicorn, I know that it does not exist, that I am making it up. But I am also aware that I am making it up from things which do exist, that I am merely rearranging contents—horses and horns—that are real. Imagination carries with it a sense of "what if . . . ?"—what if reality were different in this way or that? This question is possible only against the background of our sense of reality. Similarly, when I speculate that population growth in this country may come to a halt, I am not affirming it as a fact, but only

33. Descartes, *Meditation III*, in Ross and Haldane (eds.), *Philosophical Works*, I, 161. My argument here is similar in some respects to Sartre's "ontological proof," in *Being and Nothingness*, 21–24.

entertaining it as a possibility. I am entertaining it, however, as a possible *fact*, a possible feature of the world independent of me. Moreover, I am speculating *about* real objects, this country and its population; I am not making up the content of my speculation from scratch. When I do reach a definite conclusion as a result of conscious integration, I affirm it as a fact. The fact is experienced as independent not only of my recognition but of the processes by which I came to recognize it. I know that water will flow when I turn the kitchen tap. I had to initiate a certain modest effort of thought to grasp this fact, but I did not initiate or create the fact itself—the plumber did. If I had any suspicion that I *had* made it up, the suspicion would destroy my certainty. Hence it is self-stultifying to express a conviction while denying that what one believes is true independently of the belief.

But this sort of self-stultification infects every attempt to deny the primacy of existence. To assert that what is known depends on the knowledge of it is to offer that very thesis as something known, as something, therefore, that falls under the principle asserted, and hence as something that depends on our recognition of it. But this is manifestly not what the proponent of the thesis intends. That facts depend on our belief in them, he implies, is objectively true, a fact of reality about consciousness and its objects, made true by the nature of things, not by his believing it. Otherwise he would have to allow that realism is a fact for the realist. He would have to allow that the primacy of consciousness is both true, because he believes it, and false, because the realist denies it. To avoid this, he must assert that the realist is wrong, which means asserting the primacy of consciousness as a fact he did not create. He thereby contradicts the thesis asserted.

Of course, the subjectivist theory I have just refuted has almost never been held—the theory, namely, that "believing makes it so," that the objects of awareness depend on our conscious awareness of them in a way we can grasp from our first-person standpoints as subjects of that awareness. That is all the primacy of consciousness could mean from this perspective, which is our primary and basic mode of knowledge about consciousness. But idealists have always claimed that there is more to consciousness than meets the inner eye. In asserting the primacy of consciousness, they have said that the objects of knowledge depend not on the momentary, introspectable awareness of them but rather on the underlying subject of that awareness, that is, on its constitution as a cognitive subject, on the faculties by which it knows and their operation in producing conscious experience. In this way they have sought to make intelligible the claim that objects depend on the subject, and also to retain some distinction between objective and subjective (by defining objectivity in terms of the underlying subject) so as to avoid the immediate self-refutation of subjectivism.[34] Kant, once again the paradigm, holds that the phenomenal world is constituted by the noumenal, not the phenomenal, subject.

But the contradiction is not eliminated. It is compounded. The claim that objects depend on the subject is still offered as a truth about the nature of things, making an objective claim on our credence, and not as a truth created by him who utters it, not even by his self-in-itself. Kant's principle of (transcendental) idealism, for example, unlike the law of causality, is not offered as something imposed on the phenomenon of knowledge by some faculty of (reflective or epistemological) cognition. It is supposed to describe the independently real relationships among noumenal objects, noumenal subjects, and phenomena. But the problem here is compounded by the type of dependence he asserts.

That of which we are aware, says Kant, exists only as representation, as the representational content of our awareness of it. The implication, as he recognizes, is that we do not know the mind as it is in itself; we know only a phenomenal mind that exists as the content of inner awareness. In claiming that the world of objects exists only as the content of our awareness, however, Kant is *not* referring to the awareness we experience as an element of the phenomenal mind. He is referring to a kind of awareness whose subject is the noumenal mind. So in stating that the objects of knowledge depend on this noumenal subject, he is claiming knowledge about something which, by his own thesis, he cannot know. He describes the transcendental syntheses in which space, time, and the categories are imposed on the manifold of sensations as processes that take place behind the representational contents they create, and take place independently of anyone's awareness of them. Thus by his

34. *Cf.* Karl Duncker, "Phenomenology and Epistemology of Consciousness of Objects," *Philosophy and Phenomenological Research*, VII (1947), 535–36.

own theory he could not possibly have knowledge of them. He is not even entitled to the claim that an unknown *something* beyond experience must be posited in order to explain experience. We can make sense of the idea of explaining experience only by stepping outside it (and taking with us the category of causality).[35]

This problem is one that has plagued idealists from Berkeley onward; they have invested an enormous amount of effort in trying to circumvent it. And it is worth trying to state in its most general form, because it will lead us directly to the central problem faced by realists. In order to assert that consciousness is constitutive, one must give some meaning to the idea that its object depends on it. And the only possibilities correspond to the two perspectives we can take toward consciousness. We can view it from the inside, as its subjects. But from this first-person perspective, as we have seen, the claim that objects depend on the introspectable awareness of them is simply unintelligible. Or we can view it from the outside, from a kind of third-person perspective, as a kind of thing in the world whose faculties, operating in specific ways, give rise to the conscious awareness of objects—and, idealists claim, to the objects themselves. From this perspective, we can at least understand what is meant in calling consciousness constitutive—if we are talking about someone else's consciousness. And there is the problem. In adopting this perspective in the first place, we are implicitly adopting the primacy of existence for ourselves as third-person theorists about consciousness. We are viewing consciousness as something with an objective nature, existing independently of the subject's awareness of it, and independently of *our* theories about it. The attempt to apply this third-person perspective to ourselves while maintaining the thesis of the primacy of consciousness, produces the incoherence that pervades Kant's transcendental psychology.[36]

These dialectical arguments against the primacy of consciousness are certainly not new. They are at least as old as Plato's attack

35. *Cf.* P. F. Strawson, *The Bounds of Sense* (London, 1966), 170–74. Richard Rorty points out that experience requires a mechanism of synthesis to explain it only if one makes the assumption, not warranted by experience itself, that experience must have emerged from a manifold of unrelated sensations. *Philosophy and the Mirror of Nature* (Princeton, 1979), 152–55.

36. *Cf.* Bernard Williams, "Wittgenstein and Idealism," in Godfrey Vesey (ed.), *Understanding Wittgenstein* (New York, 1974), 78.

on Protagoras in the *Theaetetus*.[37] Then why has their force been ignored? I believe the answer lies in a certain principle concerning knowledge, one that has always been an obstacle to accepting the primacy of existence.

We can get at this principle by pursuing the distinction between first-person and third-person perspectives on awareness. These two standpoints acquaint us with two different relations between subject and object. A person is looking at a tree. From his perspective, the tree is present to him, revealed as it is; his consciousness is nothing but the revelation of it, a focus or direction upon it as the object. From our external perspective, the tree is a causal agent acting on the person; his consciousness is a certain set of capacities for being acted upon by the tree in certain ways; we observe the causal sequence from the reflection of light by the tree, to the effect on his visual receptors, to the various stages of processing in his brain. Neither perspective has any direct access to the fact grasped by the other. The person himself has no phenomenological access to the causal relation between the tree and himself. He sees the tree; he does not see the *means by which* he sees the tree.[38] We, on the other hand, have no direct access to the conscious relation to an object which is the person's awareness of the tree. Examine his cognitive apparatus how we will, we know nothing of the awareness it produces except through the subject's report of it. In other words, we have no access to it except through his access.

So far, we have an interesting phenomenon, but no apparent philosophical problem. We can integrate the perspectives easily enough, it seems, by saying that the awareness of an object must result from some causal sequence in which the object plays a role, even if, as subjects of the awareness, we are not directly aware of the causal sequence. Or, starting from the external perspective, we can say that when an object acts on a conscious agent it sets in mo-

37. Plato, *Theaetetus*, trans. John McDowell (Oxford, 1973), 170a–171d. Aristotle seems to be making a similar argument, in a more complicated form, in *Metaphysics*, trans. W. D. Ross, in Richard McKeon (ed.), *The Basic Works of Aristotle* (New York, 1941), Book IV, Chaps. 4–8.

38. In perception, we never perceive the means by which we are aware of objects. At the conceptual level, we *are* aware of the means by which we know, insofar as we consciously direct such processes as concept formation or inference, but we do so by means of cognitive mechanisms whose operations are not fully conscious.

tion a causal sequence culminating in the awareness of the object. Yet virtually every major theory of knowledge manifests some unease about how to integrate the cognitive with the causal relation between subject and object, suggesting the presence of a deep-seated problem. Philosophers in the phenomenological tradition have typically maintained that consciousness, as a direction on the world, cannot itself be an existent in the world it knows, subject to its causal laws.[39] Philosophers who have tried to assimilate the findings of scientists about the causal bases of cognition have often adopted versions of behaviorism or naturalism which *identify* the cognitive with the causal relation. They ignore or try to explain away the perspective of the subject, who does not experience his consciousness of objects as a causal relation.[40] Finally, the most common view has been a kind of representationalism which says that consciousness of objects only begins where causality ends. We are conscious, not of the external things which initiate the causal sequence, but rather of entities produced as the final stage of the sequence.[41]

The source of the difficulty here is a certain model of awareness, whose appeal is not hard to understand. We know of consciousness in the first place from the inside, as its subjects. From this perspective, the awareness of an object seems transparent, the simple presence of the object, a revelation of it. Unaware as we are, from this perspective, of the way our cognitive faculties operate to produce our awareness, it seems as if nothing but the object itself determines the way we grasp it, the way it appears. As G. E. Moore remarked, "When we try to introspect the sensation of blue, all we can see is the blue: the other element is as if it were diaphanous." As a result, this seeming "diaphanousness" comes to be regarded as essential to the nonconstitutive character of consciousness. William Earle, for example, claiming that "cognition is and must be absolutely noncreative," takes this to imply that "the subject of cog-

39. Thus when Edmund Husserl suspends the "thesis of the natural standpoint," he does not suspend the consciousness that is aware of the natural world; that is precisely the point of the *epochē*. *Ideas*, trans. W. R. Boyce (New York, 1931), 113.

40. This approach can be found in various quarters in contemporary philosophy—among causal theorists (see Chapter 4); among certain of the linguistic idealists (see Chapter 6); and among the functionalists in cognitive science.

41. For a particularly clear example of this view, see Lord Brain, *Mind, Perception and Science* (Oxford, 1951), Chap. 1.

nitive intentionality therefore is a pure spectator. . . . Apprehension is transparency."[42]

Traditional realists turned this sense of transparency into a model of consciousness as a "mirror of nature," grasping its objects by reflecting them in a transparent medium.[43] The model has been stated many ways: that awareness is a direct confrontation between mind and object, that the mind in cognition becomes identical with its object, or similar to it, taking on its form without its matter. But the different formulations have a common thrust: that the awareness of objects cannot be mediated by any process whose nature affects the way the object appears. And this means that the subject of awareness cannot have a positive nature of its own. Such a nature would be like bubbles in glass, distorting the reflection of objects outside. Thus the model says, in effect, that that of which we are not aware from the first-person standpoint—namely, the operation of specific means of awareness in causally determinate ways—cannot exist at all. It implies that consciousness as the subject of awareness cannot have an identity, if, that is, it is to give us any awareness of external objects, of things as they are in themselves.[44]

Correspondingly, every major antirealist argument confronts this model with the facts available from the external standpoint. The model itself is taken for granted, as a condition for consciousness' being noncreative, and the facts are therefore taken to mean that it *is* creative. The arguments follow two broad patterns. One—we may call it the Cartesian pattern—is based on the possibility of error. Be-

42. G. E. Moore, "The Refutation of Idealism," in *Philosophical Studies* (London, 1951), 545; William Earle, *Objectivity* (Chicago, 1955), 63, 64, 68.

43. The phrase is from Rorty, *Philosophy and the Mirror of Nature*.

44. This model has often been traced to Aristotle, to passages such as the following: the intellect "must, then, since it thinks all things, be unmixed . . . in order that it may know; for the intrusion of anything foreign to it hinders and obstructs it; hence too, it must have no other nature than this, that it is potential." *De Anima*, trans. D. W. Hamlyn (Oxford, 1968), Book III, Chap. 4, 429a18–23. It is arguable whether this actually expresses the model, but it has often been interpreted that way. See, for example, John Herman Randall's statement: "If *nous were* something—if it had a definite and determinate structure of its own—then men could not transparently 'see' and know what is, without distortion. They could not really 'know' things as they are, but only things mixed with the structure of *nous*. Such a *nous* would have turned Kantian: it would have become 'constitutive' and creative" (*Aristotle* [New York, 1960], 91).

cause awareness results from the active functioning of our cognitive faculties, there is the possibility of malfunction, leading to error, to cognitive contents that are not real. This is the fact Descartes seized upon to justify his claim that consciousness might in principle generate *all* its contents. If it can make a round tower seem square, why could it not create the appearance of the tower itself *ex nihilo*? Consciousness in these cases is clearly not a diaphanous reflector of external reality, and the Cartesian argument takes that fact as evidence that consciousness *might* never reflect reality at all. Conversely, Descartes' search for an infallible mode of knowledge is really a search for a confrontation between mind and object not mediated by any process that could go wrong.

But the deeper pattern of argument is Kant's, because it offers a reason for saying that consciousness never is or could be a diaphanous reflection. For Cartesians, an error is a local failure of correspondence between external reality and the contents of consciousness, leaving open the possibility of correspondence in the normal case. But Kant recognized that awareness is always and necessarily conditioned by the means which produce it. A faculty of cognition must have an identity which affects the content of the conscious experiences it gives rise to. The possibility of error forces us to distinguish appearance from reality, but Kant's general insight was that for us to be aware of an object at all, the object must appear to us in some way, and in a way partly determined by our faculties. Thus Kant rejects the diaphanous model, but not the assumption, implicit in the model, that diaphanousness would be a necessary condition for knowledge of things as they are in themselves.[45] And so he took as the price of his insight the implication that we cannot have such knowledge, at any level of cognition.

In this way, the diaphanous model has been common currency among competing theories in epistemology, along with the premise we uncovered at the basis of Kant's system: that if consciousness has an identity of its own, it cannot grasp the identities of things external to it. Idealists have affirmed the antecedent, hence the consequent; realists have denied the consequent, hence the antecedent. To preserve the primacy of existence, realists have traditionally re-

45. *Cf.* Norman Kemp Smith, *A Commentary to Kant's 'Critique of Pure Reason'* (2nd ed.; New York, 1962), xxxix. See also Hegel's comment on the model, in *Phenomenology of Mind*, trans. J. B. Baillie (2nd ed., 1931; rpr. New York, 1967), 131.

sisted the facts of perceptual relativity.[46] At the conceptual level, they have insisted that our classificatory hierarchies of species and genera must reflect an external hierarchy in the nature of things. And although they maintain that objects exist and are what they are independently of us, realists have refused to apply this truth to consciousness by granting it an identity. Idealists take the failure of this approach as proof of the primacy of consciousness, maintaining that consciousness creates its own contents. But to make this claim, they must step outside the confines of their thesis to observe how consciousness operates behind the scenes, offering what they observe from that perspective as a fact they did not create. So long as the basic premise is not challenged, such incoherence will be unavoidable, and epistemology will be forced to choose between two impossible positions.

The contribution of Ayn Rand's Objectivist epistemology is to challenge that premise, to reject at its root the diaphanous model of cognition. The primacy of existence she takes as axiomatic: consciousness is not metaphysically active, it does not create its own objects, it is a faculty of identifying what exists. But consciousness itself exists. It is a faculty possessed by living organisms, with a specific, determinate nature like any of their other biological systems: "Objectivity begins with the realization that man (including his every attribute and faculty, including his consciousness) is an entity of a specific nature who must act accordingly; that there is no escape from the law of identity." As a faculty with a specific identity, consciousness responds in specific ways to external stimulation, processing in specific ways the material provided by the environment: "All knowledge *is* processed knowledge—whether on the sensory, perceptual or conceptual level. An 'unprocessed' knowledge would be a knowledge acquired without means of cognition. Consciousness . . . is not a passive state, but an active process. And more: the satisfaction of every need of a living organism requires an act of *processing* by that organism, be it the need of air, of food or of knowledge."[47]

46. An extreme case was the New Realist movement, which produced the view that all sensory qualities are in the object, even contradictory ones (for example, the warmth felt by one hand and the coolness felt by the other when both are in the water). See E. B. Holt's contribution to Holt, *et al.*, *The New Realism* (New York, 1912), 303–73.

47. Ayn Rand, *Introduction to Objectivist Epistemology* (New York, 1979), 4, 110, 109.

Consciousness is not metaphysically active. It no more creates its own contents than does the stomach. But it *is* active epistemologically in processing these contents. *What* we are aware of is determined by reality—there is nothing else to be aware of— but *how* we are aware of it is determined by our means of awareness. How could there be any conflict between these facts? It is true, as we have noted, that the perceptual subject is not perceptually aware of the means by which he perceives nor can he isolate what effects his perceptual system has on the way objects appear to him. But to infer from this that his perceptual system can have no effect is to believe in magic; it is to believe that his perception of the object occurs by no means, that it literally is a revelation. The other side of this coin is to infer that because his perceptual system does affect the way things appear, he is not after all aware of the object that appears. In either case, the diaphanous model "regard[s] *identity* as the *disqualifying* element of consciousness." It holds, in effect, that because consciousness is something, it can be conscious of nothing. For that is the real meaning of Kant's basic premise. In Ayn Rand's words, "[Kant's] argument, in essence, ran as follows: man is *limited* to a consciousness of a specific nature, which perceives by specific means and no others, therefore, his consciousness is not valid; man is blind, because he has eyes—deaf, because he has ears—deluded, because he has a mind—and the things he perceives do not exist, *because* he perceives them." [48]

Ayn Rand's principle that consciousness must have identity, and her rejection of the diaphanous model, allows us to integrate the facts about consciousness—its causal nature and its relational character as the grasp of objects—within the framework of the primacy of existence, and without the difficulties faced by other theories of knowledge. As an overview of the detailed discussion to come, let us consider how that integration will proceed in the case of perceptual awareness.

Metaphysically, our cognitive faculties determine the manner in which we grasp reality, but it is reality we grasp. In perception, the way objects appear to us is partly determined by our perceptual apparatus, in ways we will explore; but the objects themselves appear, the objects themselves we are aware of by means of their appearances. I will introduce the concept of perceptual *form* to isolate

48. *Ibid.*, 106–107; Rand, *For the New Intellectual*, 32.

those aspects of appearance that result from the way our sensory systems respond to stimulation. But this form, as we will see, is not an inner object of awareness. It is not an object, but the way in which we perceive external objects. And it is not an inner phenomenon, for it is the product of an interaction between our senses and external objects. Our senses have no capacity to create objects of awareness; they can only respond, in determinate ways, to external objects.

Epistemologically, all our knowledge about consciousness is acquired within the context of our knowledge of reality, with the primacy of existence implicit as an axiom throughout. Our primary and only direct knowledge of consciousness is acquired from the standpoint of the subject, in which it appears as something noncreative. As our knowledge expands we can adopt an external perspective, grasping the causal relations between subject and object and noting the ways our faculties affect the perception of objects. But this knowledge does not undercut the first-person sense of the nonconstitutive nature of awareness. On the contrary, it confirms and deepens that sense.

Part of what we learn from the external standpoint is that certain aspects of the content we immediately perceive are the product of an interaction between external objects and our senses. But this does not mean these aspects of content are produced by the introspectable awareness experienced from the internal standpoint; they result from the processes that give rise to that awareness. Hence the experience of that content as wholly independent of our awareness of it is not wrong. The content *is* wholly independent of the introspectable awareness. From the standpoint of the subject, the nature and operation of his perceptual apparatus are features of reality external to his awareness.

And indeed that is how they must be studied. Knowledge about how the senses function is knowledge about the external world, the same world we grasp from the first-person perspective. We begin to isolate the effects of our faculties only when it occurs to us that, given what we know about external objects, certain perceived variations cannot be ascribed to the objects themselves, and so must result from the way we perceive them. It is only because we know the railroad tracks cannot really converge, the stick in water is not really bent, the colors of things do not really change when we come indoors, that we have any reason for assigning these phenomena to the operation of our senses. Similarly, we learn to explain these phenomena by studying the sensory systems as physical existents occupying the same world as the objects perceived by means of them. As our knowledge of them expands we may find (as we will in the case of colors) that certain qualitative aspects of what we perceive must be assigned to the sensory systems, not to the objects in themselves. But we discover this only by studying the causal interaction between object and sensory system, and only by identifying in the object the intrinsic features to which the senses are responding. Thus at every stage of the investigation, knowledge of how the senses function presupposes knowledge about the objects they respond to. There is no way to leap ahead of this progression, as adherents of the primacy of consciousness do, and claim that our faculties might have created all content on their own. In the nature of the case, there could not possibly be evidence that they do.[49]

The purpose of my argument has been to lay the groundwork for perceptual realism by validating the general principle of epistemological realism and removing the chief obstacles in its way. It is perhaps best seen as defining a certain approach to epistemological issues. Most epistemologists have accepted the diaphanous model of awareness in some form. That is, they have started with an assumption about how consciousness must function in order to be valid. They have then had to treat it as an open question whether consciousness *is* valid, whether it can live up to the model. The Cartesian tradition accepted the challenge, and tried to prove that we can have knowledge of an external world. The Kantian tradition has abandoned that effort as impossible and has limited itself to examining the structure of our experience and of our conceptual scheme, regarded as subjective products (though it typically redefines objectivity to avoid this label). My approach, by contrast, starts from the primacy of existence as an axiom. We know from the outset that consciousness is valid; that is not an open question. In rejecting the diaphanous model of awareness, however, we reject any a priori assumptions about how consciousness must function. That is a matter for inquiry. So let us begin our inquiry into the nature of perception and perceptual knowledge.

49. *Cf.* Duncker, "Phenomenology and Epistemology," 525–27, 530–32.

2

Sensation and Perception

I am still at my desk. Before me sits the typewriter, and around it on the desk top are the usual adjuncts to the Muse—scattered cards and papers, pens and pencils, a book, an ashtray. Across the desk I face a wall. These things all lie in different planes, the wall perpendicular to my line of sight, the desk and everything on it slanting away at an angle in a horizontal plane. The objects on the desk stand out against the desk top as distinct units. Unlike the blotches in the wood or the figures in a painting on a wall, they are separate objects; I could reach out and grasp them. They have definite edges, and if I looked around any edge I would find another side, now hidden. Most of them are rectangles, but the ashtray is round. None is moving or changing in any visible way.

The rest of the room is equally stable as I turn to view it, no matter how quickly my eyes scan back and forth, except for the leaves of plants stirring faintly in the breeze. All the leaves are green, but in countless different shades. I could not begin to name or describe them all, but I can see the differences very clearly. These colors are all in the surfaces of the plants. They have a definite texture, quite different from the filmy blue-gray of cigarette smoke. The plants have a smooth texture; the pots they stand in are rougher, about the same as the rubber eraser in my hand, though of course the eraser is flexible to the touch, and the pots look rigid.

It is dark outside, and raining. I am not aware of the rain directly, but I sense its effects. The air is moist—I can smell the moisture, and feel it against my face when there is a breeze. There are also ripples from the rain in a puddle on the ground outside, and the motion in the water's surface forms a pattern visibly different from that caused by any other sort of disturbance. And I hear the rumble of traffic in the street; it is a mixture of noises, and one of them is the peculiar rushing sound made only by tires on a wet pavement. All the sounds in the environment stand out as units to the ear—the traffic, the whir of the typewriter, a voice in the next room, an airplane overhead—and I have no trouble distinguishing them. . . .

There is much more, of course. A report of what is revealed by a moment or two of attention would fill pages. But we have enough to introduce the issues. The preceding paragraphs described various perceptible features of the world around me. They named facts I could know directly, without reasoning. It did take an inference to know that it is raining, but I inferred this from facts I knew without inference—the moisture in the air, the ripples in the puddle, the sound of the tires. Like all the rest, these were *given*. I had only to look, or listen, or smell, and they were there.

So at least it seems. But was I really aware of all this? Was I directly aware of it? The realist theory of perception says that I was. In stating the theory, we will have to examine in what sense perceptual awareness is direct, what categories of things can be perceived, and how this awareness relates to its physical causes. We will also need to consider in more detail where and why realism differs from the other theories, which claim that perception is at best indirect. Before turning to this formal presentation, however, we must examine some of the specific issues raised by the facts of the matter, issues that have been the subject of heated controversy in the philosophy of perception. The first set of issues concerns the physiological processes by which we perceive.

Sensation and Perception

To perceive an object is to discriminate it from other objects, to isolate it from its background, to be aware of it as a unit, a distinct whole. Thus the proper object of perception is the entity—the ash-

tray on the desk, the eraser in my hand. It is true that many of the
things one perceives are not entities in the usual sense of solid objects. One can see cigarette smoke and shadows, feel a breeze or the
water in the tub. Indeed, in some modalities one is never aware of
solid objects as such. One smells chemical substances carried by the
air; one hears sounds, and by means of them discriminates events.
But in all these cases, the object perceived has the character of an
entity. It is a segregated whole: it stands out from its background,
and it possesses a distinctive identity *as a unit*. I will therefore use
the concept of an entity in an extended sense to indicate this fact.

In the case of vision, psychologists describe this aspect of perception in terms of the figure-ground phenomenon. When an object
stands out as a figure against a ground, the contour dividing them
has a one-sided character. It belongs to the figure, as an edge; it does
not belong to the ground, which is perceived as extending beyond
the contour, behind the figure. Normally one sees depth at the edge.
The figure is closer, the ground more distant. A similar phenomenon occurs in the other sense modalities. The sound waves produced by events in the environment are mixed together in the air
and arrive at the ear as a single complicated wave. Yet somehow the
auditory system resolves this wave into its components, isolating the
wave train caused by tires on pavement from that produced by
the typewriter from that produced by the active vocal cords next
door.

But one does not merely isolate entities; one is aware of their
identities. Some of a thing's attributes are perceptible, and one can
discriminate different degrees of perceptible attributes. These range
from the simple and obvious examples, such as color, shape, or texture, to more complicated attributes, such as the distinct pattern
made by rain on the surface of water, or the rushing sound of tires
on wet pavement. In this respect, we discriminate attributes as well
as entities. But the two abilities cannot be separated. One could not
isolate an entity without perceiving (some of) its qualitative differences from the background. Conversely, one could not detect differences among things in respect of their attributes without isolating the things to be compared. These are two sides of the same
discriminative capacity.[1]

1. Robert Efron, "What is Perception?" *Boston Studies in the Philosophy of Science*, IV (1966–68), 148.

Perception is thus the awareness of entities as such, and the discrimination of objects requires a great deal of integration on the part of our sensory apparatus. The visual discrimination of an object involves the awareness of its shape, but that in turn requires that its contours be integrated into a single, unitary structure.[2] Perceiving shape by touch requires integrating the input from the different fingers in contact with different areas of the surface. Equally important is integration over time. The discrimination of weight is finer if one hefts the object, or tosses it from hand to hand, than if it rests motionless in the palm.[3] And of course the awareness of any event is a temporal phenomenon. One cannot hear a melody in an instant or even discriminate one voice from another; one cannot see a car moving without watching it over time. And there is a real integration here. One does not perceive the melody, or the motion of the car, as a succession of discrete stages; it is a unitary existent. Finally, there is integration between the modalities. One can turn to locate visually an object one has heard, or reach out to grasp it; one is aware of it as a single object seen, heard, and felt. I can compare the relative textures of the eraser in my hand and the pots I see across the room.

The presence of such integration suggests that perception may be a derived phenomenon, not the simplest or most elementary form of sensory awareness. One can look at an object, for example, and isolate the awareness of one of its attributes, such as its color. One can then imagine experiencing that awareness in a detached way, distinct from and unintegrated with the awareness of the whole entity and the rest of its perceptible attributes. The traditional name for this sort of awareness is sensation. Philosophers normally regard sensations as obvious and omnipresent phenomena; their role in knowledge and their relation to states of the brain have been discussed endlessly, but their existence rarely. Yet it is not easy to find examples of genuine sensations. The act of isolating an attribute of a perceived object does not produce a sensation, nor does that act fully indicate what it would be like to experience sensations as such.

2. There is a certain disorder, a form of agnosia, in which a person can see the color, brightness, and size of an object, and can even *trace* its contour sequentially, but cannot discriminate the shape as such. See Efron, "What is Perception?"

3. James J. Gibson, *The Senses Considered as Perceptual Systems* (Boston, 1966), 127–28.

For one is still aware of the isolated attribute as the attribute *of* the entity. To find genuine examples, we must look further afield.

Perhaps the most striking cases appear in the experience of blind persons whose sight is surgically restored. Such newly sighted patients have great difficulty learning to perceive and identify objects visually. The nature of the difficulty is still a matter of controversy and in any case seems to vary from person to person. Some reports, however, suggest a form of experience radically unlike our own. One doctor suggested that his patients "do not localize their visual impressions . . . ; they see colours much as we smell an odour of peat or varnish, which enfolds and intrudes upon us." Marius von Senden observed that the newly sighted appear at first not to perceive depth at all, but only patches of color in a plane field; that they cannot detect the real sizes and shapes of objects, and can barely attend to the shapes and sizes of the color patches; and that they cannot follow the motion of an object across the visual field, experiencing it instead as a transformation of the field. He inferred that there was "a total absence of relationship among virtually all visual impressions. . . . The elements initially presented to his mind constitute . . . a fortuitously given ordering of various coloured patches, more or less indistinctly separated off one from another."[4]

These phenomena, if they occur as described, may result in part from neurological damage. But it is possible to produce something like a sensation in normal subjects by presenting them with severely impoverished sensory stimuli—flashes of light, points of pressure on the skin, tones of a single frequency, saline solution on the tongue. In these conditions, the subject does not experience entities possessing stable attributes, discriminated from a background of other entities, but rather a qualitative content whose dimensions vary in close correspondence to the dimensions of the stimulus energy impinging on his receptors.

4. Marius von Senden, *Space and Sight*, trans. Peter Heath (London, 1960), 128–38 (quotations, 129, 135). Von Senden almost certainly overgeneralized his findings in the attempt to show that the blind lack any real sense of space. Some newly sighted patients do not seem to fit his description. See R. L. Gregory and J. G. Wallace, *Recovery from Early Blindness*, EPS Monograph 2 (Cambridge, England, 1963). The issue of what a blind person would see on recovering his sight was raised by John Locke, *Essay Concerning Human Understanding*, ed. Alexander Campbell Fraser (1894; rpr. New York, 1959), Book II, Chap. 9, sec. 8. For a history of the issue, see M. J. Morgan, *Molyneux's Question* (Cambridge, England, 1977).

These phenomena, and others we will encounter presently, are clearly more primitive forms of awareness than is ordinary perception, and I will use the concept of sensation to refer to them. The term actually covers a range of experiences, lying along a continuum with no sharp border line between sensation and perception. Even the sensation of a color patch involves the discrimination of it from its background, whereas the olfactory perception of an odor seems more like a sensation in comparison with the visual discrimination of entities. Nevertheless, we can define the poles of the continuum in terms of two basic features. First, a pure sensation would be the awareness of an isolated quality, such as color, pitch, warmth, sweetness. The quality would not be sensed as an aspect of an integrated whole, not grasped as the quality *of* an entity. In this respect, a purely sensory form of experience would be a welter of unrelated qualities, like the visual fields von Senden described, like the sensory manifolds posited by Hume and Kant. Second, a sensation would be a momentary experience, varying in response to the flux of stimulus energy at the sense receptors. Without perceptual integration over time, each moment would be a new experience, replacing the one before it and replaced in turn by another.[5]

With this distinction in hand, I can state my first major thesis about perception. Perception is our normal mode of experience. It is the normal result of using our senses, and the basis for our ordinary judgments about the objects around us. Sensations are experienced only in unusual circumstances, and pure sensations are probably not possible for an adult with normal faculties. Both sensation and perception are products of our sensory systems, in response to stimulation, and exactly the same stimulus might give rise to a sensation in one subject, a percept in another. But if a subject's nervous system is capable of the integration necessary for perception, his percept is a unitary product; it is not composed of sensations as real constituents; sensation and perception are distinct modes of awareness. Further, the perceptual awareness of entities

5. Von Senden's description of a newly sighted patient is again illustrative: "Although, when one passed a hand or an object in front of his eyes and said to him 'look, it's moving', he did his best to understand, he still did not succeed in grasping the meaning of the words. He took it purely as an interlude of light and darkness, without there being any awareness in his mind of a change of position" (*Space and Sight*, 136–37).

is direct. Entities are *given* as such. The perceptual integration necessary to achieve this awareness is physiological. It does not involve, and should not be conceived on the model of, conscious processes of integration—association, inference, hypothesis, calculation, or computation. The discrimination of objects may in some cases be aided by such processes, but they are not in general necessary for the perception of entities.

The major source of opposition to these theses is the doctrine of sensationalism, which maintains that only sensations of individual qualities can be given; that the perceptual awareness of entities is derived from sensations; and that it is derived by means of processes which are cognitive in the sense that they involve the logical synthesis of information given.[6] Thus in its traditional form, sensationalism held that perception involves the interpretation of what is given in sensation—interpreting a field of qualities as a world of objects. More recent versions hold that in producing a percept, the nervous system engages in processes that must be regarded as forming and testing hypotheses, decoding sensory messages, or computing data. I will follow current fashion by referring to these as computational processes.[7]

It is obviously not true that we *consciously* experience sensations, or engage in computation, in the course of ordinary perception. Sensationalists have often replied with a developmental claim: infants do experience the world in the form of sensations, as a "blooming, buzzing confusion," and must learn to integrate sensations into percepts; but these integrative processes have become so automatic that we are no longer aware of them. Now even if infants were limited to sensations, this would not mean that percep-

6. Thus sensationalism is not equivalent to empiricism, though the two are often equated (as by Joseph Agassi, "Sensationalism," *Mind*, LXXV [1966], 1–24) and though sensationalism has been accepted by most empiricists. Empiricism is the doctrine that all knowledge of the physical world comes from the evidence of the senses; sensationalism is a doctrine about the specific form in which we acquire this evidence. One can accept the former without the latter. On the other hand, one could adopt sensationalism without empiricism. Some psychologists, as we will see, hold that sensations are integrated into percepts by means of innate knowledge.

7. A typical expression of the theory in its classical form is James Sully's definition of perception in *The Human Mind: A Textbook of Psychology* (New York, 1892), 207. For a clear statement in outline of the modern version, see Jerry A. Fodor, *The Language of Thought* (Cambridge, Mass., 1975), 42–51.

tual development is a matter of automatizing computational processes. It might involve some purely physiological maturation that results in the ability to perceive entities. But infants do not in fact seem to experience sensations. A baby will track a moving object with his eyes, in a jerky way, virtually from birth, indicating some discrimination of the object as a unit. Developmental psychologists are finding that the process of perceptual learning consists not in discovering which sensations to put together into the perception of whole objects, but in discriminating finer and finer differences among the entities which the child can pick out as wholes from the beginning.[8] In any case, developmental sensationalism was never based solely, if at all, on the observation of infants, but rather on a prior commitment to sensationalism, which then suggested that our first experiences *must* have been sensations.

Then what *are* the real sources of that commitment? They are various, and we will have to take them one by one. This is as might be expected, since sensationalism does not follow directly from any of the fundamental epistemological approaches outlined earlier. It is a doctrine about the relationship between two modes of awareness, leaving open the relation between either mode of awareness and the world outside. One could thus imagine a realist version of sensationalism. Nevertheless, sensationalism has always been located within the representationalist and idealist traditions, and we will see the reason shortly. The *major* considerations which have led philosophers and psychologists to adopt sensationalism turn, implicitly, on the assumptions discussed in Chapter 1.

Sensations as Simple Ideas

Sensationalism was an integral part of modern British empiricism. It appears in Locke and Hume as a distinction between simple and complex ideas. The former are ideas of individual qualities, which the mind is given and is incapable of creating. The latter are results of the mind's own activity in compounding simple ideas. Sensationalism reappears in Kant as a distinction between the ma-

8. Eleanor J. Gibson and Elizabeth S. Spelke, "The Development of Perception," in John H. Flavell and Ellen M. Markman (eds.), *Handbook of Child Psychology* (4th ed.; 4 vols.; New York, 1983), III, 4, 25–36; T. G. R. Bower, *Development in Infancy* (San Francisco, 1974).

terial element in experience, a manifold of unrelated sensations, and the formal structures imposed on this material by the mind itself, the forms of perception and the categories. In both cases, the perceptual awareness of an individual entity was regarded as a complex idea that joins together, by means of some cognitive process, the simple ideas of the entity's individual qualities.

There are traces in Locke of all the sensationalist arguments we will consider, but we may start with the distinction itself. As we have seen, Locke views perceptual experience as a sequence of Cartesian ideas, and this gives him two different perspectives. On the one hand, ideas have a representational nature, a content, and Locke sets out to examine this content, showing the relationships ideas have to each other in virtue of it. Most of Book II of the *Essay Concerning Human Understanding*, including the distinction between simple and complex ideas, is devoted to this aim. On the other hand, ideas have a formal nature, as psychological occurrences; sensory ideas in particular are caused in a certain way by external objects. This dimension of ideas takes precedence in Book IV, where Locke is concerned with our knowledge of particular objects in reality. But Locke defines simple ideas both in formal and in representational terms, and the two definitions are not equivalent.[9]

Both are implicit in his introduction of the concept: "Though the qualities that affect our senses are, in the things themselves, so united and blended, that there is no separation, no distance between them; yet it is plain, the ideas they produce in the mind enter by the senses simple and unmixed. . . . And there is nothing can be plainer to a man than the clear and distinct perception he has of those simple ideas; which, being each in itself uncompounded, contains nothing but *one uniform appearance, or conception in the mind*, and is not distinguishable into different ideas."[10] In the first sentence, the criterion of simplicity is a formal one. A simple idea is *given*, not produced by the mind in any way; it enters "by the senses simple and unmixed." This criterion says nothing about the idea's content, and it is thus an open question which ideas can meet the criterion—ideas of whole entities or of individual qualities. In fact, Locke believes that only the latter are given, but so far he has not explained why.

9. Richard Aaron, *John Locke* (Oxford, 1955), 111.
10. Locke, *Essay*, Book II, Chap. 2, sec. 1.

The second sentence offers a criterion for simple ideas in terms of their representational content. A simple content is not distinguishable into parts or elements; it presents a single, uniform content to the mind's inspection; its simplicity is clearly and distinctly perceived. It is *unanalyzable*. Insofar as Locke approaches ideas from this perspective, he is not concerned with the way they are acquired. He is taking cognitive inventory, analyzing the contents with which the mind is already stocked. Although the ideas in question are described as ideas of sensation, being products of that faculty, Locke does not treat them as sensations. There is nothing in his discussion of the ideas of yellow, cold, bitter, and the like, which indicates that sensations of these qualities are experiences that occur at specific times, in specific circumstances. Frequently it is not even clear whether the qualities are concrete and determinate or whether Locke is dealing with abstract characteristics. Conversely, when he argues that ideas of substance are complex, it is not always fully clear whether he means the perception of individual entities or the concepts for types of substance.[11] In analyzing contents, he is abstracting from questions of how the ideas are experienced. The result is that by this representational criterion, only ideas of individual qualities are simple, but it remains an open question whether they and they alone are given.

Yet his examples show that Locke believes individual qualities are given—in effect, that sensation is the basic form of experience and that perception is derived. The belief appears to be a result of combining his two concepts of simplicity. Ideas of individual qualities are simple in the sense of being given, because they are simple in the sense of being unanalyzable. But this argument is an equivocation. One can maintain, as I do, that the perception of whole entities is given, and yet recognize that individual qualities can be isolated by an act of selective attention.

The only way to justify Locke's inference would be to show that whatever the mind can analyze into elements must have been synthesized by the mind out of those elements. This was in fact a common view at the time, something Locke may have taken for granted. The science of mind, it was supposed, should proceed as the science of matter does—discovering atoms and then explaining the

11. See, for example, Locke, *Essay*, Book II, Chap. 12, sec. 6.

properties of wholes by showing how they are compounded out of atoms. At the end of the modern period, Kant made an analogous assumption: "For where the understanding has not previously combined, it cannot dissolve, since only as having been combined *by the understanding* can anything that allows of analysis be given to the faculty of representation."[12] As applied to perceptual experience, any such principle inevitably yields sensationalism. But the principle is precisely what must be proved to give a basis for sensationalism, and any reason for rejecting the latter would be a reason for rejecting the principle. Thus the distinction between simple and complex ideas, in itself, provides no such basis.

Sensations as Appearances

Another mode of argument for sensationalism can also be found in the empiricists, especially Hume, but it is better illustrated by the sense-data theorists of this century. As a type of representationalism, the sense-data theory held that we are directly aware only of appearances, so that any awareness of external objects must be derived by inference. The general principles which motivate this view have already been rejected; the specifically perceptual arguments will be discussed later. Of interest now is the claim that perceptual appearance can be analyzed as a series of sensations. What is given, it holds, is the sense-datum, which is a qualitative content of experience and lacks the holistic and enduring attributes of entities. What we are given, says C. I. Lewis, "is either a specific quale (such as the immediacy of redness or loudness) or something analyzable into a complex of such."[13] In accordance with our distinction between sensation and perception, therefore, the sense-datum is an object of sensation; and it was typically viewed that way by those who accepted the theory.

The method used to defend this claim was based on a certain visual phenomenon. Normally we see the environment as a three-dimensional layout of objects, possessing three-dimensional shapes,

12. *Cf.* James Gibson, *Locke's Theory of Knowledge and Its Historical Relations* (Cambridge, England, 1960), 46–49; Immanuel Kant, *Critique of Pure Reason*, trans. Norman Kemp Smith (1929; rpr. London, 1953), B130.

13. C. I. Lewis, *Mind and the World Order* (1929; rpr. New York, 1956), 60.

at various distances from us. Within certain limits, we are not aware of any change in their shapes as we move them or change our point of observation; or of any change in size as they advance and retreat; or of any change in color as the illumination varies. In psychological terms, our visual awareness of the environment includes depth perception and the constancies of shape, size, and color. And they are essential elements in our ability to see entities and the enduring attributes they possess. But the sense-data theorists argued that we will see something quite different if we examine the way objects really look to us. We will not see depth, for objects will appear as patches of color in a two-dimensional visual field, the patches being projections of the objects onto a plane perpendicular to the line of sight. The edges of objects will be seen merely as lines separating the patches. The patches will not be constant in shape. A penny lying on the table will look elliptical, and the elliptical shape will change as one moves around it.[14] Similarly, the size of an object in the visual field will vary with its distance, and its color with the illumination. The sense-data theorists did not hold, with Locke, that we have separate sensations of shape, size, and color; we have a single sensation of a sense-datum that has all three qualities. Nevertheless, the awareness of a visual field is a sensational form of experience. The field does not consist of entities, any more than a painting does; it is not a world of distinct and enduring things, but a field of qualities in constant flux.

Do things really look this way? Yes and no. The railroad tracks stretching into the distance look parallel, giving no cause for alarm that a train running down them would derail; but they also look convergent. A person far away looks normal, of human size, but he also looks tiny. "You can see the pattern one way or the other at will, according to which question you ask yourself about the perception." There is no doubt that one can adopt a certain reductive focus on one's experience, intentionally disregarding the awareness of depth and the constancies. If one does, things will appear more or less as the theory describes. At least, they will look that way in *some* respects. It is easy to see the change in perspectival shape as one moves around an object. It is virtually impossible, outside a special

14. C. D. Broad, *Scientific Thought* (New York, 1923), 235ff.

laboratory setup, to see objects as moving whenever one moves his eyes. And there are degrees of difficulty between these extremes.[15]

It is equally clear, however, that this is not the only perspective one can take. Subjects in psychophysical experiments, asked to adjust a variable object so that it looks the same as a standard, will equate them on the basis of their real attributes *or* the qualities of their projections, depending on the instructions given. Both tasks are performed with roughly the same ease and accuracy.[16] It seems clear that they are shifting back and forth from one perspective to another, but that both allow judgments based on direct observation. We are directly aware of the projected shapes, as the theory holds, but the awareness of the real shapes is equally direct.

To justify its claim, then, the sense-data theory would have to show that the reductive focus has some priority: that only within that perspective can we be aware of what is actually given; that the normal perceptual focus is learned by elaborating in some way what is given; and that the processes of elaboration become so automatic that we now experience the perceptual focus as direct. But apart from the physiological facts to be considered in the next section, nothing ever was put forward to support these claims, and there is a great deal against them. The distinction between perspectives is not really applicable to the other modalities. It is impossible, for example, to experience an object manipulated by the hands as a set of changing sensations in the fingers and joints. The reductive focus is also learned after the normal one. Babies see depth and the real attributes of objects, not their projected features. Indians and Africans who were asked to equate a variable ellipse to the apparent shape of a tilted circle erred in the direction of the real circular shape more

15. Edwin Boring, "Visual Perception as Invariance," *Psychological Review*, LIX (1952), 141; see also James J. Gibson's reply to Boring, immediately following. The term *reductive focus* was suggested by Roderick Firth's discussion of perceptual reduction in his "Sense-Data and the Percept Theory," in Robert Swartz (ed.), *Perceiving, Sensing, and Knowing* (Garden City, N.Y., 1965), 233–42. See also Anthony Quinton, "The Problem of Perception" (in the same volume), 504. I have avoided calling it the phenomenological focus, as some writers do, because its use in this context is an example of bad phenomenology. It does not reveal but alters the way things appear.

16. Julian Hochberg, "Perception II. Space and Movement," in J. W. Kling and L. A. Riggs (eds.), *Experimental Psychology* (3rd ed.; New York, 1972), 509–10.

than did westerners, suggesting that familiarity with perspective paintings and drawings is part of what makes the reductive focus seem so natural to us.[17] And most people have great difficulty drawing perspective shapes. The evidence suggests, in other words, that the sense-data theorists had it backwards. It is the reductive focus that develops out of the perceptual one. The former does not reveal the given; it is a new and sophisticated ability that develops after and on the basis of the perceptual focus in which entities are given.

Of course, there are reasons why representationalists might be disposed toward the sensationalism of the visual field. The visual perception of objects includes the awareness of features that, in one sense, do not appear in the visual field. The perception of motion, as I noted, requires integration over time, resulting in the awareness of a movement as a unitary existent. This means that at any moment, one is aware of a moving object as being about to be in a different place. Similarly, the perception of an edge involves a sense of the object as possessing a hidden side beyond that edge. Thus perception involves the awareness of the object as extending beyond the temporal and spatial bounds to which a sensational form of experience would be limited. Such phenomena would naturally create unease in anyone inclined to a diaphanous view of the directly given. But these considerations do not constitute a commitment to sensationalism on the part of representationalists. If one is going to posit a spatial manifold inside consciousness, there is no compelling reason against positing three dimensions instead of two. Roderick Firth, for example, attacked the sensationalism of the sense-data theory, claiming that what are given are "ostensible physical objects" as wholes. But as the term *ostensible* indicates, these are still appearances. Firth accepts the usual arguments against any direct perception of *external* objects.[18]

17. T. G. R. Bower, "The Visual World of Infants," *Scientific American*, CCXV (December, 1966), 80–92; see also Eleanor J. Gibson's discussion of constancy in *Principles of Perceptual Learning and Development* (Englewood Cliffs, N. J., 1969), 363–68; M. H. Segall, D. T. Campbell, and M. J. Herskovits, *Influence of Culture on Visual Perception* (New York, 1966), 55–58.

18. Firth, "Sense-Data and the Percept Theory," in Swartz (ed.), *Perceiving, Sensing, and Knowing*. For the same reason, H. H. Price allowed that a sense-datum could have three-dimensional features, in *Perception* (1932; rpr. London, 1964), vii.

In any case, the fact that we can adopt a reductive focus in vision provides no support for sensationalism. So let us turn to what has undoubtedly been the major source of the doctrine.

Sensations as Receptor Functions

Unlike the sense-data theorists, most perceptual psychologists recognize that we do not see objects as items in a two-dimensional array. Within limits, an object will look the same regardless of distance, angle of orientation, and illumination. These are the constancy phenomena, and they have been known for over a century. As for depth vision, the great nineteenth-century theorist Hermann von Helmholtz pointed out that the "perception of depth is fully as vivid, direct, and exact as that of the plane dimensions of the field of vision."[19] Yet most theorists, Helmholtz preeminent among them, have accepted the thesis of sensationalism, maintaining that perceptual phenomena such as these are derived from sensations together with some process of inference or association. The reason is a certain interpretation frequently put upon the physiological facts.

The argument goes back at least to Locke. In perceiving a globe, Locke argues, one is not directly aware of its spherical shape or uniform color. The sensory idea one is given is "of a flat circle, variously shadowed." He does not explain this assumption further, but the reason for it is indicated by a parallel argument from his *Examination of Malebranche*: "The idea we have of [external objects] and their grandeur being still proportioned to the bigness of the area, on the bottom of our eyes, that is affected by the rays which paint the image there." That is, the invariant size of the object cannot be given, since the image on the retina varies with distance. The parallel argument concerning depth was made by Berkeley: "distance, of itself and immediately, cannot be seen. For *distance* being a line directed end-wise to the eye, it projects only one point in the fund of the eye, which point remains invariably the same, whether the line be longer or shorter."[20] In all such arguments, the claim is that cer-

19. Hermann von Helmholtz, *Popular Scientific Lectures*, ed. Morris Kline (New York, 1962), 158.
20. Locke, *Essay*, Book II, Chap. 9, sec. 8; John Locke, *An Examination of P. Malebranche's Opinion of Seeing All Things in God*, in *The Works of John Locke*, ed. J. A. St. John (Freeport, N.Y., 1969), sec. 11; George Berkeley, "An Essay Towards a New

tain features of the object cannot be given, because they are not present as such in the proximate stimulus.

The discovery of the sensory receptors produced a new version of the argument, one that could be generalized to cover the other senses, which lack anything analogous to the retinal image. Individual nerve cells of specialized types, in the sense organs, begin the process of perception by transforming the physical energy that impinges on them into electrical impulses. But these cells do not respond to the perceived features of the world. Rods and cones in the eye are sensitive to the intensity and wavelength of light energy. Receptors in the ear are stimulated by the motion of the basilar membrane, which vibrates in accordance with the same properties of sound waves. Some tactual receptors are stimulated by pressure on the skin, others by heat. There are no receptors that respond to shape as such, or size, or texture; no receptor distinguishes between two voices or detects the motion of a car. The properties of energy to which they respond can be correlated only with such object properties as color or warmth. Even here the correspondence is a distant one. Receptors really are sensitive to *changes* in energy. A cell that received a uniform flow of energy would soon adapt and return to its resting state.

All this implies that the output of the receptors must be integrated somehow by the nervous system. If there is anything in the stimulus that corresponds to the invariant features of external objects, it can only be relational patterns across the whole array of stimulus energy—perhaps even relationships between the stimuli for different senses. These patterns must be extracted from the flux at the receptors by higher, integrative mechanisms. Many theorists have inferred from this, as Locke and Berkeley did from the retinal image, that the properties of external objects cannot be given because they are not represented at the receptor level. In light of this, sensations have been defined as correlates of receptor responses. And the integrative mechanisms have been regarded, on the model of conscious integration, as types of inference, ways of processing information. The result is a version of sensationalism.

Helmholtz developed the archetype of such a theory. Our only

Theory of Vision," in A. A. Luce (ed.), *The Works of George Berkeley* (7 vols.; London, 1948), Vol. I, sec. 2.

immediate awareness, he says, is the sensations aroused by receptors; to perceive, the nervous system must interpret these sensations; and the principle of interpretation is causal. We infer what cause was necessary in these conditions to produce this sensation. The percept is therefore a conclusion, and although the operations that produce it are not conscious, "we really have here the same kind of mental operation as that involved in conclusions usually recognized as such." In the case of lightness constancy, for example, what we *perceive* is the object's reflectance, the proportion of incident light it reflects, and this is constant despite variations in the level of incident light. A piece of coal looks black in sunlight, even though it may be reflecting more light than a sheet of paper in dim illumination, which still looks white. If a subject is shown an isolated patch of light against a black background, however, he will experience sensations of brightness proportional to the intensity of light. To explain this paradox, Helmholtz assumes that in every case we have sensations of brightness proportional to the intensity of light reflected from object to eye, but that the nervous system also notes the level of illumination falling on the objects outside, and then uses these two quantities to solve the equation for reflectance.[21]

The difficulties with such a theory are notorious; they have been stated many times, and nowhere more forcefully than by Helmholtz himself. In the first place, he admits that the sensations are difficult to isolate, and in some cases they are not and cannot be conscious at all. For example, he explains depth vision largely in terms of retinal disparity—the slight differences between images of an object received by the two eyes. He claims that these cause different sensations, and that the nervous system calculates the distance of the object necessary to produce just that disparity. But we do not experience two sensations of an object, unless it is far enough away from the point of focus. Helmholtz himself points out that the disparity *at* the point of focus would have to be increased twenty or thirty times before one would actually experience double images.[22]

In this respect, Helmholtz represents a transition in the history

21. Herman von Helmholtz, *Treatise on Physiological Optics*, trans. and ed. J. P. C. Southall (3 vols.; Rochester, N.Y., 1924–25), III, 2; Helmholtz, *Popular Scientific Lectures*, 178; Julian Hochberg, "Perception I. Color and Shape," in Kling and Riggs (eds.), *Experimental Psychology*, 397.

22. Helmoltz, *Popular Scientific Lectures*, 162–65.

of sensationalism. Sometimes he speaks with the classical theorists, who regarded sensations as conscious states produced by receptor responses. If the doctrine is understood in this way, then our inability to isolate sensations consciously is an objection to it. Elsewhere, as we have just seen, Helmholtz seems to *identify* sensations with receptor responses, eliminating any connotation of consciousness from the meaning of the term. This is the meaning of *sensation* that has been employed by most, though by no means all, twentieth-century theorists, and our phenomenological abilities do not constitute an objection against sensationalism so understood. Indeed, there could be no objection on this score (except to say that using the term in this sense is misleading). There is no question that receptor responses occur, or that they are in some way the input to the perceptual systems. But even this purely physiological sensationalism interprets the processing of this input by the nervous system as a kind of inference or computation, and there are ineliminable difficulties in any such view. These difficulties are evident in Helmholtz' account.

For one thing, the inferences are irreversible. In illusions, for example, Helmholtz would say we make the normal inference in abnormal conditions, producing a false conclusion, the illusory appearance. But this happens even when we know that the conditions are abnormal and the "conclusion" false. The knowledge has no effect on the appearance, even though the latter is explained in terms of (unconscious) beliefs. Second—and this is the more important epistemological problem—Helmholtz acknowledges that the perceiver does not have in any clear sense the knowledge necessary for his inferences to be justified. The perception of depth, for example, is supposed to involve a calculation of depth from the retinal disparity. This calculation would require use of the principles of geometrical optics, just as an astronomer uses these principles to calculate a star's position from a parallax effect.[23] But the astronomer consciously knows the principles. We can explain how he learned them and why he is justified in accepting them. None of this is true of the perceiver.

The difficulty here is masked somewhat by the interaction of the senses. Helmholtz claimed that sensations are interpreted in light of

23. Helmholtz, *Physiological Optics*, III, 28, 4.

past experience. His favorite example was the pressure phosphene. If one presses the eyeball on the outside, he will experience a patch of light on the opposite side, apparently over the nose. The reason, Helmholtz says, is that it normally takes an object there to stimulate the retina on the outside. How do we know this? Because in the past, when we were stimulated there, we had to reach in the opposite direction to grasp the object. Thus, following the tradition set by Berkeley, he believed that vision is tutored by the sense of touch. But how do I know that my arm has moved to the right to grasp an object stimulating my retina on the left? According to sensationalism, the motion of the arm should be experienced, initially, as a set of kinesthetic sensations in the muscles and joints. It would take an inference to translate these sensations into a percept of the *direction* in which the arm is moving in objective space. And this raises the same question, How did I learn that only a motion of the arm to the right will cause just this set of kinesthetic sensations?[24]

The problem is that Helmholtz has no way to account for the perceiver's knowledge of the principles employed in his perceptual inferences. Despite his opposition to nativism, he would be forced to consider some of that knowledge innate, or at least a priori. (This is a special case of the general representationalist problem of justifying the inference to an external world. How can we acquire knowledge of the connection between experience and reality, knowledge necessary to make the inference, prior to the knowledge of reality which that inference is supposed to explain?) Helmholtz indeed accepts this consequence for the most general principle involved. In order for any such inference to be possible, the perceiver must assume that his sensations have *some* cause. And in order to benefit from past experience, he must assume that the same cause will have the same effects. For this reason, Helmholtz argues that the law of causality is innate; he follows Kant in regarding it as a category that the mind brings to experience.[25]

In view of all these difficulties, why would anyone maintain the theory? The presence of philosophical problems in Helmholtz' theory indicates the presence of underlying philosophical assumptions. The physiological facts, about the retinal image, the behavior

24. *Ibid.*, 26; *cf.* M. T. Turvey, "Contrasting Orientations to the Theory of Visual Information Processing," *Psychological Review*, LXXXIV (1977), 83.
25. Helmholtz, *Physiological Optics*, III, 32.

of receptors, the neural mechanisms, can be established only by experiment. But the interpretation of these facts, including judgments about what is given and what inferred, rests on philosophical premises, which we will now examine.

Detection Versus Computation

The two theses I formulated earlier were (1) that perception is a unitary form of awareness, distinct from sensation, and not composed of sensations as real constituents; and (2) that perceptual awareness is direct, not the product of computational processes. We can now see that (2) is the basic issue. The phenomenological evidence supports (1), and contemporary forms of sensationalism do not accept the older claim that sensations are conscious (and consciously isolable) components of the percept. Hence the only basis for denying (1) would be to deny (2), *i.e.*, to claim that the percept is produced *unconsciously* out of some more primitive cognitive state. The key question, then, is whether the physiological processes of integration that make possible depth perception, the constancies, and other features distinguishing perceptual from sensational awareness provide any reason for considering perception indirect. I will argue first that they do not provide any such reason. We can then turn to the sensationalist arguments for the opposing view. Along the way, we will need to pay careful attention to the meaning of the term *direct*, to the sorts of evidence adduced to support claims that perception is or is not direct, and to the ways in which both are affected by epistemological assumptions.

Let us begin with the phenomena to be explained. Perception is a form of awareness; we discriminate objects and their attributes. This cognitive dimension of the percept can be measured by determining the range of objects and attributes we can discriminate, and the specificity of our discriminations. Subjects can be asked to report whether they detect a given object, and the physical conditions necessary for them to do so can be isolated, as in measuring the absolute thresholds. Subjects can also be given two objects and asked to judge whether they are the same or different. If the conditions are set up properly, this will determine whether they are sensitive to a given attribute at all, and if so, with what specificity they can detect different degrees of it. These relationships have been explored extensively in psychophysics for the simpler variables of objects, corresponding to the features of isolated sensations such as hue, brightness, saturation, pitch, timbre, loudness, and so on. Less has been done with the more complicated attributes we *perceive*. These variables are more difficult to isolate, and psychologists have also assumed that perception is not a form of direct discrimination but a product of inference from sensations—but this assumption in turn is produced by the philosophical premises to be explored here. In any case, there is no reason in principle why a similar psychophysics of perception could not be carried out.[26]

Once a given discriminative capacity has been established, the task is to *explain* it, and among the various problems this poses, our philosophical question is, In what conditions would such an explanation require us to posit an inference or some other form of computational integration? Two sorts of *external* factors have been taken as marks of inference. The first are reasons for thinking that what is discriminated cannot, by its nature, be present to a perceiver. Some poultry workers, for example, can separate male from female day-old chicks simply by looking at the genitalia. At this age, the gross differences between them have not yet developed, and to an untrained observer they all look the same. The workers can only describe what they discriminate by saying it is male or female. Yet they obviously do not *see* the functional or genetic differences that define the sexes. What they actually discriminate must be some yet-to-be identified physical difference. But this sort of case raises none of the relevant questions. In calling the discrimination of male from female indirect, we still assume that there is a direct discrimination of something physical, some attribute of the external object. And the reason for calling the one indirect has nothing to do with the nature of neural integration.

Second, it is often assumed that any type of discrimination that is learned must involve inference. But this is not true in general, as

26. For a fuller discussion of this project, see Efron, "What is Perception?," 147–49, 150–55; and James J. Gibson, "Perception as a Function of Stimulation," in Sigmund Koch (ed.), *Psychology: A Study of a Science* (6 vols.; New York, 1959, 1962), I, 464–68. In his last work, *The Ecological Approach to Visual Perception* (Boston, 1979), 149, Gibson rejected the idea of a perceptual psychophysics, on the grounds that it suggests a passive subject. But such passivity, which did characterize much of classical sensory psychophysics, does not seem essential to this project.

we can see by distinguishing interpretive from discriminative learning. When a car makes a right-hand turn, an experienced driver in the car behind can tell—almost the instant the other car begins to move—whether its driver intends to proceed down the street or pull into the curb. There is clearly interpretation here. What the second driver actually sees is the angle at which the car is turning and its rate of acceleration, and he interprets these as signs of the other driver's intentions. Similarly, we can see the difference between a nervous and an insincere smile on another's face. The nature of this ability to "see" psychological states in facial expressions is complex and controversial, but a good case can be made that interpretation is involved here as well.

In other cases, however, such as tasting wines, perceptual learning is acquiring the ability to discriminate finer and finer differences in regard to some perceived attribute. If the perception of that attribute with any degree of specificity is direct, then the capacity to discriminate its degrees with greater specificity should also be regarded as direct, unless there is some other reason for doubting this. Similarly, in learning to listen to music, one learns to detect more subtle and more complicated patterns in the sound than one could before; but if such patterns are the sort of thing one can hear directly, the increased ability is also direct. These enhanced capacities for discrimination require a process of selective attention, which may in turn be aided by conceptual knowledge of what one is looking for, but no inference is required to explain the content which a person thereby becomes aware of. What sort of inference, indeed, would be possible in such a case? The role of attention is to focus awareness, not to provide premises for a conclusion. A type of discrimination that is learned, therefore, is indirect only if it results from interpretive learning. And since our chief reason for holding that interpretation has taken place would be that what is discriminated cannot actually be present to the senses, the fact of learning does not add a new criterion of directness.[27]

Let us consider, then, the neural processes by which we discriminate. Is there anything we might discover about them that would require us to label as indirect the discrimination they me-

27. See E. J. Gibson, *Principles of Perceptual Learning*, Chaps. 5–6, for an analysis of the types of discriminative learning. I will later discuss the claim that perception is "theory–laden" (see Chapter 7).

diate? Conversely, does the claim that a given type of discrimination is direct commit one to anything about the neural processes that mediate it? The only such implication that can be established with any certainty is that there must be something in the proximate stimulus that is specific to the attribute discriminated. The physical process by which we perceive must preserve the specificity of what is discriminated. If it did not, then the percept *would* involve something like hypothesis or sheer guessing. And so this specificity must be present in the proximate stimuli to which sensory systems respond. If a visual discrimination is to be direct, for example, there must be something in the array of light energy striking the retina that is specific to the constant shapes, sizes, colors, and motions that we see. If two objects gave rise to exactly the same proximate stimulus—the same in *every* respect—there would be no way for the system to detect the difference between the objects.[28] This does not imply, however, that the relevant stimulus feature must be anything like the qualities of the retinal image, or something to which an individual receptor might respond. These are specific types of stimulus features, and the drift of experimental research has been to show that taken alone they are not very important. It is only philosophical assumptions, to be discussed presently, which could have given them special prominence.

The work of James J. Gibson provides a wealth of examples of the sort of stimulus feature that can be found if one rejects those assumptions.[29] Gibson observes that although the energy at a single point in the sense organ varies only along such simple dimensions as wavelength and intensity, the array of stimulus energy has a far richer structure. The array of light striking the retina, for example, is reflected from objects with different shapes, slants, sizes, colors, and textures. As a result, it is structured into visual solid angles with relationships among them—there are borders in the light, and re-

28. The specificity need not run in the opposite direction. There may be many stimulus features specific to a single attribute of the object. This is almost certainly the case in depth perception.

29. In addition to the works already cited, see James J. Gibson, "A Theory of Direct Visual Perception," in J. Royce and W. Rozeboom (eds.), *The Psychology of Knowing* (New York, 1972), 215–27, and "New Reasons for Realism," *Synthese*, XVII (1967), 162–72. For a good overview of Gibson's theory, see Claire F. Michaels and Claudia Carello, *Direct Perception* (Englewood Cliffs, N.J., 1981).

lations between the borders. And he claims that we can find relational properties there that are specific to the attributes of the objects reflecting the light. He points out, for example, that distance in our environment is not a "line directed end-wise to the eye" but a surface stretching away to a horizon and projecting across the retina from top to bottom. The texture of the surface—the floor, the earth, a city street—projects a pattern on the retina; the texture of more distant parts of the surface projects a more densely packed pattern; thus the density is specific to distance. Similarly, a given object covers the same amount of texture regardless of distance, so long as its size remains constant. There is therefore a relational feature in the stimulus array whose invariance corresponds to the invariant size of the object. And our own motion produces yet other invariants: "A great many properties of the array are *lawfully* or *regularly* variant with change of observation point, and this means that in each case a property defined by the law is *invariant*."[30] Such a property might then be specific to the invariant shape of the perceived object.

It is important to emphasize that Gibson presents his theory about invariants in the stimulus array as a way of explaining the direct, noninferential perception of external objects. We are aware of the real, constant attributes of those entities *by means of* the invariants in the array. But we do not perceive the invariants themselves: "We do not see our retinal images. We see the environment." D. W. Hamlyn objects that this makes perception indirect: "It seems extremely implausible in any case, to say the least, that we get to the features of the real world through the features of the pattern of stimulation; this would imply that we always make some form of inference in perceiving the world."[31] Hamlyn's argument obviously presupposes that whenever we perceive one feature by means of another, the relation between them is that of premise to conclusion, or sign to significate. But this assumes that we can be directly aware

30. On the perception of size and distance, see J. J. Gibson, *Ecological Approach*, 159–64. J. J. Gibson, "Theory of Direct Visual Perception," in Royce and Rozeboom (eds.), *Psychology of Knowing*, 221.

31. J. J. Gibson, "Theory of Direct Visual Perception," in Royce and Rozeboom (eds.), *Psychology of Knowing*, 224; see also J. J. Gibson, "New Reasons for Realism," 168; D. W. Hamlyn, "The Concept of Information in Gibson's Theory of Perception," *Journal for the Theory of Social Behavior*, VII (1977), 7–8.

only of the last stage in the causal sequence, and that our awareness of it must occur by no means, must be diaphanous—assumptions we have already rejected.

In vision, many features of the optic array are reflected in the visual field. As a result, there may be cases in which it is difficult to determine whether the stimulus feature is isolated physiologically by the nervous system and thereby serves as the means of directly perceiving the external attribute or whether the corresponding element in the visual field functions as a sign or cue for the attribute, mediating an indirect awareness of the latter. A case in point is aerial perspective, which makes distant objects look foggy. But this is not true in general. More often, the perceiver is not aware at all of the stimulus features. They function only as means by which he is aware of the external attribute.

The discovery of relevant stimulus features, of course, is only part of the explanation of perceptual discrimination; there must also be neural mechanisms that isolate and detect these features. Are there any constraints here on what is required for direct awareness? We know on general grounds that some neural process is involved—we do not perceive by magic. But there is no *particular* neural process that we can say ahead of time is required. Neurophysiologists may someday discover a particular type of mechanism that is always correlated with direct perception, but they could do so only by correlating the mechanism with the discriminations that we take on other grounds to be direct. There is no a priori condition one could set forth. With what is known at present, we cannot even say that there must be some overall state of the nervous system that is specific to the relevant stimulus feature, except in the vaguest sense of *state*. The neural basis might instead be some sort of modification in ongoing activity.

The basis for these claims about stimulus features and neural processes is implicit in the concept of direct awareness. In calling a mode of awareness direct, we cannot mean that it is unmediated by *any* causal process. That would equate direct with diaphanous awareness, and I argued there could be no such thing. We can understand direct awareness only by contrast with knowledge that results from consciously directed processes of integrating information. And by that criterion, perception clearly seems direct. Indeed, we normally determine whether something could be the object of direct awareness by asking whether it could be perceived. Of course, an adult's perceptual capacities are integrated with his other cognitive skills, so that seemingly direct observations may actually contain interpretive elements. We must therefore be open to the considerations, mentioned above, that provide evidence of interpretation. In rejecting the diaphanous model, however, we have rejected any a priori assumptions about what sort of causal process underlies direct awareness. Hence nothing we discover about the process could, in itself, show that perceptual awareness is indirect.

In particular, the fact that individual receptors cannot detect the sorts of stimulus features Gibson describes is simply irrelevant. If there were some reason to do so, we could distinguish between features that receptors can detect (such as wavelength at a point) and those that can be detected only higher up in the sensory pathways or the cortex. We could even define a concept of physiological directness to mark the distinction. But it would be an equivocation to argue from physiological to cognitive indirectness. And that is exactly what sensationalists have done. They have formed the concept of physiological directness, in effect, by drawing a sharp line at the receptors. But they have merged that concept with the ordinary meaning of directness, by assuming that any processing of receptor responses must involve computation or inference.

The implication of the argument so far, then, is that only one sort of physiological discovery would bear on the directness of perception—the discovery that there is no stimulus feature specific to a given external attribute or object we can discriminate. And this is precisely what most sensationalists have assumed or tried to show: that the sensory stimuli really underspecify the objects we think we perceive, and so must be supplemented either by past experience or by innate knowledge. But they have not reached this conclusion by studying the stimulus arrays exhaustively and meeting with failure. They have assumed ahead of time that the sensory stimuli could not possibly be specific to the attributes we perceive. And we can trace this assumption to the basic models of cognition. The Kantian view that an active process of cognition must constitute its object has led many to hold that a sensory stimulus, by definition, is what an individual receptor can respond to, since anything detected by processing would be a constituted product, not a stimulus. The representationalist model has led others to assume that, in vision at least, the only relevant stimulus features are those of the retinal image. It is time to explore these arguments in more detail. I will also examine separately the information-processing approach, which, though it adds nothing fundamentally new to the issue, does recast the issue in an illuminating way.

1) Helmholtz explicitly adopted the Kantian model of cognition:

> Our apperceptions and ideas are *effects* wrought on our nervous system and our consciousness by the objects that are thus apprehended and conceived. Each effect, as to its nature, quite necessarily depends on the nature of what causes the effect and on that of the person on whom the effect is produced. To expect to obtain an idea which would reproduce the nature of the thing conceived, that is, which would be true in an absolute sense, would mean to expect an effect which would be perfectly independent of the nature of the thing on which the effect was produced.

A form of awareness that is "true in an absolute sense," in other words, would have to reproduce the external object in a mirrorlike way. This would require that it be diaphanous, not dependent in any way on the nature of the faculty by which one is aware, and it is therefore impossible. This is Kant's basic argument in miniature. Putting it a different way, Helmholtz argued that our awareness of external objects cannot be direct, because we do not perceive "at the place of the objects themselves."[32] For us to perceive a distant object, some causal sequence must cross the spatial gap, and the effects of that sequence will depend on our mode of sensitivity to it. Direct awareness can occur only after the causal chain has run its course, and our receptors have responded; and then we can be aware only of that response.

A second Kantian principle, however, explains the distinction between the receptors and the mechanisms of neural integration. Kant's basic principle was that any cognitive faculty must have some identity and, as a result, must constitute its own objects. Consciousness, in his view, is metaphysically active. But he also distinguished between active and passive faculties in another sense, calling sense

32. Helmholtz, *Physiological Optics*, III, 18; Helmholtz quoted in Nicholas Pastore, "Helmholtz on the Projection or Transfer of Sensation," in Peter Machamer and Robert Turnbull (eds.), *Studies in Perception* (Columbus, Ohio, 1978), 372.

perception a faculty of receptivity, the intellect a faculty of spontaneity. This does not mean that perception is metaphysically passive, that it mirrors reality while the intellect does not. The point is rather that the objects of the intellect are doubly constituted—by the form of the receptive faculty, which provides the materials, and by the intellect, which imposes various relationships on this material. This means that although sensory experience does not mirror reality, it is in a sense closer to it than are the finished products of the intellect. Sense perception is the given; intellectual knowledge involves interpretation of the given.

In the tradition represented by Helmholtz, this distinction was applied to the sensory pathways. As Nicholas Pastore notes, Helmholtz' view about sensation and unconscious inference "represents a continuation of the classical tradition that had evolved, namely, that the mind is passive in respect to sensation but active in respect to perception."[33] It was therefore important to distinguish between the responses of the receptors, which could be regarded as passive, providing us with the given; and the neural processes of integration, which are active and therefore constitutive. In effect, Helmholtz identified receptor firings with the sensory atoms of Kant's manifold of sensations.

These same assumptions motivate many of Gibson's critics. R. J. Richards points out, for example, that "neural input is processed at several levels in the nervous system," and that this processing is required to isolate relationships in the stimulus array. He infers that the active processing must partly constitute the relationships: "Relations, at least those to which Gibson here refers, are not real features of the physical world. To use the older jargon, they are *entia rationis cum fundamento in re*; that is, they demand a mentating observer as well as certain physical situations in order to exist."[34] More generally, the distinction between active and passive has introduced confusion into the very concept of a stimulus. As Gibson

33. Pastore, "Helmholtz on Projection," in Machamer and Turnbull (eds.), *Studies in Perception*, 355. See also Nicholas Pastore, *Selective History of Theories of Visual Perception 1650–1950* (Oxford, 1971).

34. R. J. Richards, "James Gibson's Passive Theory of Perception," *Philosophy and Phenomenological Research*, XXXVII (1976), 229, 224. Considering the stress that Gibson places on the *activity* of the perceptual systems, it is revealing that Richards calls his theory a passive one.

uses the term, it refers to the whole array of energy that is given to a sensory system, available for active exploration by it. His critics agree in thinking of a stimulus as something *given*, but assume that the only features given are those that individual receptors can respond to, since anything detected by exploration, by processing, would be constituted and thus not given. The stimulus is therefore equated with the response of the receptors, and the two sides talk past each other. Correspondingly, without this Kantian distinction between active and passive, there would be no basis for claims that the perceived world is constructed, elaborated, enriched, or built up out of sensations—instead of being discovered or detected by the active brain.[35]

2) The older representationalist tradition has also played a role in perceptual theory, especially in regard to vision. The nature of this role can be seen in Locke's argument concerning the globe, which set the pattern for most theorists of the nineteenth century. Locke draws a conclusion (about what is given) from the features of the retinal image cast by an object. But the image is only one element in the stimulus array. Indeed, it is a distinctive element only from the perspective of an observer looking at the retina, not from that of the perceiver behind it.[36] Why, then, should its attributes determine what can be given? The assumption is intelligible only in the context of the Cartesian theory of ideas.

The correspondence of ideas to reality was supposed to be partly a function of a similarity between their representational contents and the objects they represent. This similarity, in turn, was to be explained in terms of the causal sequence producing the idea. That sequence had therefore to be viewed in a certain way. It could not be regarded simply as a series of physical events, to be understood on their own terms. It had to be seen as the reproduction of a series of physical images of the object, preserving the features of the latter so that the final stage—the idea—might resemble it. The retinal image, then, is one stage in the series, and its features as an image are crucially important. It transpires, of course, that it is a poor reproduction—the third dimension has been lost somewhere, along with the constancies, and other shortcomings were discovered later.

---

35. *Cf.* Eleanor J. Gibson and James J. Gibson, "Perceptual Learning—Differentiation or Enrichment?" *Psychological Review*, LXII (1955), 32–41.

36. *Cf.* James J. Gibson, *Perception of the Visual World* (New York, 1950), 116.

Hence the idea can do no better. What has been lost cannot be regained except by inference, so the idea given us must be two-dimensional and fluctuating.

It is not likely that anyone would still explicitly accept this doctrine concerning the retinal image, or the reasoning behind it. But both survive in a methodological vestige—the use of impoverished stimuli or two-dimensional drawings to test visual capacities. The problem lies not in the use of such stimuli per se but in the inferences drawn from experiments involving them, and the problem can be illustrated by an extreme case. In connection with a drawing of an ambiguous figure, R. L. Gregory argues: "Here perception fluctuates between two possibilities. This is important, for it shows at once that perception is not simply determined by the patterns of excitation at the retina. There must be subtle processes of interpretation." Gregory claims that these examples reveal "the ambiguity of sensory data." Therefore perception "involves a kind of inference from sensory data to object-reality. . . . So perception involves a kind of problem solving—a kind of intelligence."[37]

Consider the logic of this argument. The reversals experienced with ambiguous figures are certainly real phenomena, and although there is at present no satisfactory explanation for them, it is reasonable to suppose that something like interpretation is involved. The reversals can be made voluntary to a degree, and then it does feel as if one is interpreting the figure first as one object, then as another. But why does Gregory generalize from this to the case of normal perception? The only ground he offers is physiological: "Any two-dimensional image could represent an *infinity of possible three-dimensional shapes*."[38] But how is this relevant? In ordinary perception, we do not see two-dimensional images in drawings; we see the three-dimensional world. Gregory must be assuming, then, that even in ordinary perception, the visual system has available to it only the retinal image—the same retinal image that would be provided by a two-dimensional drawing of the object from that perspective. Apart from the representationalist model, there is no basis for this assumption. The features of the retinal image form only one aspect of the total stimulus, and not, apparently, the most important part.

37. R. L. Gregory, *The Intelligent Eye* (New York, 1970), 15, 25, 30.
38. *Ibid.*, 25.

Correspondingly, if the ambiguous figures are constructed as three-dimensional objects, most lose their ambiguity immediately and the rest lose it as soon as one moves. Hence the reasonable hypothesis would be that when certain information normally present in stimulation is missing, we make up for it by elaborating what little *is* given; when the information is there, we need not do this.

The latter point applies more widely. Even with a three-dimensional object as the distal stimulus, it is possible to impoverish the stimulus conditions by reducing illumination, presenting the object against a black background, preventing the subject from moving his head or using both eyes. These conditions eliminate the relational features of the stimulus array which, according to Gibson, are the effective stimuli for depth, slant, and the constancies. One of two things then tends to happen, and each gives rise to a generalization analogous to Gregory's. In most cases, the subject simply does not see depth, slant, constancy; the visual field appears two-dimensional, and the appearance of objects in the field varies in accordance with their retinal images. The generalization is that this is how objects would appear in normal perception were the information in the retinal image not elaborated inferentially by other information present in the normal stimulus—the information eliminated by impoverished conditions. This generalization obviously depends on a representationalist assumption that only the retinal image and its features are genuine stimuli, detectable without inference. Otherwise, there is no basis for discriminating between features of the image and relational features across the array, both of which are effective stimuli in normal cases.

In other cases, however, subjects perceive objects as having constant shapes or sizes, despite variations in their retinal images and despite the elimination of relational features that would specify constancy. This tends to happen when the objects are familiar ones, so that here, as in the ambiguous figures, perception appears to be influenced by interpretation or background knowledge. The problem here lies in generalizing beyond the class of impoverished stimuli. The fact that information normally present is supplied in these cases by background knowledge does not imply that that source is tapped in normal cases, when the information *is* present in the stimulus array. Unlike the generalization in the last paragraph, the faulty inference here does not necessarily depend on a representationalist assumption about the retinal image as stimulus, but it does rely on an analogous premise, as we can see by spelling out the argument.

Gibson claims that in normal conditions, stimulus features uniquely specify the object features we perceive. That is, a given stimulus invariant S is lawfully related to a given object feature O such that S occurs if and only if O is present. What about the relation between S and the perception of O? For S to be an *effective* stimulus, it must actually cause the percept. But there will not in general be a one-one relation between S and the percept. On the one hand, the causation must proceed by means of some neural mechanism for detecting S, and that mechanism may require perceptual learning to develop. On the other hand, there may be cases of impoverished stimulation in which S is absent but the subject still seems to see O. In the latter case, the mechanism of detection is presumably not elicited, and so there must be another mechanism that gives rise to the ostensible awareness of O. Perhaps that other mechanism involves inference from background knowledge; let us assume it does. The important point of this: to assume that because these other processes occur in the impoverished case, they must also occur in the normal one, is to assume that the mechanism of detection elicited by S in the normal case is not sufficient to give rise to the perception of O. But that in turn would imply that S is not after all an *effective* stimulus, and hence that the effective stimulus is the same in normal and in impoverished cases. This is merely a generalized version of the representationalist assumption.[39]

3) At an abstract level, the error of representationalism might be described as the attempt to integrate two aspects of perception— the cognitive and the causal—in an illegitimate way. Thus because the awareness of external objects was analyzed in terms of Cartesian ideas whose contents resemble the objects, the causal sequence was viewed as the reproduction of images. A contemporary version of this same pattern is the information-processing model of percep-

39. This way of formulating the argument was suggested by the concept of an effective stimulus in Jerry Fodor and Zenon Pylyshyn, "How Direct is Visual Perception?" *Cognition*, IX (1981), 172ff. It is not clear whether Fodor and Pylyshyn make the inference criticized in this paragraph; their point seems to be rather that cases of underspecification are more frequent than Gibson allows. But the only evidence they cite is the phenomenon of phoneme restoration. I will discuss this and other cases of alleged cognitive influences on perception later (Chapter 7).

tual integration, which interprets the physiological process not as a sequence of images but as a flow of information being transformed, integrated, processed, stored. The model is constructed, of course, by analogy with the computer. The problem with it arises from taking the analogy literally.

At a minimum, this would mean ascribing intentional content to discrete stages of the neural sequence, *i.e.*, regarding the neural states as *descriptions* of the stimulus or the object.[40] It would also mean treating the causal transition from one stage to another as being in some real sense an inferential transition, governed by rules formulated in terms of the intentional contents. In a computer, such ascription of content is necessary to understand the causal processes that occur. The computer is a human artifact. The settings of its various switches have been assigned a representational content by its programmers—that is a fact of the matter about them. The physical processes of the computer have been organized by its programmers so that physical states representing premises will give rise causally to other physical states representing conclusions. That too is a fact of the matter. Thus one can argue that something is lost if we regard a computer solely in physical terms, on the model of a power station, as a system in which current flows through various circuits as determined by the settings of various switches. The representational content is necessary to understand why those switches have been set that way. There is no programmer present in the nervous system, however, to assign representational content to the firing of nerve cells. And so some other reason must be offered for ascribing content to them.

We have already considered the Kantian reasons that led Helmholtz to believe that perceptual integration must be inferential. We have also considered the Kantian and Cartesian reasons for holding that the stimulus underspecifies the perceived feature of the object, and so must be elaborated by processes sensitive to information. What reason remains for ascribing content? It may well be that the computer is useful as an analogy in trying to understand what neural processes could serve to isolate the stimulus features that are specific to the object features we perceive.[41] But that is not

40. *Cf.* Irvin Rock, *The Logic of Perception* (Cambridge, Mass., 1983), 16.
41. This is Shimon Ullman's major argument in "Against Direct Perception," *Behavioral and Brain Sciences*, III (1980), 373–81.

an argument for ascribing content in any literal sense, for the same strategy may be necessary in understanding the nervous system's regulation of the heartbeat, or the operation of a petroleum refinery, or any system that responds selectively to complex features of its environment.

Jerry Fodor has argued that insofar as Gibson admits the need for neural processing to extract stimulus invariants, he is committed to "the same sorts of inferences from inputs that empiricist [sensationalist] theories assumed"; and that insofar as he denies the existence of such inferences, he is evading the problem of explaining how the invariants are extracted.[42] Either way, Fodor's assumption is that any neural processing is *ipso facto* computational. But that is just what needs to be shown. There is a distinction between physiological and informational integration, and the inference from the one to the other is precisely what is at issue. In their classic receptive-field studies, for example, D. H. Hubel and T. N. Wiesel found cells in the visual pathways that respond only to lines of a certain orientation in the stimulus array. This response can plausibly be explained by synaptic connections among neurons in the pathway, so that the simultaneous firing of certain receptors will cause the higher cells to fire.[43] This is a type of physiological integration, but there is no reason to treat it as a type of inference. There is only the causal connection among neurons.

In a critique of Gibson's theory, Fodor and Zenon Pylyshyn raise a different issue. Even granting that stimulus invariants might be detected noninferentially, they argue, inference is still required to answer the question, "How (by what mental process) does the organism get from the detection of an informative property of the medium to the perception of a correlated property of the environment?" This appears to be yet another instance of the representationalist argument that if we perceive X (a property of the environment) by means of Y (a property of the medium), we must really be

42. Fodor, *Language of Thought*, 49. It should be noted that Gibson gives some grounds for this argument by his use of the term *information*. But information, for him, only means "specificity to something" (*Senses Considered as Perceptual Systems*, 187). On this point, see also Peter Machamer, "Gibson and the Conditions for Perception," in Machamer and Turnbull (eds.), *Studies in Perception*, 440.

43. D. H. Hubel and T. N. Wiesel, "Brain Mechanisms of Vision," *Scientific American*, CCXLI (September, 1979), 150–62.

directly aware of Y and then infer X. If so, the answer I have given before still applies: the awareness of any object must occur by some means; to assume that we can be directly aware only of the means is to assume that awareness must be diaphanous. But remarks elsewhere in Fodor and Pylyshyn's paper suggest that they are making a different point.[44]

To say that perceptual awareness must occur by some physical means is not to explain how the operation of the physical process—in this case, the neurological mechanism that registers the presence of the stimulus invariant—can give rise to the awareness of an object in the external environment. Or rather, I have not explained this fully—and could not, without a theory of how conscious experience in general relates to physiological processes. In short, Fodor and Pylyshyn are raising a mind-body issue, to which I have no general solution. But the inference they posit is no solution either. The general problem is one of understanding how the relational character essential to consciousness—the fact that it is of or about something, that it has a content—can arise from the causal interactions of neurons. One cannot solve this problem by treating the state of awareness in question (*e.g.*, the perceptual awareness of an object's shape) as the conclusion of an inference, with the content of the conclusion derived from the contents of the premises, because then one must explain how the premise (*e.g.*, the "belief" that a certain stimulus feature is present) acquires *its* content from the causal transactions of neurons. The inferential view merely shifts the mind-body problem to a different place in the nervous system, and if my argument is correct, it is the wrong place.[45]

The computer analogy, then, adds nothing to the traditional reasons for accepting an inferential view of perception. But it does not escape the problem that plagued Helmholtz. An inference requires knowledge of the connection between premise and conclusion, and hence an inferential view must explain this knowledge. We saw that Helmholtz had to credit the perceiver with the knowl-

44. Fodor and Pylyshyn, "How Direct is Visual Perception?," 167, 188ff.

45. Fodor and Pylyshyn suggest (*ibid.*, 190) that the content can be ascribed to neurological states on the basis of their functional role. Apart from the fact that this theory remains entirely promissory, it is likely to encounter the same difficulties as other causal theories about the objects of intentional states. I will discuss those theories in Chapter 4.

edge of geometrical optics. More recently, P. H. Lindsay and Donald Norman suggest that the visual discrimination of figures is mediated by cells which, because of the way they are wired to certain receptors, are sensitive to different types of angles in the visual stimulus. The responses of these cells are then integrated in accordance with rules ("a program") to yield a percept of the whole figure. But these rules represent knowledge of the world—knowledge of which angles are normally found in the contours of objects and which are not. Apart from such knowledge, there is no reason to call them rules; they would merely be causal connections, as in Hubel and Wiesel's discovery. The problem is to explain where this knowledge came from, and since some "rules" are necessary for any awareness of external objects, some of this knowledge would have to be innate. It is small wonder that this normally results in the view that "perception is not a passive taking-in of stimuli, but an active process of synthesizing or constructing a visual figure."[46]

I have argued that the basic level of ordinary experience is the perceptual. We perceive entities and their constant attributes, and we perceive them directly. We can of course focus selectively on individual qualities. We will need to do so in discussing issues of sensory qualities in the next chapter, and for the sake of economy of expression I will use the concept of sensation in this context: I will speak of sensations of red as well as of perceptions of red objects. But this does not imply that the awareness of the individual quality occurs in isolation from the perceptual awareness of the object. It is also possible in the laboratory to produce simpler sensory states— the awareness of patches of color, isolated tones, and the like—and I will continue to call them sensations as well. These artifacts of the laboratory yield knowledge about the sensory systems, including an appreciation of how much integration the nervous system must accomplish to produce the perception of whole objects and their invariant properties.

It is clear on phenomenological grounds, however, that such sensations are not the atomic constituents of perception, and that

46. Cf. Rock, Logic of Perception, 15–16; P. H. Lindsay and Donald Norman, Human Information Processing (2nd ed.; New York, 1977), 22–26; Ulric Neisser, Cognitive Psychology (New York, 1967), 16. Neisser has since rejected the processing model for precisely this reason. See his Cognition and Reality (San Francisco, 1976), 15–18.

perception is not the product of conscious cognitive processes which combine or interpret sensations. The only way to support sensationalism, therefore, is to show that such cognitive processes must be posited at an unconscious level in order to explain perception. But we saw that every attempt to justify this hypothesis relied either on an equivocation between physiological and information processing or on a premise to the effect that the stimulus for perception underspecifies the objects we perceive, and must therefore be elaborated by processes that integrate information. And we saw that that premise, in turn, rests on Kantian or Cartesian assumptions, not on an examination of the stimulus itself. Perception, then, is a unitary product of *physiological* causes.

3

Sensory Qualities

The last chapter dealt with what might be called a horizontal issue, the relation between sensation and perception as two modes of awareness. There remains a vertical issue, the relation between an external object and its appearance to a subject—in sensing or perceiving. An appearance is always an appearance to someone, just as a percept is always a perception of something. Appearance and perception are correlative terms, describing, from different directions, the same cognitive relation between subject and object. Yet it is a commonplace that the appearance of an object may vary when the object itself does not. The moon looks larger near the horizon than overhead, food tastes different if one is sick, a healthy face turns ghostly pale under a streetlamp. In these cases, the object appears in a way that is relative to the means by which we perceive it, and such relativity exists in regard to every perceptible attribute of things, in every modality of sense. That fact poses a central problem for the philosophy of perception. As we have seen, for example, perceptual relativity was widely used by modern philosophers to support representationalism in perception. They turned appearance from a relation between subject and object into a separate object of awareness constituting a veil that prevents us from perceiving external objects after all.

To avoid this misuse of the facts of perceptual relativity, contemporary philosophers have often tried to explain them away. J. L. Austin, for example, dismissed the argument from perceptual relativity as the product of linguistic confusion, criticizing the misuse of *real* and *delusive* in arguments such as the following, from A. J. Ayer: "If I gradually approach an object from a distance I may begin by having a series of perceptions which are delusive in the sense that the object appears to be smaller than it really is." Austin was certainly right that there is nothing at all delusive about this phenomenon. But Ayer's mistake is not really linguistic. It is the assumption he makes, inspired by the diaphanous model, that a veridical perception of an object's size must somehow reproduce that size. Given the assumption, *delusive* is an appropriate word choice. The problem, in other words, lies in the philosophical interpretation of the facts of relativity, and indeed the core of Austin's own counterargument consists in a number of penetrating and nonlinguistic objections to Ayer's interpretation.[1] The critique of the traditional argument, however, still leaves us with the need to formulate an alternative account of the facts, and this Austin did not provide.

One linguistic point made by Austin and others is that the term *appears* (or *looks*, *sounds*, etc.) sometimes refers to an inclination to believe or judge something about an object. "This looks red to me" sometimes means "I am inclined to believe it *is* red, though I'm not sure" or "I would be inclined, though I know better." In this context, the term does not pick out any phenomenal quality that is relative to the perceiver; it indicates the perceiver's hesitation in judging something about the qualities of the object itself. Accordingly, some philosophers have tried to dispense with the phenomenal aspect of appearance, and the problem of relativity it poses, by claiming that appearances are nothing but inclinations to believe propositions about external objects.[2] In some cases, this view was inspired by the thesis that all awareness is conceptual, so that any cognitive dimension of perceiving must be analyzed in propositional terms—a thesis whose roots we will explore in Chapter 6. Apart from that

1. A. J. Ayer, *Foundations of Empirical Knowledge* (London, 1940), 8; J. L. Austin, *Sense and Sensibilia* (Oxford, 1962), 45, Chap. V.

2. This view is defended by George Pitcher, *A Theory of Perception* (Princeton, 1971); D. M. Armstrong, *Perception and the Physical World* (London, 1961); and Wilfrid Sellars, "Empiricism and the Philosophy of Mind," in *Science, Perception and Reality* (London, 1963), 127–96.

thesis, the only positive argument ever offered for the view is that it provides a way to avoid the introduction of sense-data, sense impressions, or other versions of the veil of perception. But it is certainly not reasonable to ignore the phenomenal aspects of perceptual relativity in order to avoid an unwanted explanation of them; nor do they require any such explanation once we have rejected the diaphanous model.[3]

With few exceptions, then, contemporary philosophers have skirted the problem of perceptual relativity, or else they have adopted some variant of the representationalist solution to it. My critique of that solution will occupy the next chapter. Here, I will try to isolate in neutral terms just what the facts of perceptual relativity are, and then show how they can be understood in light of a concept of perceptual form. With that foundation, we can go on to consider the problematic status of sensory qualities such as colors, and the traditional distinction between primary and secondary qualities.[4]

Form and Object

As a result chiefly of the representationalist tradition, the concept of phenomenal appearance has acquired an almost inexpungible connotation of subjectivity, appearances being conceived as effects of objects on a perceiver's consciousness. So strong is the connotation that the admission of the concept has seemed tantamount to accepting a representationalist veil of perception, and it is understandable that those who would reject the latter have tried to dispense with the former. We need to untie this connection if we are going to develop a realist alternative, and the only way to do so is

3. See especially Armstrong, *Perception and the Physical World*, 89–90; and Pitcher, *Theory of Perception*, 61–62. For a critique of Pitcher and Armstrong, see Alan Goldman, "Appearing as Irreducible in Perception," *Philosophy and Phenomenological Research*, XXXVII (1976), 147–64; and my "Specificity of Perception," *Philosophy and Phenomenological Research*, XL (1980), 401–405.

4. A recent article by Maurice Charlesworth, "Sense-Impressions: A New Model," *Mind*, LXXXVIII (1979), 24–44, is one such exception. See also Anthony Quinton, "The Problem of Perception," and G. N. A. Vesey, "Seeing and Seeing As," both in Robert Swartz (ed.), *Perceiving, Sensing, and Knowing* (Garden City, N.Y., 1965), 497–526, 68–83. The concept of form and the view of perception it expresses were originated by Ayn Rand.

to form the concept of appearance from the beginning, to see what it is in perceptual experience that forces us speak, not merely about the way things are, but also about the way they look, sound, feel, taste, and smell. If anything we discover forces us to interpret appearances as mental or subjective facts, so be it; but we will not start with that assumption.

The way an object appears is a joint product of the object itself and of the means by which we perceive it. But we have no *perceptual* way of distinguishing the contributions of these two causes. We are certainly not aware of two items, the object and the appearance. When I look at the ashtray across the desk, I see a single, unitary form in my visual field. It is true that in one sense the ashtray looks round and in another it looks elliptical. But it is crucial to be clear about what this difference comes to. I do not have two shapes before me. My ability to switch from the normal perceptual focus to a reductive one is an ability to grasp two *relationships* in the same visual field. In one respect, what I see is similar to other round things seen from various angles. In another respect, it is similar to other round or elliptical objects that have the same projection on a plane perpendicular to my line of sight.

Normally we do not notice the second axis of similarity; we have no reason to. But even when we do, we do not have any direct awareness of a dependence on our own senses. We still experience the world as a unitary field of objects, possessing various qualities and relationships, all external to our awareness of them. Noticing the second axis of similarity serves only to isolate a certain aspect of the field which we are forced to *interpret*, in light of what we know about the objects themselves (from noticing the first axis, or from background knowledge), as an effect of the way we perceive them. On the one hand, we can notice that things are similar in a respect in which we know they are not similar in themselves, *e.g.*, an ellipse in the perpendicular plane and a circle seen at a slant, or a thumb held at arm's length and a tree in the distance. On the other hand, we can notice that a single object is different at different times (in different conditions, to different perceivers) in a respect in which we know it has not changed, *e.g.*, the circular ashtray as we move around it. Or we can notice that two objects differ in a respect in which we know they do not differ in themselves, *e.g.*, two sheets of white paper, one in sunlight and the other in shade. In these ways we can isolate those aspects of the field which, on the basis of background knowledge about objects, we know are relative to factors outside the objects themselves; and we use concepts of appearance to describe them. The ashtray looks elliptical, the paper in shadow looks gray. Hence it is no accident that appearances exhibit such relativity, for it is only when we notice the relativity that we are led to form the concept of appearance. (It is also worth recalling that the existence of relativity could not possibly place the existence of an external world in doubt, since it is only knowledge about external objects which forces us to interpret certain similarities and differences as being merely apparent.)

We can, of course, go on to identify the causal factors, external to the objects themselves, to which appearances are thus relative. Some of those factors are themselves observable, such as the angle from which we see an object, the level of illumination, the motion of an ambulance whose siren seems to change pitch. Others, including all those having to do with the conditions of our own perceptual systems, we know about less directly—dizziness, for example, or prior adaptation to stimulation. We thus have a body of common knowledge about the effects, on the way things appear, of conditions external to the things themselves; and this knowledge is woven into our ordinary concepts of perceptible attributes. Psychophysical measurements expand this knowledge in certain directions, even though they deal with more rudimentary modes of sensory awareness, in conditions of impoverished stimulation. They discriminate more finely among the dimensions in which appearances can vary—such as the hue, brightness, and saturation of colors—and they establish more detailed correspondences between those dimensions and the attributes of physical stimuli. The study of the sensory neural mechanisms takes us even further, in ways we will explore.

Such, then, are the facts of perceptual relativity. We do not experience appearances as distinct from external objects, but we do notice patterns of similarity and difference, among the objects we perceive, that are not intrinsic to the objects themselves. And we can explain these patterns by reference to causal factors in the processes by which we perceive. In ordinary life, we make our way among these facts well enough by means of the concept of appearance. But that concept has too many uses, answering to the varied needs of

ordinary discourse, and too long a history of misuse by philosophers, to serve us well in providing a philosophical account of the
facts. I will therefore introduce the concept of perceptual form, to
designate those aspects of the way an object appears which are determined by the manner in which our senses respond to the object
in the particular conditions at hand. Thus if perception and appearance are correlatives, the *form* in which we perceive an object is the
correlative term for the *relative* aspects of appearance, and *form* will
give us a verbal means of referring individually to those aspects. I
will say, then, that we perceive the ashtray's shape in different forms
as we view it from different angles; that we perceive an object's color
in different forms as the illumination varies; that we perceive the
temperature of the water in different forms when our hands are differently adapted to prior stimulation; and so on.

Given what I have said so far about perceptual relativity, it is
clear that we have two methods for isolating particular forms of perception. From the inside, we can notice the respects in which the
field we are directly aware of varies in a way not assignable to the
objects themselves. It is not that we can identify particular attributes as forms. We cannot say, for example, that shape as such is a
variable aspect of the objects we perceive, and thus a form in which
we perceive them. What we notice is that some of the relationships
among objects *in virtue of* their shapes are variable while some are
not. We will therefore have to speak in a highly abstract way about
aspects or dimensions of the attributes we perceive in objects. In addition, we cannot expect that every dimension of perceptual relativity will reveal itself to us from the inside. The examples mentioned
so far are dimensions of relativity that result from variations in the
particular conditions of perception at a given moment, but there may
well be deeper levels at which appearances are relative to the basic
unchanging nature of our perceptual apparatus. These could only
be discovered from the outside, by studying the causal process of
perceiving. The concept of perceptual form must therefore be regarded as open-ended, as a framework for identifying successive
levels of relativity as we acquire evidence of them, including those
to which we have no phenomenological clue.

The possibility of isolating perceptual forms, however, does not
mean that we experience them in isolation, and there are two crucial
points to be made in this regard. The first is that isolating a form re-

quires a process of selective attention to an object perceived as a whole. Objects appear as entities, not as collections of unintegrated attributes, so there is a unity among the forms in which we perceive their attributes. But there is also a narrower point concerning the constancy functions, which, as we have seen, are essential to our perception of entities. A form is a product of the way a perceptual system responds to stimulation, but the forms isolated thus far as examples are variable features of appearances, reflecting variable features of the stimuli for the attributes perceived by means of those forms. And we saw that the perception of a given attribute in an object is mediated by *invariants* in the stimulus array. That fact is reflected in the constancy phenomena: despite the variable form in the visual field, the ashtray in another sense looks round from any angle, the paper looks white in sunlight or shade. This is another reason why perceptual relativity is rarely noticed in ordinary experience, and we need to see how the concept of form applies to it.

The ashtray looks elliptical, in a certain respect, because of the shape of its retinal image. But that shape is only one aspect of the stimulus feature relevant to the perception of shape in external objects. If James J. Gibson is right, for example, there is a higher-order invariant relationship between the variable shape of the image and the variables specifying slant.[5] That relationship is paralleled in the form with which we perceive shape. I see the ashtray in a unified total form, aware at once of its shape, slant, and other features. The variable ellipse is nested within an overall appearance of the ashtray at any moment, determined by my visual system's overall response, which includes its response to the invariant features of the optic array. The way the object appears changes in certain respects as I move around, but is invariant in others. Thus perceptual constancy does not mean that one experiences a constant object through a shifting haze of appearances that float in front of it; it means there is a unity among the transformations in appearance as conditions vary.

So long as any aspect of an object's appearance remains invariant in this way, we have no phenomenological reason for regarding the invariant dimension as a form of perception. But constancy

5. James J. Gibson, "A Theory of Direct Visual Perception," in J. Royce and W. Rozeboom (eds.), *The Psychology of Knowing* (New York, 1972), 215–27.

mechanisms function only within certain ranges of conditions, the ones we call normal conditions of perception. In abnormal conditions, many normally invariant aspects of an object's appearance do vary, resulting in what we call perceptual illusions. In all normal conditions of perception, for example, a stick has an invariant straight look about it, but when it is placed in water, the refraction of light makes it look different in just that respect. Thus illusions reveal a deeper level of perceptual relativity. They force us to isolate certain normally invariant aspects of appearances as variable forms in which we perceive the attributes of things. The normal "straight look" of the stick is revealed as a form in which we normally perceive physical straightness, the absence of angles or curvature; it is revealed as such by contrast with the form in which we perceive that shape in abnormal conditions. Conversely, the illusory "bent look" is a case, not of nonveridical perception, but of perceiving physical straightness in an unusual form.

The latter statement, however, is likely to inspire some protest. When the stick looks bent, how can we be perceiving its straightness? In order to answer, I need to make explicit an interpretation of the facts of perceptual relativity that has been implicit all along in the concept of form. First, the form in which we perceive an object is not subjective or "in the mind" in any sense. Second, the form is not an object of awareness, or an intrinsic feature of any inner object, but the means by which we are aware of the external object and its attributes. Third, we can perceive the same object, and the same attributes of objects, in different forms. Each claim requires some elaboration.

1) A form of perception is obviously not subjective in the ordinary, commonsense meaning of the term—it is not something we make up arbitrarily, something we see because we want to see it. It is an inexorable causal product of the interaction among the object perceived, the physical organs of perception, and the external conditions in which they operate. Of course, that commonsense meaning is not what philosophers have had in mind when they called appearances subjective. They have given the term more technical meanings, based on conceptions of physical reality and models of mind in relation to it. This is not the place to review these theories, since our primary interest in perceptual relativity is epistemologi-

cal, not metaphysical. But there are two essential points to be made here.

A form of perception is not "in the mind" in the only phenomenological sense we can give that phrase. It is not in or an aspect of our direct awareness of objects. We experience it on the side of the objects perceived, as the form in which they appear. Phenomenologically, we are not aware of appearances in addition to external objects; we experience a unitary field of objects. And it is only against those objects that we can distinguish our awareness of them and give a meaning to the "in here" as opposed to the "out there." Of course, the facts of perceptual relativity show that forms are not intrinsic properties the objects possess apart from us. As products of the interaction between the objects and our senses, forms are relational features of what we perceive. And that is the basis of the second point. Relational features by nature cannot be located in—as intrinsic attributes of—any of the relevant *relata*. The weight of an object (unlike its mass), for example, is not in the object apart from the earth, or in the earth as opposed to the object; it cannot, in this sense, be located at all. Analogously, the elliptical look of my ashtray is not in me or in my awareness apart from the ashtray, or in the ashtray apart from me, or somewhere in between.[6] It is the very shape of the ashtray, as seen from here.

But what about the privacy of appearances to perceivers? The form in which a subject perceives an object is something directly observable only by him. No one else is aware of it in the way he is. A scientist studying a perceptual system is of course himself a perceiver, so that he sees the objects he presents to the subject, and sees them in specific forms. But he has no direct access to the way those objects look to the subject. The scientist must rely on some report from the subject, such as a judgment of similarity between the test object and a standard. This disparity in access to a phenomenon, this "privileged access," has often been regarded as a criterion for saying that the phenomenon is mental. But the criterion does not apply in this case—or, rather, the case shows that the criterion is not decisive. We are asking how an object appears to a subject. Its appearing the way it does is a fact in the world, produced by physical causes. The subject does not have the same cognitive access to this

6. *Cf.* Hans Reichenbach, *Experience and Prediction* (Chicago, 1938), 167.

fact that other people have; in this respect an appearance is unlike other facts in the world. But this is not because it is a mental fact or because his awareness of it is introspective. It is because the subject is a part of the fact in a way that no one else is. He *is* the perceptual system that interacts with the object to produce an appearance of it. It is not surprising, then, that he has a different mode of access to the appearance.

The outside observer can certainly acquire the same conceptual grasp of the facts that the subject can, for both *know* that the subject is perceiving a given object in a given form. What the external observer cannot do is *perceive* the form in which the subject perceives the object. But of course he cannot. It is a category mistake to suggest that he could, a mistake that can be exposed without any reference to the mental. The observer sees the external object himself, in a form determined by the conditions in which he perceives. To see the form in which the subject perceives it, he would therefore have to see the form as a separate object. The form would have to be something which can be seen; that is, it would have to reflect light and be perceivable in a form. But that is incoherent. The form in which the subject perceives the object is a dimension of a relationship between him and the object, not an object in its own right. One would have to reify the form into a separate object of awareness before one could argue that because only one person can be aware of it, it must be a mental object. And it is not a separate object of awareness—a point which brings us to the second thesis.

2) As I said at the outset, appearance and perception are correlative concepts. When we perceive an object, it is the object itself that appears and is discriminated from its background as a unit with a distinctive identity. But now we have found that various aspects of the way it appears, in respect of the attributes constituting its identity, are relative to our means of perceiving it. To reconcile this fact with our awareness of the object as it is in itself, we appeal to the fundamental principles used throughout. We have no diaphanous access to the world; the concept of such access is incoherent. We perceive by specific means, a fact which requires that we distinguish between *what* we perceive and the *way* we perceive. And when we identify some feature of perception as an aspect of the way we perceive, only the diaphanous model could justify our treating it as the real object of awareness, standing between us and the external

object. We have seen that physiologically, perception must involve the response of sensory systems to features in the stimulus arrays that are specific to the external attributes perceived; and on basic realist principles, I rejected the argument that we must therefore really be directly aware only of the stimulus feature. The same argument applies to the aspects of appearances we have identified as forms. Indeed, it is simply an extension of the argument. The variable forms in which we perceive an object are effects of variations in the physiological means by which we perceive, and therefore *must* be regarded as features of the way we perceive. It is this very fact—that forms of perception are physiologically determined—which tells us they are not objects of perceptual awareness, but aspects of the way we are aware of attributes in the external object.

Consider the following passage from C. D. Broad, in which he is preparing the way for the introduction of sense-data:

> The difficulty is to reconcile the different appearances with the supposed constancy of the penny, and the ellipticity of most of the appearances with the supposed roundness of the penny. It is probable that at first sight the reader will not see much difficulty in this. He will be inclined to say that we can explain these various visual appearances by the laws of perspective, and so on. This is not a relevant answer. It is quite true that we can *predict what particular appearance* an object will present to an observer, when we know the shape of the object and its position with respect to the observer. But this is not the question that is troubling us at present. Our question is as to the compatibility of these changing elliptical appearances, however they may be correlated with other facts in the world, with the supposed constancy and roundness of the physical object.

The argument offers a nearly pure example of the effects of the diaphanous model on reasoning about perception. Once we can explain and predict how the penny will appear, by reference to the laws of perspective, what question is left to trouble us—apart from the assumption that our perception of a constant object cannot vary no matter how we vary our position? Once we have correlated variations in appearance with changes in position, what further problem remains of correlating appearance with object—apart from the assumption that the appearance ought to reproduce the object as though in a mirror? It is only the diaphanous model, with its a priori assumption about how perception must work if it is to be valid, that could lead one to dismiss in this way the causal explanation of how it does work. If we reject the model, then the point that Broad puts in the mouth of his reader is the whole truth of the matter.[7]

Thus the forms in which we perceive an object, like the stimulus features or physiological processes in perception, are aspects of the way we perceive. The first are no more the objects of awareness than are the second, and the same philosophical argument applies to both. There is of course a phenomenological difference here. In a sense, we *are* directly aware of the form, whereas we are not perceptually aware in any sense of the physiological factors. But there is no phenomenological basis for saying that we are aware of the form *as opposed to* the external attribute of the thing perceived. A form is only a respect in which an object's appearance is causally dependent on factors external to the object. Certain forms can be isolated phenomenologically, as we have seen, by distinguishing variable from invariable dimensions of an appearance. In these cases, it is particularly clear that a form is merely a dimension of the way objects appear in respect of their attributes, not a separate qualitative content. When I note that a tree in the distance looks the same size (in one respect) as my thumb held at arm's length, what *is* that size? It is the size of the tree itself, and the thumb itself, as they look from here. I could not reify that aspect into a separate object of awareness, without ignoring or denying the other respect, equally evident to me, in which they look very different in regard to size.

There are other dimensions of appearances which we cannot isolate phenomenologically in this way, but which nevertheless can be shown to be dependent on the physical processes of perception, and which must therefore be identified as forms of perception. In these cases, there is no phenomenological basis whatever for saying that we are aware only of the form, and not of the external attribute we discriminate by means of it—as we shall see in the case of colors. In either case, what we perceive is the attribute-in-a-form; a form is an aspect of the way an object appears in regard to an attribute.

3) A direct corollary is that we can perceive the same objects and attributes in different forms. That, after all, is what happens in any case of perceptual relativity. The same determinate characteristic of an object is perceived in forms that vary in familiar ways with the

7. C. D. Broad, *Scientific Thought* (New York, 1923), 235–36.

conditions of perception. But the same thing occurs when the conditions are unusual, and the form varies in the ways we regard as illusory. Let us now return to the bent stick in water.

When a person sees a stick that is half in water, it looks bent. But he still sees the stick. He also sees the shape of the stick—the whole contour is visible to him. And in fact the shape is straight. Hence what the person sees is a straight shape in an unusual form. That form is apt to be misleading, and the person may make the wrong perceptual *judgment* about it, since our concepts for the perceptible attributes of things are tied to the forms with which we normally perceive them. But such illusions are not failures of *perceptual* awareness. There is—there could be—no such thing as a nonveridical percept. The normal look of the stick and the refracted look are simply two different forms in which one can perceive the same external attribute. Both are potential effects the object has in virtue of its intrinsic shape; either can be actualized, depending on conditions; either allows us to discriminate the actual shape from different ones.

Psychologists, for example, have experimented with lenses that refract all incoming light in this way, altering the apparent shapes of all figures. After a period of disorientation, subjects adjust to this new form of perception, coming to experience it as normal and regaining the ability to discriminate the presence or absence of angles and curvature in the objects themselves. The adjustment does involve some compensating activity that makes the objects look less bent than at first—it is an adjustment back toward the old form of perceiving them. But this compensation is never complete, and is not apparently very significant. The chief adjustment seems to involve simply getting used to the new look of things, learning to identify objects and move among them in terms of a new form of perception.[8]

8. For summaries of the experiments with distorting lenses, see Eleanor J. Gibson, *Principles of Perceptual Learning and Development* (Englewood Cliffs, N. J., 1969), Chap. 10; and Robert B. Welch, *Perceptual Modification* (New York, 1978), Chap. 9. Because the retina is a curved surface, there is a respect in which, even in ordinary vision, the visual field conforms to a Riemannian geometry, not the Euclidean geometry of the external world. We see a quadrilateral figure, for example, in such a way that its internal angles are greater than 360 degrees. See R. B. Angell, "The Geometry of Visibles," *Nous*, VIII (1974), 87–117.

In addition to illusions, there is a more familiar example of the phenomenon—the "common sensibles," attributes that can be perceived through more than one sense modality. I can feel as well as see the size of an object, for example. The form in which I am aware of that attribute differs more radically between the modalities than it does within either; yet I am aware of the size in both cases. Here again we can perceive the same attribute in different forms. Any form that allows us to discriminate the attribute is a form in which we can be aware of it, and no form is more or less right or valid than another. To be sure, a given form of perception may not allow one to discriminate degrees of an attribute with as much specificity as another. I can tell a quarter from a nickle by sight but not by touch. But we always perceive an attribute with *some* finite specificity, and are aware of the attribute as long as we perceive it with *any* specificity.[9] Different forms of perception may also make different axes of similarity among objects accessible at the perceptual level, so that perceivers with different sense organs might begin by forming different concepts, classifying objects in different ways. But they would still be aware of the same objective world, and they would recognize that fact once they reached the scientific level and could classify objects in abstraction from the forms in which they perceive them (a point considered at greater length in Chapter 7).

The concept of form, then, provides a general theory of perceptual relativity, a theory that integrates the causal with the cognitive dimensions of perceiving, in a manner consistent with the primacy of existence. The discussion thus far, however, has been highly abstract, designed to apply to all the varieties of relativity. So let us now consider a particular case, that of color.

There is another reason for discussing color in particular at greater length. So far I have dealt only with the types of perceptual relativity identifiable at the commonsense level, arising from variations in the determinate state of the conditions of perception. Correspondingly, the forms identified so far have been *quantitative* dimensions along which appearances can vary independently of the object. A tree will look larger or smaller, depending on our distance

9. Most subjects are better at matching a test shape to a standard shape if both are seen than if one is seen and the other felt; but the tactile-visual matches are better than the tactile-tactile ones. See Lawrence Marks, *The Unity of the Senses* (New York, 1978), 21–22, for a review of the experimental evidence.

from it; water will feel warmer or colder, depending on prior adaptation. But scientific knowledge about physical objects seems to show a much more radical sort of dependence on our means of perceiving. At the commonsense level, for example, we know that the apparent color of leaves varies in one respect with the illumination, though the operation of the constancy mechanisms makes them look invariant in another respect. But there are scientific reasons for thinking that the attribute of the leaf itself in virtue of which it looks the way it does is the atomic structure of its chlorophyll, which causes it to absorb certain wavelengths of light and reflect others. Thus it seems that even in its invariant aspect, the sensory quality green— the quality we experience as a cool color—is in part a product of our visual system, and thus a form of perception. We need to see how the concept of perceptual form applies to this deeper level of relativity. It should be emphasized, however, that the reasons for taking this view of colors are entirely scientific. Nothing in the concept of form as such implies that colors are forms of perception, that they do not exist in objects apart from us. The concept is only a framework within which we can assimilate the scientific evidence for thinking so.

Colors

The view that colors do not exist in external objects apart from perceivers has been common since the scientific revolution of the Renaissance, based less on hard evidence than on an intuition that colors (and analogous qualities in the other modalities) are not on a par ontologically with the attributes of mass, extension, motion, and the like. That intuition was formalized in Locke's distinction between primary and secondary qualities, and it is probably still shared by a majority of scientists and philosophers. Locke's positive theory about the location of colors and other secondary qualities—that they exist as the inner, representational content of sensations—is also still widely accepted. The evidence for saying that colors do not exist in objects apart from us is taken to mean that they are subjective, the contents of mental states. Indeed, colors as phenomenal qualities are often taken as paradigms of the mental. Here again, as with appearances in general, we need to look at the facts without any such presuppositions, and then ask how they are best conceptualized.

There are two sets of facts to be integrated, pertaining to the physical and physiological bases of color and to the psychology of color vision. When we examine both sets of facts, and then consider how the basic realist approach should be applied to them, we will find they are best conceptualized in terms of perceptual form.

The stimulus for color vision is light, and it arrives at the eye by various routes: directly from luminous sources, by reflection from mirrors, by diffraction from particles in the air, by passage through translucent substances, and by reflection from the surfaces of opaque objects. In the last case, the light is altered by the surface, and various properties of the surface determine the way it is altered; I will call them reflectance properties. To understand them in functional terms, one can plot the proportion of incident light that is reflected for each wavelength of light.[10] An object with a high reflectance at each wavelength will look white; it will look black if the reverse is true. The chromatic colors—red, yellow, green, blue, and their combinations—occur because some objects reflect different proportions of light at different wavelengths. But this gives us only a dispositional concept of reflectance properties, as capacities to reflect light. What are the actual properties in virtue of which objects have those capacities? Of the various properties involved, the basic level is the atomic structure of the surface, in particular the arrangement of electrons in shells around the nuclei of the various atoms in the surface. These are chiefly responsible for the differential reflection of light, and thus for colors.

But no matter how the light arrives as a stimulus, the visual system responds to it in essentially the same way (so far as color is concerned). The evidence indicates that two basic stages are involved, beginning with the receptors themselves. There appear to be three light-sensitive pigments in the retina, each contained in a different type of cone. Each pigment absorbs some light at every wavelength but the amount absorbed differs with wavelength, and each pigment has a different wavelength-absorption function. Thus light at any wavelength on the spectrum gives rise to a specific triad of responses from the cones. The triad is unique to that wavelength, although the proper mixture of three other wavelengths, at different intensities, can produce the same triad and will look the same.

10. This is called a spectral reflectance curve. Examples for a variety of common objects are given in Gunter Wyszecki and W. S. Stiles, *Color Science* (New York, 1967), 181–82.

In that sense, the eye is a very limited instrument for resolving wavelengths.[11]

It is a matter of some controversy how the output of the cones is processed, but the evidence seems to favor a system of "opponent" responses. These are neural mechanisms receiving input from the receptors; they are called opponent because they have a resting level of activity that can be either increased or decreased by that input. Thus a white-black system receives positive input from all three types of cones; it registers the general level of luminance. Red-green and blue-yellow systems, by contrast, are affected positively by some cones and negatively by others; their responses are therefore complicated products of the light absorption by different pigments, and vary markedly with wavelength. The attractiveness of the opponent theory is its ability to explain a number of color phenomena.[12] For our purposes, however, only two are important.

The first is that all the colors we experience are experienced as mixtures of the six primary colors posited by the theory. The spectral colors are mixtures of red, yellow, green, and blue. None of these can be reduced further to any combination of the others. The other, nonspectral colors can be obtained by adding black or white. Brown, for example, is a mixture of orange and black, pink a mixture of red and white. There is no physical reason why light should be experienced in the form of just these six primaries—the spectrum is a continuous band of electromagnetic energy. But the fact *is* explained by these neural mechanisms. Second, normal subjects agree fairly well on the location of the pure hues on the spectrum: pure blue at around 465 nanometers, green at 505, yellow at 575.[13] Again,

11. Robert Boynton, "Color Vision," in J. W. Kling and L. A. Riggs (eds.), *Experimental Psychology* (3rd ed.; New York, 1972), 315–68; Gerald S. Wasserman, *Color Vision* (New York, 1978), Chap. 7. For some wavelengths, matching requires that two of the other wavelengths be mixed and the third added to the given wavelength. For an excellent theoretical explanation of these facts, see T. N. Cornsweet, *Visual Perception* (New York, 1970), 155–75.

12. See Wasserman, *Color Vision*, Chap. 6, for a summary of these phenomena. The modern opponent theory derives from the work of L. M. Hurvich and D. Jameson, "An Opponent Process Theory of Color Vision," *Psychological Review*, LXIV (1957), 384–404.

13. There is no pure red on the spectrum. It can be obtained, however, by mixing red from the long end of the spectrum, which contains some yellow, with blue-red from the short end. The blue and yellow will cancel each other if the intensities are adjusted properly.

there is nothing in the physical stimulus that makes these wave-lengths special. The reason a unique hue is experienced at 505 na-nometers is that the yellow-blue system is at the zero point there, leaving only the contribution of the red-green system. This in turn is to be explained by the mathematical relations between the cones and the opponent processes, a matter of their neurological wiring.

The foregoing outline of the physical bases of color is enough to show that if this scientific account is true, colors are dependent on the visual systems of perceivers and do not exist in objects apart from them. We can explain the various attributes of color only by reference to the physiological mechanisms of color vision. These mechanisms explain not only the *awareness* of color and the varia-tions in experienced color with changes in the illumination, but also the attributes of color itself, in particular the existence of just six pri-mary hues across the spectrum and the location of the pure hues. There is nothing in the objects themselves, or in the light they re-flect, that would account for this. If so, there is no reason for attrib-uting colors to objects apart from our visual systems. Our only rea-son for believing in colors is that we perceive them. And if, in examining that mode of perception, we find that the intrinsic prop-erty of objects to which the senses are responding is a reflectance property, we have no reason left for attributing sensory colors to those objects, except as relational features, dependent on our re-sponse to the reflectance properties. Nor have scientists found that physical objects have any sort of causal influence on each other that would require them to posit intrinsic color properties. So far as we know, the scientific account of the inanimate world is complete (or can be completed) without the introduction of intrinsic colors.[14]

Of course, we have been assuming that sensory colors are at-tributes distinct from any reflectance properties, on the ground that the latter, as dispositions, are to be identified with atomic structures and other microscopic features of surfaces. But it may be suggested that sensory color can nevertheless be identified with those fea-

14. See Frank Jackson, *Perception* (Cambridge, England, 1977), 121–28; and Morland Perkins, *Sensing the World* (Indianapolis, 1983), 237–38. Nothing in current physics, however, makes it *impossible* for colors to exist intrinsically in objects above and beyond the properties we have scientific evidence for. See James Cornman, ''Can Eddington's 'Two' Tables Be Identical?'' *Australasian Journal of Philosophy*, LII (1974), 22–38. But attributing intrinsic colors to objects would still be an arbitrary posit.

tures. A full discussion of this view would require an analysis of the conditions for treating apparently different attributes of things as identical, a complex matter. As it happens, however, there is a simpler way to see that the supposition is false. For a given color property to be identified with any property of objects definable without reference to the visual system, the latter property would at least have to be coextensive with every experience of that color. And there is no such external property, no single attribute of things with which color can be correlated. In conditions of impoverished stimulation, a given color is the visual system's response to features of the light impinging on the retina. In normal perception, it is the response to reflectance properties of objects, regardless of the light they are actually reflecting to the retina. In other modes of color vision, it is a response to the diffractive properties of particles or the light-emitting properties of luminescent bodies. Thus color could at best be identified only with a disjunctive property embracing all of these, but the only single feature uniting the disjuncts would be that the visual system responds to them in the same way. It is clear once again that sensory color—the unitary quality we directly experience—is dependent on us and is distinct from any intrinsic feature of objects.[15]

But what does all this tell us about the status of colors? We know that color cannot be located in external objects as an intrinsic property, since it depends on a relationship. Thus Aristotle was right in saying that the occurrence of color is a joint actualization of a capacity in external objects and a capacity in the perceiver, so that objects have the quality only in a potential sense when unperceived.[16] In this respect, color may be considered a relational property of the object, analogous to weight as opposed to mass. But the facts do not justify locating color anywhere else. When an object looks red, the red is not in the light, the eye, or the nervous system. And we cer-

15. See Keith Campbell, "Colours," in Robert Brown and C. D. Rollins (eds.), *Contemporary Philosophy in Australia* (London, 1969), 132–46. Campbell goes too far, however, in arguing that objects with the same reflectance property have different perceived colors (with different illuminations). One aspect of perceived color changes with illumination while another does not. Constancy mechanisms make objects with the same reflectance property look alike in this second respect.

16. Aristotle, *De Anima*, trans. D. W. Hamlyn (Oxford, 1968), Book III, Chap. 2.

tainly have no basis for saying it exists in the *mind* of the perceiver. The facts show only that it results from the interaction of two physical systems, the external environment of objects and light, and the physiology of a perceiver.[17] Indeed, as the product of an interaction, color cannot be located anywhere, as an intrinsic property of some participant in that interaction—any more than the weight of an object or the violence of an automobile collision can be so located.

We have examined color so far from the standpoint of the physical scientist studying a physical interaction. But one element in the interaction is the nervous system, a faculty of conscious awareness. There is thus another perspective on color, that of the perceptual subject. We can hardly say that this cognitive standpoint is less valid or informative than that of the physical scientist. On the contrary, the latter relies on the subject's report of color to establish his own conclusions about the causal basis. To know even that color depends on the visual and not the auditory system requires testimony from the subject. We must therefore examine the psychology of color vision.

Because light is structured in different ways on its path to the eye, there are different modes of color vision, classified by the Optical Society of America into five categories. The simplest is *film* color, which is produced in such a way that it cannot be seen as the color of any surface. For example, a screen with a small aperture (a reduction screen) is placed before the subject, and objects behind it are more brightly lit than the screen. If it is arranged so that the subject cannot focus through the aperture on the objects behind it, he will see the color of what is behind the screen, but will experience it as a textureless, two-dimensional expanse of color. It will not be seen as the color of any surface, or as being any particular distance away. And the color will vary in close correspondence with the character of the light coming through the aperture—its hue with the wavelength, brightness with intensity.[18]

17. To be sure, if the term *physical* is reserved for attributes employed by contemporary physics in its account of inanimate matter, then colors are not physical. *Cf.* P. E. Meehl and Wilfrid Sellars, "The Concept of Emergence," in Herbert Feigl and Michael Scriven (eds.), *Minnesota Studies in the Philosophy of Science* (Minneapolis, 1956), I, 239–52. But to define the term *physical* this narrowly is to remove any justification for regarding everything nonphysical as mental.

18. Committee on Colorimetry, Optical Society of America, *The Science of Color* (New York, 1953), 146; Jacob Beck, *Surface Color Perception* (Ithaca, 1972), 17–19.

The film mode of color vision is closer to sensation than to perception; the other modes are clearly perceptual. One is the perception of *illuminant* color when a person looks directly at a light source.
More important for our purposes is *illumination* color, the perception of light in the environment. The most vivid example is the shaft
of sunlight one sees when dust is in the air. But one can also discriminate the illumination, including its wavelength composition,
by such things as shadows and reflections from glossy surfaces. One
is normally sensitive to the general level of illumination, as opposed
to the amount of light reflected from any one object. There remain
two modes connected with physical objects: *volume* color, seen as
occupying the volume of a transparent or translucent object; and
surface color.

Psychologists have noted that surface color differs markedly
from film color in two respects. First, although surface color has the
dimensions of film color—such as hue and brightness—they correspond not to the dimensions of the light but to the reflectance
properties of the object. This is the phenomenon of color constancy,
parallel to the shape and size constancies discussed earlier. Second,
surface color varies along certain other dimensions as well, corresponding to other reflectance properties of surfaces.

Color constancy may be viewed as a mathematical problem.
Understood functionally, a reflectance property is a ratio between
the intensities of incident and reflected light at each wavelength. But
the eye, it seems, can register only the reflected light. How does it
detect the ratio? For reasons discussed in the last chapter, many theorists have assumed that what is given is a sensation corresponding
to the reflected light, and that color constancy results from inference. But there are automatic mechanisms which can achieve this
result. For example, the receptors adapt to the level of stimulation.
When the lights are turned up, the room looks brighter at first but
then returns to its normal appearance. When a person wears tinted
sunglasses, objects at first take on the tint of the glass but after a time
look normal again. Besides adaptation, there is simultaneous contrast. The effect of light from a given object will depend on the light
reflected by neighboring objects; the eye is sensitive in this way to
relationships within the optic array.

Contrast mechanisms apparently serve to provide information
about the level of illumination. In a classic experiment, A. Gelb

placed a black surface against a dimly lit background and then il-luminated the surface with a bright light in such a way that the light fell only on the surface and cast no visible shadow. The surface looked white, presumably because it was reflecting more light than anything in the background, and there was no clue that the illumi-nation on it was different. But as soon as an actually white object was placed against the surface, the latter immediately "turned" black—the contrast informed the eye of the real illumination.[19] (This cannot be taken as evidence for the inferential view of perceptual integration, for when the white object is taken away, the black sur-face again looks white, despite one's knowledge of its real color; the mechanisms involved are automatic.)

But color constancy cannot be separated entirely from the other constancies, as the result of an independent mechanism. If a white card is folded so that one side faces the light and the other faces away, the two sides will appear to have the same shade or degree of white-ness, although one looks brighter than the other.[20] Were they both viewed through a reduction screen, there would be a single sensory dimension corresponding to the intensities of light they reflect, and one would look brighter than the other. But with surface color, there are two dimensions; the whiteness of the surface is distinguished from the brightness of the illumination. This visual distinction re-quires that the surface be seen *as* a surface, as having a certain shape, slant, angle of orientation to other surfaces, texture, and distance. A surface color, in other words, is fully integrated with the spatial attributes of the object. In particular, it is integrated with depth. To have color constancy one must see objects at a depth, as having a distance and an orientation in three dimensions. Conversely, to see objects at a depth one must be able to discriminate contours, shad-ows, texture gradients, all of which are borders between colors that are seen at that depth. Color vision and depth vision are two aspects of a single, integrated awareness of objects. Color, depth, and the other attributes are experienced as integrated features of a single object.

Surface color exhibits other qualities as well, besides those it shares with film color. Silver and gray wool reflect light that is sim-

19. For a description of Gelb's experiment, see Julian Hochberg, "Perception I. Color and Shape," in Kling and Riggs (eds.), *Experimental Psychology*, 404ff.
20. Beck, *Surface Color Perception*, 106–107.

ilar in wavelength composition, but they look utterly different. Silver has a liquid appearance and a luster that make it glow even when the lights are dim; the wool is rough and matte, almost visibly trapping light. A velvet fabric has a sheen that makes it look quite different from cotton of the same hue. A face and a piece of blond furniture may reflect roughly the same wavelengths, but differ markedly in "complexion." These dimensions of surface colors correspond to reflectance properties other than atomic structure, chiefly the microscopic geometry of the surface.[21] The awareness of them derives from more complicated forms of perceptual integration.

For our purpose, the phenomena of color vision reveal two important points. The first is that color is experienced as external. From the perspective of the subject, color is a feature of *what* he sees, not of his awareness of it—we do not have red sensations or percepts. We are aware *of* color; it is something detected and discriminated as an object of awareness. Moreover, unlike interoceptive phenomena, color is experienced as being in physical space outside the body. Even the vaguest film color is seen as being out there somewhere. Thus the facts of color vision provide no evidence that color is in the mind, any more than do the facts about the physical basis of color.

But a more specific conclusion is also justified. Color is experienced as being located at the place of whatever the subject discriminates by means of it. In the mode of film color, a relatively primitive response to impoverished stimulation, the color is experienced as having a determinate direction but not a determinate distance. And by means of film color, we discriminate the attributes of the light, which also has a determinate direction but is not an object at any particular distance. In normal conditions of perception, the mechanisms of perceptual integration that underlie surface color perception function, as it were, to bend this primitive response to a more sophisticated end: they allow us to discriminate features of the objects that reflect light. And the experienced result is that color takes on a specific location in the third dimension. It appears as a quality of the surfaces of objects, at a specific depth and orientation in space. It is experienced as being located at the place of the objects and attributes discriminated by means of it.

We have now examined two sets of facts about color, each

21. *Ibid.*, Chap. 8.

grasped from a different perspective, each yielding a different conclusion. The philosophical problem is to integrate the conclusions,
and the essential precondition is that the diaphanous model of
awareness be rejected at the outset. For if it is accepted, it will render the two conclusions inconsistent and force us to choose between them.

The diaphanous model can be expressed as the thesis that if the
means by which we perceive affect the way things appear in perception, then we cannot perceive things as they are, but only their
effects on us. This is the meaning, for perception, of the wider thesis that if consciousness has an identity of its own, then it cannot
grasp the identities of things external to it, but only objects it itself
has constituted. And the narrower version, like the general one,
forces us to choose between two impossible positions. On the one
side, naïve realism regards perception as the awareness of what exists independently of the perceiver, and in this respect it is consistent with the experience of color as external. Because it accepts the
diaphanous model, however, it must deny even the ordinary types
of perceptual relativity. It must certainly deny the relativity of color
as such, and thus ignore the scientific facts which imply such relativity.[22]

On the other hand, the Kantian mode of argument recognizes
that our means of cognition do have an identity that affects the
way things appear, and is thus open to the facts concerning the
physiological bases of color. But those facts, together with the diaphanous model, imply that we cannot perceive the attributes of external objects. So the Kantian approach can find no room for our
conclusions about the psychology of color vision. Thus C. W. K.
Mundle argues: "According to the Selective theory [naïve realism],
the function of the relevant processes in the C[entral] N[ervous]
S[ystem] is to reveal things and their properties which exist independently of the observer. But the states of his CNS form one of the
factors which determine the phenomenal colours of a thing. . . . We
cannot then claim for colour-vision that the observer's CNS *reveals*

22. This was one motive for instrumentalist views of science. There is, however, no need to discuss instrumentalism, since none of my philosophical conclusions depend on the scientific view of colors. Suffice it to say that with this approach
to sensory qualities, we can defend perceptual realism without having to abandon
scientific realism.

qualities which things have independently of being perceived by creatures like us."[23] Because colors are relative to us, in other words, color vision cannot be the awareness of any external attribute of objects. The natural next step of the argument is to say that color vision acquaints us only with inner representations constituted by our own faculties. Its exponents are, in effect, frustrated naïve realists, retreating to a level of inner objects when it transpires that external objects cannot be perceived diaphanously. But that step leaves us with no hope of understanding the experience of color vision as the discrimination of features in external objects.

If we reject the diaphanous model, however, we can see that there is no contradiction between the conclusions we have reached, because they do not speak to the same issue. The physical scientist can show that color depends on the nervous system of a perceiver, but he cannot relate color to the awareness that arises from the same cause, or determine the role of color in perceptual cognition. The subject does have an insight into this relation; but he cannot, qua subject, relate color to the physical means by which he perceives. Although he does not experience color as a product of those processes, he cannot meaningfully claim that it appears to him as something which is not such a product. He experiences color as nonrelational in regard to every relation he can perceive. More precisely, when he distinguishes between the dimension in which color changes with the illumination and the dimension in which it is invariant, he experiences the latter as nonrelational in regard to every perceptible relation. But he does not—he could not—perceive the relation on which color in fact depends, and so his experience of it as nonrelational does not contradict that fact.[24]

This latter point has often been denied, not only by naïve realists, but also by representationalists. Indeed, the assumption that color must be an intrinsic property of *something* defines what has

23. C. W. K. Mundle, *Perception: Facts and Theories* (Oxford, 1971), 146–47.
24. Wilfrid Sellars has argued that there is a conflict between the perspectives along another dimension. A colored object such as a pink ice cube "presents itself to us as something which is pink through and through, as a pink continuum. . . . It presents itself to us as *ultimately homogeneous*" in respect of color, and cannot therefore be identified with a system of discrete particles ("Philosophy and the Scientific Image of Man," in *Science, Perception and Reality*, 26). But we do not experience objects as being homogeneously colored beyond the limits of visual acuity; that would be to experience something we cannot see.

been called the ostensive introduction of sense-data. As one of its clearest exponents, H. H. Price, argued: "Suppose I have the experience commonly called seeing something red. . . . *Something* must be red, for whatever else is uncertain it is certain that there exists at that moment an actual red particular." He makes clear that by an "actual red particular" he means one that possesses that color as an intrinsic quality, and his basis for claiming certainty about its existence is direct inspection of his experience. But the appeal to inspection is invalid, for it offers the testimony of the subject on something he cannot witness, the relational or intrinsic character of color (in the sense I have defined).[25] Nor can sense-data be introduced by stipulative definition, as bearers of colors or other sensory qualities, in the way A.J. Ayer and others have suggested.[26] The definition assumes that they are intrinsic qualities of something. It would be analogous to recognizing that weight is not an intrinsic feature of massive objects, since their weight varies depending on their proximity to various other massive bodies, and then introducing "weight-data" as the intrinsic subjects of the attribute.

Our problem, then, is to integrate the relational character of color with its role in perceiving and discriminating external objects. And let us begin by pursuing the analogy with weight. An object's mass is an intrinsic property and is thus independent of its relation to other massive objects, but the weight it has in virtue of its mass depends on such relations. Similarly, an object has various reflectance properties independently of its relation to any perceiver, but the color it has in virtue of those properties depends on such relations. But what about our awareness of these attributes? In lifting

25. H. H. Price, *Perception* (1932; rpr. London, 1964), 105. See also G. E. Moore, *Some Main Problems of Philosophy* (London, 1953), Chap. 2. *Cf.* Broad's assumption that if something looks *F* to a perceiver, then something *is F* intrinsically (*Scientific Thought*, 239). For a critique of Broad's principle, see Winston H. F. Barnes, "The Myth of Sense-Data," in Swartz (ed.), *Perceiving, Sensing, and Knowing*, 138–67. T. L. S. Sprigge, for example, argues against the relational view of colors on the ground that "one cannot notice a relational property without noticing the relation upon which it rests" ("The Common Sense View of Physical Objects," *Inquiry*, IX [1966], 348). That premise may be true of some such properties (*e.g.*, being to the left of), but the examples of weight and color here show that it is not true in general. Sprigge offers as justification an appeal to direct inspection.

26. Ayer, *Foundations of Empirical Knowledge*, 58ff. See also Mundle, *Perception*, 11–12.

an object, we perceive its weight but not its mass. It would not feel the same on the moon as on earth; the way it feels allows us to discriminate the relational property on earth but not the intrinsic mass. Can we say similarly that we see the color of an object but not the atomic structure, the relational but not the intrinsic property?

Here the analogy fails, in two crucial respects. In the first place, we perceive the weight of an object because it feels a certain way in virtue of its weight. The way it feels can be analyzed in terms of sensations of pressure, stretch and motion in the fingers, muscles, and joints. The analogy would then lead us to expect that we perceive the sensory color of an object because it looks a certain way in virtue of its sensory color, and that the way it looks can be analyzed in terms of sensations of—what? Color already *is* the way an object looks in virtue of certain properties. Second, weight is an attribute that one object has in relation to another *external* object; it would exist were there no conscious subjects to perceive it. But an object has a color in relation to a nervous system, to the means or faculty of perception itself. It would not exist without the subject who perceives it. So in relation to perceptual awareness, the analogue of weight is the reflectance property, and sensations of pressure are the analogue of color.

We must therefore go back a step. Color is a relational feature of external objects. The physical scientist is right this far. And this is as far as he goes. For him, the nervous system of a perceiver is an object like any other in the natural world. What he sees is the interaction of two natural systems; color, for him, is perfectly analogous to weight. But his is not the whole story, and color is not just a relational property. To consider its relation to our perceptual awareness, we must shift to the perspective of the subject, and this means that we are no longer looking from the outside at the interaction of two natural systems. We are looking at one system *by means of* the other. The subject is not aware of the means by which he perceives. He is not a disembodied spirit detached from his senses, watching the effect of objects on them as he might watch the effect of sunlight on a photoelectric cell. He *is* the system in interaction with which external objects produce colors.

Two essential points follow from this, and they will allow us to integrate the perspectives. The first is that in surface color vision we are aware of the reflectance properties of external objects, including their atomic structure. These are what the visual system responds to and discriminates. The diaphanous model has taught us to assume that if we perceive objects in virtue of their effects on us, we can only perceive those effects; that awareness occurs only after the causal sequence has run its course, and that we are aware only of the finished product. As we have seen, however, this is false. What the object causes is the awareness of that object. The causal sequence depends in part on the nature of our own means of perception, and these must therefore affect the way the object appears. But it is the object that appears, the object that we discriminate by means of its appearance. It is the object that we perceive. In the case of surface color vision, objects act on us as they do because of their reflectance properties; hence we perceive those properties.

Does accepting this first point mean that we are not aware of the sensory color? Certainly not. We are aware of it. If our faculties suddenly changed, so that objects looked different in respect to their reflectance properties, we would notice the change. But this does not mean that we are aware of the reflectance property in virtue of a prior awareness of the sensory color, so that the perception of the first is indirect.[27] This would be true only if we were aware of the sensory color *as opposed to* or distinct from the reflectance property, and my second point is that that is not the case. From the subject's perspective, these are a single attribute. For him to perceive one as opposed to the other, they would both have to affect his senses and look some way as a result. But the color *is* the way an object with that reflectance property affects his senses; it is the way it looks. He discriminates the one by means of the other—a color is the way or manner in which he perceives a particular reflectance property. Hence he does not perceive the red as opposed to the reflectance property, for he does not perceive the way he perceives. A given color *is* a certain reflectance property, as perceived by this subject, in these conditions.

We can therefore integrate the two perspectives, without having to deny any of the conclusions reached within them, or invent any new objects. The physical scientist is given his due with the recognition that color is a relational property, produced by an interaction between external objects and the nervous system. And we can

27. Perkins, *Sensing the World*, 233–34, makes this claim.

now see that the subject is indeed aware of something external to and independent of him. In the case of film color, he is aware of light and its attributes, which he discriminates by means of color. In the case of surface color, he is aware of surfaces and their attributes, for the same reason. We found that he was registering these properties, detecting differences among them. We can now say he was directly aware of them. And we found that he experiences color as external, a property of surfaces that *seems* independent of his awareness of it. We can now see why.

Color itself, as distinct from the reflectance properties, is not independent of him. But it was not the color itself, as distinct from the reflectance properties, that he experienced as independent. He cannot distinguish them. The reflectance property of the object *is* independent of his perception. So in perceiving it as red, he *must* experience the red as an external property of the object. The common claim that this experience is deceptive assumes that there ought in the nature of the case to be some way for the subject to grasp that color is a relational property, dependent on his own nervous system.[28] But that is not the way sense perception works. To be perceptually aware that color is relational, he would have to perceive the relation on which it depends. Then he would have to perceive this relation by some means, it would have to appear some way to him, raising the same questions all over again. So there is nothing deceptive about this experienced externality.[29] On the contrary, color is the way he perceives something that *is* external and independent of him. Experiencing color as external is the only way he *could* experience the externality of the reflectance properties. Given the necessity of perceiving by specific means, he experiences color in just the right "place"—the place of the attribute he is aware of by means of it.

Given the currency of the diaphanous model of awareness, it is likely that C. D. Broad's objection will be a common one: "When I see a pin that of which I am immediately aware is [not] colourless atoms . . . ; and this is a matter of simple inspection." Broad is right, of course, that we do not perceive colorless atoms—if that means perceiving atomic structure as distinct from color. But we do di-

28. *Cf.* J. L. Mackie, *Problems From Locke* (Oxford, 1976), 11.
29. *Cf.* Hermann von Helmholtz, *Popular Scientific Lectures*, ed. Morris Kline (New York, 1962), 142.

rectly perceive the atomic structure *as* color. Broad denies this on the grounds of simple inspection, and this can only mean that what we see does not look like an atomic structure. How should that look? We all have a picture from physics of a swirl of little gray particles. Well, atomic structure *might* look like that—to atomic-size perceivers. It would then be merely another way that a given attribute could appear to perceivers with specific means of perception, and their philosophers would ask the same questions. Where is the gray? How can we see the real size of the atoms if their apparent size changes with distance? But in this context the picture is obviously an attempt to step out from behind our own senses to see the world diaphanously—to see how it looks apart from any effect it might have on us. And this is a contradiction. The way a thing looks *is* its effect on a perceiver with a specific nature. A thing acts differently on sense organs of different types, and looks different as a result. There is no right way for it to look in abstraction from a specific type of sense organ. Colors are the way atomic structure looks to us.[30]

I can now summarize these conclusions about color in terms of the concept of form. As we have seen, the variable aspects of experienced color—those due to illumination changes, for example, or adaptation—are forms of perception. We can now see that the color *qualia* themselves are also forms. The relativity of the *qualia*, unlike the relativity of their variations, is a fact to which we have no phenomenological clue; it is an example of the deeper sort of relativity I anticipated in the last section. Nevertheless, it is a fact and it requires us to identify the *qualia* as forms, since they are aspects of the way objects appear to us which are determined by our means of perceiving them. The preceding discussion has shown, moreover, that the theses concerning form apply to color as well.

Color is not in the mind in any sense. From the standpoint of the subject, color is not in or a feature of his perceptual awareness. The physical facts show that color is a relational property of objects, arising from an interaction between them and our visual systems. As with other relational properties, there is no reason to locate them at all. And our rejection of the diaphanous model removes any philosophical reason for viewing color as subjective. As for the sec-

30. C. D. Broad, *Perception, Physics, and Reality* (Cambridge, England, 1914), 3. *Cf.* Campbell, "Colours," in Brown and Rollins (eds.), *Contemporary Philosophy in Australia*, 150–51.

ond thesis, colors are not separate objects of awareness, or qualities of inner objects, but aspects of the way external objects appear to us in respect of their reflectance properties. They are thus aspects of the means by which we are directly aware of those properties. Finally, it is clear that these reflectance properties could be perceived in different forms, if our perceptual apparatus were different. Certain types of color blindness, for example, seem to result from abnormal wiring in the opponent systems. In these cases, there is slightly poorer discrimination among wavelengths, but the chief difference is that subjects make different matches among combinations of wavelengths, suggesting that those combinations simply look different to them. It is only an extension of this phenomenon to imagine retinal inputs to the opponent systems reversed, so that what we now perceive as blue we would perceive as yellow, and so on. And though colors are "proper sensibles" and reflectance properties are normally perceived only by vision, there are rare cases of synesthesia in which subjects respond to optical stimulation with sensations of sound or pressure.[31] (More often, the cross-modality connection runs the other way. The most common form of synesthesia is "colored hearing," in which tones are perceived in the form of colors.) Were the synesthesia thorough enough, these sensations might enable a subject to discriminate reflectance properties.

Primary and Secondary Qualities

The conclusions that color is a relational property of external objects and is a form of perception can apparently be extended to other items on the traditional list of secondary qualities. At least, there are scientific grounds, analogous to those examined in the case of color, for holding that the feeling of warmth or coolness is the form in which we detect the kinetic energy of the molecules in substances touching the skin; that sensations of sound are the form in which we perceive certain events in the environment; and that flavors and odors are the form in which we discriminate the chemical composition of what is tasted or smelled. There is thus a basis for the traditional distinction between those sensory *qualia* and the primary qualities of size, shape, motion or rest, number, and position—a basis, at any rate, for the division itself, though not for the tradi-

31. Marks, *Unity of the Senses*, 83–98.

tional interpretation of it. As we have seen, there is nothing deceptive or illusory in color vision just because sensory color is a relational property of objects, dependent on our visual systems. The
same is true of the other secondary qualities, and so there is no in-
vidious comparison to be drawn between them and primary qualities in terms of veridicality. Given the concept of perceptual form,
we can only say that in regard to the primary qualities, certain quantitative dimensions of the way objects appear in respect of them are
to be identified as forms. For the secondary qualities, not only the
corresponding quantitative dimensions but also certain qualitative
ones—the sensory *qualia*—are forms. The only difference is in degree of relativity to our senses.

Nevertheless, it will be worthwhile to explore the difference
further, and to do so we need a more clearly defined terminology.
To stress the similarity which underlies the differences, I will use
primary quality and *secondary quality* as Locke did, to refer to intrinsic
attributes of external things, the objects of perceptual awareness as
opposed to the forms.[32] Thus the primary qualities are physical
shape, size, and the rest; secondary qualities include reflectance
properties, kinetic energy of molecules, and so on. For the purposes
of this discussion only, the terms *color, sound, warmth*, and so on, are
restricted to the sensory *qualia* identified as forms in which we perceive secondary qualities. Finally, I will use the ordinary concepts
of appearance to indicate the quantitative dimensions that vary in
ordinary cases of perceptual relativity.

To begin with, then, there appears to be a rough correspondence between the primary-secondary and the perception-sensation distinctions. If there were such a thing as a pure sensation, it
would be the experience of color, warmth, or other sensory *qualia*
without any awareness of primary qualities. Of course a color must
have some size and shape, even as a patch in the visual field. But
von Senden's investigations of newly sighted patients seemed to reveal some who simply could not detect or attend to the figural as-

32. Actually, as Reginald Jackson has shown, in "Locke's Distinction Between
Primary and Secondary Qualities," *Mind*, XXXVIII (1929), 56–76, Locke's use of the
terms is more complicated. Locke uses *secondary quality* to refer to what he elsewhere
calls a power, not a quality; it is a power to produce sensations of a certain type. I will
use the term to refer to the actual properties to which (as Locke believes) such powers
can be reduced when we understand their causal workings.

pects of the field, and they experienced colors merely as qualitative presences of indeterminate extent.[33] The perception of size, shape, position, motion, and number seems to require enough perceptual integration to isolate as units the objects which possess these attributes. Given the nature of this integration, moreover, it would be impossible to perceive any primary quality without some awareness of a secondary one. We see shape as a contour between areas of different hue or brightness. We hear objects moving in terms of variations in the *qualia* of sound. Even in olfaction we can detect the direction of an odor, a primary quality, but we could not do so without an awareness of the *qualia* of smell. Thus it seems that the awareness of secondary qualities first occurs at the level of sensations, but the awareness of primary qualities requires the perceptual level and necessarily includes some awareness of secondary qualities.

One difficulty in this thesis occurs in applying it to the sense of touch. After sight, touch provides us with the most information about the primary qualities of objects. What secondary qualities and *qualia* are involved in the tactile perception of these attributes? Texture is perhaps the most natural answer, but it will not survive a closer look. In a narrower sense, texture consists in minute and regular variations in the surface of an object. In that respect, it is a primary quality—an aspect of shape—and can be seen as well as felt. In a broader sense, texture includes any surface quality that can be perceived by touch, including many that are not accessible to vision—a texture can be sticky or slippery, moist or dry. These may seem to be distinct sensory *qualia*, serving as forms in which we perceive various microscopic features of the surfaces. They may seem, in other words, analogous to color. However, they could not be detected in isolated sensations. The awareness of any texture quality requires integration over time as one actively explores a surface. Passive momentary touch yields no sense of texture, only the bare awareness of contact.[34] Moreover, these texture qualities do not seem to be distinct sensory *qualia*, but are experienced instead as patterns in the way the feeling of contact varies as one moves the hands over

33. Marius von Senden, *Space and Sight*, trans. Peter Heath (London, 1960), 128–38.

34. James J. Gibson, "Useful Dimensions of Sensitivity," *American Psychologist*, XVIII (1963), 4–8.

the surface (or that feeling of contact combined with qualities of warmth or coolness).

Then what of the feeling of contact itself? Touch receptors (other than those for temperature) are stimulated by mechanical deformation of the skin when an object touches it. Thus the external quality involved is the object's resistance to its own deformation, its hardness, a feature ultimately of the chemical bonds among its molecules; and the hardness is perceived in the form of the *qualia* we describe as the feeling of contact or pressure. This is the closest we can come to an analogy with color. But it is not close enough. Color differences can be detected even at the sensational level. They are the forms in which we discriminate the reflectance properties of surfaces. But any discriminating awareness of hardness would be perceptual, involving integration over time. We detect an invariant relation between the degree of indentation (in the object or in the skin) and the amount of force applied (as detected by kinesthetic input) as the object is actively pressed. The simple feeling of pressure involved in any tactile perception is merely a limiting case of this. Thus in the sense of touch, there is at best a very imperfect correlation between the primary-secondary and the perception-sensation distinctions.[35]

Another, deeper problem emerges when we examine the underlying causes of the correlation, and the problem cuts across all the modalities. Let us begin again with color. Why is it that we cannot see shapes without seeing colors? We see shapes by means of forms and patterns in the optic array that are isolated by the visual system. But these "extensive" features could not be isolated unless there were differential responses on the part of the system to the "intensive" features of the stimulus energy at each point in the optic array. Color as a form of perception arises from the response to these intensive features—wavelength and intensity—in the cones and opponent systems, and so is naturally involved in any perception of shape. We can generalize from this and say that sensory *qualia* in all the modalities are forms resulting from the response to intensive features of the stimulus, but the forms in which we perceive the primary qualities of objects arise from the way our sensory systems detect extensive patterns across the arrays. Hence it is not surpris-

35. On the sensation-perception distinction in touch, see James J. Gibson, *The Senses Considered as Perceptual Systems* (Boston, 1966), Chap. 7.

ing that the perception of any primary quality involves some awareness of sensory *qualia*, whereas the latter can occur without the former if the perceptual integration necessary for detecting extensive
features has not occurred.

But here is the problem. If perceptual integration does not occur, so that there is no awareness of the primary qualities of objects,
then the sensory *qualia* which remain are not the forms in which we
are aware of secondary qualities in objects. In the film mode of color
vision, as we saw, the color *qualia* were forms in which we are aware
of attributes in the light itself. Only in the context of perception,
through the operation of constancy and other mechanisms, is that
primitive response to light bent to the discrimination of reflectance
properties in the objects themselves. Thus the awareness of either
a primary or a secondary quality is possible only at the perceptual
level, and neither is possible without the other. *Qualia* such as colors, warmth, odor, sounds, pressure are not forms in which we perceive secondary qualities in objects unless we can discriminate those
objects as units, with some more or less definite distance and/or direction from us in space. That requires some awareness of spatial
attributes, which are primary.

Nevertheless, the distinction between the intensive and extensive features of the stimulus arrays does suggest the proper formulation of the distinction between primary and secondary qualities in objects, as well as the explanation for the differing degrees of
relativity in our perception of them. Even in the context of perception, the sensory *qualia* arise from the way perceptual systems respond to the intensive features of stimulus energy—however much
this response may be affected by their response to extensive features. And the qualities in the object that determine the intensive
features of the stimulus are *microscopic*. Given the illumination, reflectance properties determine the mixture of wavelengths stimulating the eye; molecular kinetic energy determines the heat flow
which stimulates temperature receptors; and so on. On the other
hand, the *macroscopic* qualities of objects determine the extensive
features of the stimulus array, the borders and edges, structures and
relations across the array. Thus the distinction between primary and
secondary is at root a distinction between macroscopic and microscopic qualities.[36]

36. R. Jackson, "Locke's Distinction."

It is true of course that the primary qualities as physical attributes exist at the microscopic as well as the macroscopic level. Indeed, any nondispositional understanding of secondary qualities would presumably involve some reference to microscopic size, motion, and the like. Conversely, a secondary quality could not be perceived unless it existed across a minimally perceptible extent of an object. But these facts are not relevant to the distinction. In distinguishing primary from secondary qualities, we are referring only to the macroscopic sizes, shapes, positions of whole physical objects and their perceptible parts, for these determine the extensive features of the stimulus array. But it is not the macroscopic extent across which a secondary quality exists that explains the sensory *qualia* by which we perceive it. For us to perceive either a red or a green surface, light must be reflected from a large enough region of the surface to be perceived. But the difference between red and green is to be explained by the microscopic features of the surface in that region. This is why the secondary qualities are continuous and not discrete. They must occupy some extent in order to be perceived, but no particular extent; and they exist at any point across the region they occupy. (The primary qualities, by contrast, are discrete. Their instances are objects as wholes. A square object is not square in every part, at every point, nor is a large object large throughout.)

We can summarize the distinction, then, as follows. An object appears as a unified whole, as an entity. The way it appears in respect of any one of its attributes is affected by the way it appears in respect of the others. Hence the appearance, with all its qualitative dimensions, is a unitary product of a perceptual system's total response to the object, with all *its* attributes. Nevertheless, we can single out the qualitative dimensions of the appearance and correlate them in a rough way with the attributes of the object, establishing causal relations between the dimensions of appearance and the way the perceptual system responds to the external attributes. When we do this, we find that certain dimensions can be explained by reference to the macroscopic attributes of objects. With other dimensions, however, we cannot find the intrinsic feature of the object itself, to which the senses are responding, unless we proceed to the microscopic level. In both cases, though, we are perceiving attributes of the object, and the object itself cannot appear *as* an object unless we perceive *some* attributes from both categories.

Since we necessarily perceive objects in a form that is relative to our means of perceiving, such relativity is not incompatible with veridical perception, but rather a necessary aspect of it. Hence differing degrees of relativity do not imply different degrees of veridicality—there is no distinction to be drawn on this score between primary and secondary qualities. And as we have just seen, there is no way to perceive one sort of quality without perceiving the other; the sensory *qualia* are required for the perception of either. On the traditional distinction, therefore, I need only add a few comments.

There *is* a further difference at the level of our concepts for the qualities. Since the perception of primary qualities is subject—so far as we know at present—only to the ordinary sorts of perceptual relativity, it is easy to abstract the qualities themselves from the variable forms in which we perceive them. Moreover, since the primary qualities are macroscopic, it is easy to measure them as they are apart from the forms in which we perceive them. There are rulers and protractors for size and shape, counting for number, slightly more sophisticated measures for the others. And as "common sensibles," they can be perceived through more than one sense, facilitating the abstraction of the qualities themselves. As a result, ordinary concepts of these qualities identify the intrinsic attributes of external objects. Concepts of the secondary qualities also abstract from the ordinary sorts of relativity—we distinguish between an object's being red and its merely looking red—but they do not abstract the intrinsic attribute fully from the form in which we perceive it. Because the intrinsic attributes in this case are microscopic, it takes a scientific theory to isolate them and scientific instruments to measure them. Hence the concept of red picks out a class of objects which in fact possess certain reflectance properties in common, as well as the relational property of being perceived in a certain form by ordinary perceivers in ordinary conditions. But the concept does not distinguish the intrinsic from the relational property. I will argue in Chapter 7, however, that this makes no difference whatever to the justification of perceptual judgments in which the concepts for the qualities are employed to identify the objects we perceive. And in any case, this distinction at the conceptual level is not directly relevant at all to the nature of our *perceptual* awareness of the qualities.

Locke's major claim in distinguishing primary from secondary qualities was that the ideas of the former resemble the external attributes they represent while the ideas of the latter do not.[37] He concluded that ideas of primary qualities are veridical in a way that ideas of secondary qualities are not. This claim is incompatible with my argument here.

First, as indicated by the term *idea* in the statement of the doctrine, it presupposes that the forms of perception are intrinsic qualities of certain inner objects of perception. Resemblance is a relation between two or more items that have the attribute in respect of which they are similar. In the case of Locke's thesis, this would require that there be something, besides the external object, which has the primary quality as an intrinsic feature. (And for the sake of contrast, there must be something which has the secondary qualities, so that we can meaningfully deny similarity in their case.) But my argument has been that the forms in which we perceive both primary and secondary qualities are relational phenomena; there are no entities of which they are intrinsic qualities. Second, the doctrine presupposes the diaphanous model of awareness. It is really suggesting that if we could step out from behind our senses, we would see that the shapes of objects are quite similar to their apparent shapes, but that their atomic structure looks nothing like color. But this is contradictory. Neither the objects of awareness apart from the forms, nor the forms apart from the objects, could look *any* way to us. The form *is* the way the object looks.

Thus it is not possible to defend Locke, as J. L. Mackie does, merely by distinguishing the way things are from the way they appear. Mackie admits that the doctrine of resemblance presupposes a type of representationalism, but it is an innocuous type, he says, because the inner objects it speaks of are intentional objects, used not to explain or analyze appearance but merely to redescribe it. All that the doctrine of resemblance means, then, is that in certain respects (the primary qualities) things are as they appear, but in others (the secondary qualities) they are not. That formulation, however, cannot have the intended meaning without a stronger version of representationalism, one that involves actual inner objects in such a way as to be incompatible with my analysis of appearance. For on the basis of that analysis, objects necessarily "are as they appear,"

37. Locke, *Essay Concerning Human Understanding*, ed. Alexander Campbell Fraser (1894; rpr. New York, 1959), Book II, Chap. 8, sec. 15.

in all respects. They have the attributes we are aware of by means of the form with which we perceive them in particular conditions. To allow for a doctrine of resemblance, appearances must involve some real inner object that could have (or be meaningfully said to lack) the property possessed by the external object. And Mackie seems to assume such an object when he explains perceptual relativity in the case of primary qualities. He says that the object as seen and the object as it is are different determinations of the same determinable shape.[38] For that to be possible, the object as seen must be distinct from the actual object, and it must be the sort of thing that could have a shape distinct from the actual shape.

In addition, the doctrine loses whatever initial plausibility it has when we consider the "common sensibles." Most of the primary qualities can be perceived by more than one sense. If the forms in which we perceive them are similar to the qualities perceived, therefore, the forms in which we perceive them by different senses should themselves be similar. And they are not—or, rather, since no comparison of similarity can be made, we should say there is no temptation to say they are similar. The tactual form in which one perceives shape is quite different from the visual form. Nor does the difference lie solely in the secondary qualities involved—sensations of color in the one case, of pressure in the other. I *see* the roundness of the ashtray on my desk by discriminating the figure from its background, and this involves a color difference. But the form in which I see the shape itself is the respect in which it looks similar to an ellipse. I *feel* its roundness by touch. I put my hand over the ashtray and grasp it from above, my fingers touching various points on the contour. This involves sensations of pressure at those points, but the form in which I perceive the shape itself is a peculiar feeling of the arc across my fingers and palm as they form a cupola with a circular base. I could also feel the shape by tracing the contour with a finger. In this case, I would perceive the shape in the form of a complicated relationship among the motions of the wrist, elbow, and shoulder. There is no temptation to say that either of these tactual forms is similar to the visual form.

It should be emphasized finally that the distinction between primary and secondary qualities is drawn entirely on scientific

38. Mackie, *Problems From Locke*, 47–51.

grounds. I have discussed it here solely in order to show that the concept of perceptual form is capable of assimilating any sort of perceptual relativity that science provides evidence of, and that the concept allows us to classify the different levels of relativity. Nothing in this analysis of relativity as such commits us philosophically to the relativity of sensory *qualia*. Nor would the analysis be refuted should future scientific discoveries provide evidence that at a still deeper level, even the primary qualities, even the entire spatial world, is relative to our senses.[39] We can imagine, for example, that properties of extension and location in space are not causal primaries, that they depend on some underlying energy phenomenon, and that they exist only as products of an interaction between external instances of that phenomenon and the instances we call our senses. We would then have to say that shape, size, and position are forms in which we perceive those underlying properties of energy. This would not show that our perceptual experience of a spatial world is illusory, any more than current scientific theories show that our experience of a colored world is illusory. It would only show that shapes and colors are more similar than we thought.

I began this chapter by resolving to take seriously the reality of phenomenal appearance, and the problem of perceptual relativity that arises in connection with it; and to try to explain them without explaining them away. The concept of form gives us a way to describe the facts of perceptual relativity that are accessible at the commonsense level. It provides a way to conceptualize scientific findings which explain these facts and which reveal deeper levels of relativity. And it gives us a way to formulate the realist interpretation of relativity. Given that we perceive by means of physical organs which interact with the objects we perceive, we necessarily perceive objects in a form determined by that process. That fact is only the manifestation, in perception, of the wider truth that consciousness has an identity. And once we reject the diaphanous model of consciousness, it is evident that that fact is not incompatible with the validity of the senses.

39. I am indebted to Leonard Peikoff for this point.

4

Representationalism

Representationalism, as we have seen, is a cluster of doctrines which, taken together, constitute a certain model of cognition. The doctrines are a mixture of realist and idealist premises, but the model represents a distinct view of cognition, with its own characteristic tendencies and problems. In the most general terms, it involves a separation between an internal content of awareness and its external object, the former being the content of our experiences or beliefs, which in turn are regarded as subjective states. It is assumed that these states, with all their contents, could exist or occur without their external objects, no matter how closely the two are normally related. Thus cognition may involve a kind of relation between mind and reality, but the relation is not seen as essential to either. This is simply an epistemological expression of Descartes' belief that mind and matter are autonomous realms (although the epistemological expression has survived among philosophers who reject the metaphysical side of Cartesian dualism). In making the case for epistemological realism, I argued against the model at this level. It is time now to consider the influence of this model on theories of perception.

The most obvious and straightforward version of perceptual representationalism is the sense-data theory. In its classical form, the theory held that we are directly aware of certain internal objects—

sense-data, or *sensa*—but not of physical objects, and that sense-data can occur with or without physical objects as their causes. The theory therefore defines perception in terms of two distinct and partially independent conditions. There must be an awareness of sense-data, and the latter must be caused in a certain way by external objects. Perception is, then, a species of a genus that also includes imagination, dreams, and hallucinations, all of which involve the awareness of sense-data and thus satisfy the first condition. It is the second condition alone that distinguishes perception from the nonveridical states. In the latter, the veil of perception is made up out of whole cloth; in perception, it is a product of external things.

The sense-data theory no longer enjoys the popularity it once had. It has been attacked by many philosophers, for many reasons. But the broader representationalist pattern which the theory exemplifies is still implicit as a framework in most contemporary discussions of perception. It is important to identify the pattern as clearly as possible and consider the arguments typically used to support it.

The Representationalist Model

The sense-data theory's main rival, and the chief beneficiary of its demise, is the adverbial theory espoused by C. J. Ducasse and Roderick Chisholm. By comparing the theories, we can isolate one aspect of the model. Adverbialism holds that sensory qualities are not qualities of internal objects, but ways in which external objects appear. Chisholm argues that when a thing looks red, there is no entity that has redness as an intrinsic quality. The external object is appearing redly, the adverbial form indicating that redness is the way it appears or the way we perceive it. Redness is a feature of the process of appearing. So far, the view is similar to the analysis I offered in the last chapter. But Chisholm goes on to argue that from the subject's point of view, what happens when the object appears redly can also happen when there is no object present. The status of the sensory quality is therefore better described by eliminating any reference to the object. We should say that the subject is appeared to redly, or that he senses or experiences redly. The sense-data and adverbial theories are really, then, theories of sensory *experience*, seen as a subjective pole of perceiving. The one accepts and the other rejects an act-object analysis of the experience. But what of the external thing, which all sides agree is the object of *perception*? Chisholm would agree with the sense-data theory that we perceive the object that is causally responsible for the experience. To perceive a thing is to sense in a way that varies in correspondence with variations in that thing.[1]

Although the two theories differ in their view of sensory experience, the common element is precisely that they are theories *of experience*. Neither is an analysis of perception as such. In both cases, a causal relation must be added to have a percept of an external object. Both see experience as a generic element common to perception, dreams, and hallucinations, and the theories are intended to explain experience in all these forms. Both regard an experience as a state of the subject, something that should be described without reference to the external objects that may cause it. All the contents of experience—colors, sounds, apparent shapes and sizes—are held to be contained within the experience as a state of the perceiver. And the state as a whole is nonrelational, even if, as the sense-data theory posits, it contains a relation within it. For the state could occur in the absence of any object.

Indeed, the two theories may be seen as variants on the Cartesian theory of ideas, which was introduced to cope with a problem that arises for this view of experience. Descartes claimed that modes of consciousness are nonrelational. They are properties or states of consciousness and do not depend on anything outside consciousness. To maintain this view, however, he had to read the qualitative content of experience into the experiential state. If the mode of consciousness is merely a state of awareness, it will be inherently relational. Awareness is always awareness *of* something, and it can be described and individuated as a state only in terms of what one is aware of. *What* we experience must therefore be part of the experiential state. But what, then, is its status? Redness, apparent shape, and the like are not properties of consciousness in the way objective shape is a property of external objects. Consciousness is not red, nor is it even apparently square. The concept of ideas is then introduced

1. Roderick Chisholm, *Perceiving* (Ithaca, 1957), Chaps. 8, 10, and *Theory of Knowledge* (Englewood Cliffs, N.J., 1966), Chap. 6. In a more recent work, *Person and Object* (La Salle, Ill., 1976), Chisholm defines perceptual objects in terms of perceptual beliefs.

to allow a distinction. The idea has a formal nature as a mode of consciousness and, in this respect, may be described as a state of awareness, of experiencing or sensing. But it also has a representational nature and thus has the qualities of sensory appearance as internal contents, as parts of its identity.[2]

The theory of ideas, however, reformulates the problem without solving it. The relation between the two natures must still be explained, and the sense-data and adverbial theories represent opposite extremes on this issue. The former separates the natures into distinct elements, treating the representational nature as an internal entity standing over against the awareness of it. Thus G. E. Moore argued, in "The Refutation of Idealism," that this object, the sense-datum, is independent of the awareness of it. And Russell speculated that *sensibilia* may exist when no one is aware of them. The adverbial theory takes the opposite side. Ducasse argued, in reply to Moore, that what really exists is only the act of sensing or experiencing, considered formally. *What* is sensed, the qualitative content, is the internal identity of the act. When we experience a bitter taste, the bitterness is not an object upon which the act of sensing is directed; it is the character of the act itself; it is what distinguishes a sensation of bitter from a sensation of sweet, and could not possibly exist apart from the sensation itself.[3]

In polemical terms, each theory grasps one horn of a dilemma implicit in the theory of ideas.[4] The dilemma lies in the attempt to say that the qualitative content of appearance both is and is not a feature of consciousness. Each theory, in avoiding one side of the dilemma, faces the other in a particularly clear form. The sense-data theory avoids having to describe awareness itself as red, bitter, apparently square, by making these qualities *objects* of awareness. But if they are objects, it becomes difficult to see in what way they are features of consciousness, or *mental* phenomena. They come to be seen as replicas of external, physical objects, and a host of puzzles

2. *Cf.* T. L. S. Sprigge, *Facts, Words and Beliefs* (New York, 1970), 35.

3. G. E. Moore, "The Refutation of Idealism," in *Philosophical Studies* (London, 1951), 1–30; Bertrand Russell, "The Relation of Sense-Data to Physics," in *Mysticism and Logic* (New York, 1929), 145–79; C. J. Ducasse, "Moore's 'The Refutation of Idealism,'" in P. A. Schilpp (ed.), *The Philosophy of G. E. Moore* (Chicago, 1942), 223–51.

4. For a related view of the dilemma, see George Pitcher, "Minds and Ideas in Berkeley," *American Philosophical Quarterly*, VI (1969), 198–207.

arises because it seems appropriate to ask questions that apply to physical objects. Do visual sense-data have backsides? How wide is my visual sense-datum of the table—as wide as the table itself? a few inches? how would we decide? Do sense-data exist in space? And if so, how does that space relate to the objective space of physical objects? Can they exist unperceived? Are sense-data, like other entities, fully determinate? If so, why are we not aware of their full determinacy—as when we experience an object as having many sides but no particular number of sides?[5]

The adverbial theory avoids these puzzles by denying that sensory contents are objects or entities of any kind, thus emphasizing that they *are* features of sensory awareness. But it does this at the cost of raising the other problem. If sensory qualities constitute the identity of acts of sensing, then the latter will themselves be red, bitter, and so on. Ducasse denied this by claiming that a quality like bitterness does not stand to the act of sensing as attribute to subject, but rather as species to genus—"tasting bitter" is a species of "tasting."[6] But this does not avoid the problem. The species "tasting bitter" must be differentiated from other species of the genus "tasting" on the basis of some distinguishing characteristic possessed by instances of "tasting bitter." If this distinguishing characteristic is not precisely the quality bitterness, so that the act of gustatory sensing is itself bitter, then what is it?

Hence the problems these theories encounter, as well as their conception of the problem they are trying to solve, derive from one central feature of the representationalist model: the assumption that

5. *Cf.* Chisholm, *Perceiving,* 119; Winston H. F. Barnes, "The Myth of Sense-Data," in Robert Swartz (ed.), *Perceiving, Sensing, and Knowing* (Garden City, N.Y., 1965), 145–47. Most sense-data theorists have distinguished a subjective space, in which sense-data exist, from physical space, and have been troubled by the question of how they are related. For a brilliant analysis of the problem, see H. W. B. Joseph, "The Psychological Explanation of the Development of the Perception of External Objects," *Mind,* n.s., XIX (1910), 305–21, 457–69. Frank Jackson has recently offered a sense-data theory that locates sense-data in physical space. Although he says they are mental entities, he claims that they exist at various distances from the perceiver. He implies that in nonillusory perception, they are located at the very places, oddly enough, where the objects they represent are located (*Perception* [Cambridge, England, 1977], 102–104).

6. Ducasse, "Moore's 'Refutation of Idealism,'" in Schilpp (ed.), *Philosophy of Moore,* 236, 247.

what is experienced must be contained in the experiential state, which is considered a state of the perceiver. This in turn is required by the prior assumption that any perceptual experience could occur, with just the content it has, in the absence of the external object—so that experiential states are generic elements common to veridical and nonveridical experiences.[7] And this assumption also dictates the other central feature of the model. What distinguishes veridical from nonveridical experiences is some de facto, noncognitive relation that obtains between the veridical experience and the external object. The sense in which this relation must be noncognitive can be spelled out as follows.

If, from an external point of view, the relation is not necessary for the occurrence of the experiential state, then it cannot be present from an internal standpoint—it cannot be present to the subject, cannot be given to him in the way the qualitative content of the experience is given. All forms of representationalism would allow that my present experience of the cup on my desk could occur, with just this content, even if the cup were not present to my senses. In certain conditions the cup could be removed, breaking whatever relation makes the present experience veridical, and I would not detect the absence of the relation. Hence I do not now grasp its presence; it is not given. This seems to be H. H. Price's point in saying that "in this sense, perceiving is not a specific form of consciousness . . . ; it does indeed involve a specific form of consciousness, namely sensing (acquaintance with sense-data), but that which it involves in addition is not a form of consciousness at all—it is a merely *de facto* relation." The point of calling the relation de facto appears to be that it is something which happens to an experience, but is not relevant to a description of it as a phenomenon of consciousness. Conversely, the cognitive aspect of the experiential state, my awareness of the item in my visual field, cannot be a real relation to an external object, since it could occur without the existence or presence of the

7. This same feature is present in some physicalistic accounts of perception. Peter Machamer, for example, defines "O sees I" in terms of a physical state which he assumes is common to perceiving and hallucinating ("Gibson and the Conditions for Perception," in Peter Machamer and Robert Turnbull [eds.], *Studies in Perception* [Columbus, Ohio, 1978], 449–50). See also Fred Dretske's definition of a percept, in "The Role of the Percept in Visual Cognition," in C. Wade Savage (ed.), *Perception and Cognition* (Minneapolis, 1978), 109.

real object. The cup as I am aware of it is an intentional object, and my awareness is not a transitive relation to the real cup.[8]

The relations suggested by representationalists have been non-cognitive in this sense. As we saw in Chapter 1, a basic pair of alternatives is allowed by the theory of ideas: experience can be related to its external object either formally or representationally. *Causal* theories take the first alternative, since the causal relation holds between the external object and the experience as a conscious occurrence. *Similarity* theories take the other alternative. The relation is one of picture to original, in which the content of the experience is qualitatively similar to the nature of the object. But causality and similarity are de facto relations that do not extend awareness to the external thing. Thus there is a causal relation between the cup and my experience of it. But the experience is also causally related to every other stage in the sequence by which it was produced—to the receptors, to the optic array, to the light bulb illuminating the cup, even to the manufacturer. If the fact of a causal relation does not make me aware of these other factors, how could it make me aware of the cup, which is only one stage in the sequence, somewhere in the middle? On the other hand, if it were true that my experience is similar to its object—and I argued earlier that it is not—then the experience would be similar to every other cup made from the same mold, and to every other experience of the cup by other perceivers. If the fact of similarity to these other things would not make me aware of them, it cannot make me aware of the real cup.[9]

What is the point of conflict between causal and similarity theories? Presumably each could agree that the relation favored by the other side *exists*. They must disagree about which relation should be used to define—what? There is a dilemma here, just as there was for the first part of the representationalist model. The representationalist wishes to say both that external objects are and that they are not objects of cognition. We have just seen the sense in which his model prevents him from saying they are objects of cognition. But he also wishes to define a sense in which we are nevertheless

8. H. H. Price, *Perception* (1932; rpr. London, 1964), 23; *cf.* R. J. Hirst, *Problems of Perception* (London, 1959), 294–95; and J. L. Mackie, *Problems From Locke* (Oxford, 1976), 47–51.

9. See Jaegwon Kim, "Perception and Reference Without Causality," *Journal of Philosophy*, LXXIV (1977), 606–20.

indirectly aware of external objects; or in which perceptual experiences are veridical, that is, true to the object; or in which they are experiences of the object. And all of these are *cognitive* relations. They would make no sense if one really believed that in perception a certain internal conscious state occurs which bears various relations to external objects, relations of the sort that natural objects can bear to each other.

The dilemma is particularly clear in regard to causal theories of perceptual objects. When a rock breaks a window, there is a sequence of events from the motion of the vandal's arm, to the flight of the missile, to contact with the window and the shattering of glass. To understand the effect, we relate it to all the causal factors—to each preceding event, as well as to standing conditions such as the hardness of rock, the brittleness of glass. Each is a cause of the effect, in a different way and with a different degree of proximity. But it would be senseless to single out any one factor and say that the breakage was true to that factor or was *of* or *about* it. Causal theorists wish to apply the same naturalistic analysis to perception.[10] But they also want to allow that there is a special relation—of the sort that would never be applied to the breaking of a window—between the effect (the experience) and one particular stage in the causal sequence (the object). To do this, they have tried to find some role that the physical object alone plays in that sequence.

H. H. Price suggested, for example, that the physical object alone is a differential cause, one whose variations explain variations in the experience. But the same is true of the optic array or of any proximate stimulus. It has become clear that to isolate the objects of perception from all other causal factors, one has to compile an *ad hoc* list of all the various roles played by the different objects of the different senses. Something is said to be the object of perception if it reflects light, if it is not too far away, if there is nothing between it and the eye, or if it causes vibratory motions in the air, and so on through the other modalities.[11] But this is not an analysis of the cognitive relation to an object; it is merely a list of the various ways in

10. *Cf.* Fred Dretske's reply to Kim, "Causal Theories of Reference," *Journal of Philosophy*, LXXIV (1977), 621.
11. Price, *Perception*, 70. Price finally rejects the causal theory, but he thinks this distinction frees it from the problem at hand. See also H. P. Grice, "The Causal Theory of Perception," in Swartz (ed.), *Perceiving, Sensing, and Knowing*, 438–72.

which things that we know *antecedently* are objects of cognition act on the senses.

In any case, we now have before us the representationalist model. Its two central features define an approach to perception that is broader than the traditional sense-data theory but still inconsistent with realism. In the realist view, that of which we are directly aware is the external object itself; our awareness of it is a real, transitive relation to something independent of us; the qualitative content of experience is reality itself. There is no issue about what relation obtains between experience and external object, for awareness is that relation. And there is no issue about how the qualitative contents of experience can be contained in or be features of consciousness. They are not. The only problem a realist faces on either issue is that of perceptual relativity, and I have already dealt with this in distinguishing form from object.

Despite its internal problems, the representationalist theory has had a profound influence on theories of perception. We should therefore examine carefully the arguments offered in support of it. In defending the primacy of existence, I argued that representationalism rests fundamentally on the diaphanous model of awareness. In the next section, we will see that model at work in the specifically perceptual arguments for the theory.

Arguments for Representationalism

The oldest and most important of the traditional arguments for the sense-data theory is the classical argument from perceptual relativity, based on the fact that the same object can appear differently to different perceivers and in different conditions. It is the most important argument because the fact of perceptual relativity applies to every perception of every perceptible attribute and manifests one essential aspect of perceptual awareness—it occurs by specific means.

The argument's structure is made clear in the following passage from Hume's *Inquiry*: "The table which we see seems to diminish as we remove further from it; but the real table, which exists independent of us, suffers no alteration. It was, therefore, nothing but its image which was present to the mind." The argument turns on the fact that the appearance of the table varies with a change in the conditions of perception, but the table itself does not. Since this phenomenon occurs with every object of perception, the argument may be generalized:

1) The object of immediate awareness in perception varies with certain conditions.

2) The external object does not vary with these conditions.

Therefore, the external object is not the object of immediate awareness in perception.

Although this tells us only what the object of immediate awareness is *not*, Hume's statement indicates the positive theory waiting in the wings. What we immediately perceive is an image—or idea, sense impression, sense-datum.[12]

Given the distinction between form and object, however, it is not the object of awareness that varies with conditions, but rather the form in which we perceive the object. Apart from the diaphanous model of awareness, there is no justification for reifying the form into a separate object that is perceived in place of the external thing. Hence premise (1) is false—indeed, it begs the question. The fact of perceptual relativity is that appearances vary with the conditions of perception. To take this as meaning that what varies is the object of immediate awareness is to assume that we are (immediately) aware only of appearances. But this is precisely the representationalist conclusion that the argument is intended to support.

Nor do the facts of perceptual relativity force us to adopt the broader pattern of the representationalist model, as some have suggested, by revealing a distinction between the external object and appearances as states of the perceiver.[13] Within the perceptual situation, we must distinguish the subject's awareness from what he is aware of. But that awareness, which could in a sense be described as a state of the subject, is inherently a relational state, directed upon something that is not a state of the subject. We must also distinguish those respects in which the way the object appears depends on the object itself, from those in which the way it appears depends on conditions external to the object. The latter, variable respects—

12. David Hume, *An Inquiry Concerning Human Understanding*, ed. Charles W. Hendel (Indianapolis, 1955), sec. 12.

13. *Cf.* Sprigge, *Facts, Words and Beliefs*, 4–5.

that is, the forms of perception—cannot be regarded as states of the subject. From the subject's point of view, the form is distinct from his awareness in just the way the object is, because it is the form in which the *object* appears. From the outside, we can distinguish form from object, but the form then has a relational status, as the product of an interaction between perceiver and object, and is not a state of one as opposed to the other. We cannot then move, as Chisholm does, from the object's appearing a certain way, to the subject's sensing a certain way, and thereby remove all reference to the object. And in fact Chisholm's reason for doing so follows from the logic of the argument from hallucinations, not from any considerations of relativity.

Before taking up hallucinations, however, we should consider two other arguments for representationalism. The notorious time-lag argument turns on the fact that the causal sequence in perception takes time, and in the extreme case of seeing the stars, it may take years for the passage of light from object to eye. Suppose, then, that I look at a speck in the nighttime sky, but that the star itself has exploded since emitting the light now striking my retina. What am I perceiving? Something is present to my perceptual awareness now, but it cannot be the star itself because that no longer exists. Is it the light I perceive?[14] Another time lag stands in the way of this answer. There is a very brief lag between the stimulation of the retina, or any other sense organ, and the conscious awareness it produces. And this is true in all perceiving, of any object no matter how close. Here too it is conceivable that the object might perish in the interval. Even if it does not, I do not perceive it as it is at the moment of perception. Something is present to me now, at the moment of awareness, but it is not the object as it is now. My senses provide information about the object as it was a split second ago. What I am aware of must then be some object produced by the same process as the awareness, occurring at the same moment. It must be a representation.

This argument might be questioned on the grounds of its concept of the present. One could argue that time does not consist in mathematical instants, and that the present can be understood only in terms of the interval during which perceptual integration occurs.

14. This would be a more reasonable interpretation in any case, since starlight is closer to the film mode than to the object mode of color vision. A better example would be the sun or the moon, which we do discriminate as objects.

But this excursion into metaphysics would be unnecessary, because the argument also contains an equivocation. That my awareness occurs now, at a given moment, does not mean that its object, qua object of awareness, must also exist now. This is not true of memory, or historical knowledge generally; and the time lag in perception shows that it is not true of perception either. The objects of perceptual awareness, I have argued, are real—they exist. But there is no reason to assume a priori that they must exist at the moment of the awareness of them, or that at that moment they must be exactly as they are perceived to be. Perceptual awareness is a natural phenomenon, occurring as the result of definite causes. By the nature of those causes, we could not possibly be aware of the object as it is *after* it has set in motion the causal sequence that produces our awareness of it. By what right, then, do we assume that for perception to be valid, its object must be given in some other way?

The same sort of objection applies to the argument from double images. If I press one eyeball in a certain way, I will "see double"—I am holding a single pencil in my hand, but I seem to see two pencils a short distance apart in my visual field. The phenomenon is certainly real, and the argument that employs it runs as follows. There are two items in the visual field. They cannot both be the real pencil, since then the latter would be double, would be in two places at once, etc. Nor can we identify one item, and not the other, as the real pencil, since they are perfectly similar and the choice between them would be arbitrary. There are two *somethings*, then, in the visual field, and they must be images or representations of the real pencil. What else could they be? This is the intermediate conclusion, but there is one more step to take. Seeing double is an aberration; normally there is only one item in the visual field for every external object. But the two items in double vision are phenomenally similar to the single item that normally appears. If the items are images in the case of double vision, therefore, we should conclude that the same is true in the normal case, that images always make up the visual field. The argument is thus an instance of a logical pattern characteristic of representationalism. To explain a perceptual aberration, we must, it is said, embrace a theory that has implications about perception in normal cases.

But we are not forced to accept any such theory of seeing double. It will be recalled that the normal visual system employs two sense organs—two eyes. The system normally integrates the input from them in such a way as to produce a single percept. We experience a single visual field and see each object as one thing. But the integration is never complete. It occurs within a narrow range determined by the angle of convergence of the eyes; double images occur elsewhere in the field, although they are normally not noticed. And the integration is easily disrupted by poking the eye (or drinking too much, being hit on the head, etc.). When this happens, it does not create two objects of perception; it creates two percepts of the same object. Which "image" is the real thing? They both are. The same thing is seen twice. We should interpret this in the same way we would interpret seeing and touching the same object. The only difference is that with double vision, enough integration remains that only a single visual field is experienced. Hence there appear to be two items next to each other. But this is just what one would expect. Pressing the eyeball does not eliminate binocular fusion altogether; it merely throws off the delicate calibration by which retinal inputs are matched. That is how vision works, and again we must ask, By what right do we expect it to work any differently?

This brings us to the argument from hallucinations, which is based, by the same logic, on a much more radical sort of aberration. Hallucinations do not belong in the same category as illusions. The latter are extreme cases of perceptual relativity, such as the stick that looks bent in the water. An object is perceived in unusual circumstances and thus in an unusual form, but there is still an object present and discriminated from its background. Illusions are therefore cases of perception. But in hallucinations, there is no object present at all, or objects that are present are embellished in ways that do not correspond to any of their attributes. Thus the reports of subjects on drugs are full of walls toppling or flowing, kaleidoscopic bursts of color, music and voices coming from nowhere. Illusions arise from the interaction between object and perceiver, but hallucinations are apparently produced by wholly internal sources, from neural activity touched off by abnormal causes such as drugs, intense emotions, subconscious fears, epileptic seizures. Hallucinations, then, are not perceptions, and there is no apparent reason to think they will tell us anything about perception.

Yet the argument from hallucinations denies this; indeed, the importance of the phenomenon for representational theories of perception can hardly be overstated. And the pattern here is parallel to that of the argument from double images. Thus the first step is to claim that hallucinations are phenomenally similar to percepts; from the subject's point of view they are indistinguishable. The second step is to draw an implication from this about the objects of immediate awareness. As Ayer puts it: "If, when our perceptions were delusive [Ayer refers to any experience, veridical or not, as a perception], we were always perceiving something of a different kind from what we perceived when they were veridical, we should expect our experience to be qualitatively different in the two cases." The difference in kind that Ayer means is a difference in ontological status. If the object were external in one case and internal in the other, we would expect some qualitative difference between them. If we assume, then, that there is no such difference, the objects of perception can be no more external than those of hallucination. In formal terms:

1) If the objects of perceptual awareness had a different status from the objects of hallucination, there would be a qualitative difference between the experiences.

2) There is no such qualitative difference.

Therefore, the object of perceptual awareness has the same status as the object of hallucination.

3) The object of hallucination has the status of an image, not of an external object.

Therefore, the object of perceptual awareness has the status of an image, not of an external object.[15]

This argument has been criticized so exhaustively by others that a summary will suffice.[16] Premise (2) is a psychological claim and could be supported only by judgments of similarity by actual sub-

15. A. J. Ayer, *Foundations of Empirical Knowledge* (London, 1940), 6; see also C. D. Broad, *The Mind and Its Place in Nature* (New York, 1925), 155–57. In presenting his version, Ayer denies that it is intended to prove the existence of sense-data as matters of fact; it is only a pragmatic reason for accepting the sense-data language. But J. L. Austin shows, in *Sense and Sensibilia* (Oxford, 1962), Chap. VI, that Ayer in fact takes the argument as proving a factual conclusion.

16. *Cf.* Austin, *Sense and Sensibilia*, Chap. V; and Hirst, *Problems of Perception*, 37–45.

jects of hallucinations. These judgments have been made often enough, but they cannot be taken at face value. Hallucinations occur in conditions of extreme malfunction, from causes that distort the judgment as well as the sensory processes of the brain. Although it is beyond doubt that some vivid imagery occurs, we cannot take the report of subjects as evidence about the degree of similarity between hallucinations and perception. Premise (1), by contrast, is a philosophical thesis—that a difference in status between the objects of hallucination and perception would manifest itself as a qualitative difference in content. Ayer admits that this assumption requires some justification.[17] But he offers none, and neither have other proponents of the argument. It is thus an arbitrary assumption.

The argument, finally, is circular. Suppose that we could accept the first two premises, and thus the intermediate conclusion that the objects are the same in perception and hallucination. If we approached the matter without presuppositions, this would put us in a quandary. Common sense tells us that what is experienced in hallucinations is not real. This is expressed as premise (3), and it forces us to a conclusion about perception. But common sense also tells us that what is experienced in perception *is* real. And if this were put in place of premise (3), it would force us to conclude that the objects of hallucinations are after all real. There is no reason to prefer premise (3) over this alternative, since they have the same basis. The claim that hallucinated objects are not real is asserted, and could only be understood and justified, by contrast with the assumption that the objects of perception are real. Without this, there is no contrast to be drawn between them, and thus no meaning to the claim that hallucinated objects are unreal. A presuppositionless reasoner would therefore feel some hesitation about how to proceed from the intermediate conclusion. But there is no such hesitation on the part of the argument's proponents. They must have already rejected the possibility that external things are the objects of perceptual awareness—and that was the conclusion to be proved.

There is more to be said, however, about the role hallucinations have played in perceptual epistemology. The argument from hallucinations was stated above as an argument for sense-data—the act-

17. Ayer, *Foundations of Empirical Knowledge*, 12.

object analysis of sensory experience was incorporated into the conclusion. But we saw that the representationalist model was more
general. It rests fundamentally on the assumption that perception
consists in an experiential state, however it is to be analyzed, which
could occur in the absence of the external object. And it is clear that
this assumption requires some argument. I am looking at the cup on
my desk again. If the cup is taken away, there seems to be nothing
left of the experience; the experience is nothing but the awareness
of the cup. The representationalist, then, must offer some evidence
that the experience *could* remain in the absence of the object, and
that it would consist in a state also present in normal perception.[18]
Hallucinations are typically cited in this regard, as a way of showing
ostensively that something is left after the object is subtracted. Roderick Firth has argued, for example, that by comparing percepts and
the corresponding hallucinations, we can isolate a "sensory constituent" common to both, and that we can do so prior to choosing
between act-object and adverbial analyses of the constituent.[19] But
hallucinatory phenomena will not support even this generalized
conclusion unless they are interpreted in light of an antecedent
commitment to the representationalist model.

Whether or not premise (2) of the argument is true, there is
doubtless *some* similarity between a hallucination and the actual
perception of the corresponding objects. The question is, What is
necessary to explain this similarity? Without an answer to this question, there is no basis for Firth's conclusion. The key to any answer
is the fact that a hallucination is the experience of sensory contents
that cannot be identified with any object present to the senses. How
is this possible?

We know that the perceptual awareness of a scene can be retained and reexperienced in a certain way. I picture to myself the
face of a friend. The experience is not a perceptual one; I am not
fooled into thinking I am seeing her again. Yet it is not a purely con-

18. This assumption also requires support if the experiential state is identified
with a physical state. Indeed, Machamer's theory contains a piece of a priori neurophysiology in its assumption that perceptions and hallucinations involve the same
neural states ("Gibson and the Conditions for Perception," in Machamer and Turnbull [eds.], *Studies in Perception*, 449–50).

19. Roderick Firth, "Austin and the Argument from Illusion," *Philosophical Review*, LXXIII (1964), 375–77.

ceptual memory, either. I picture details—a wave in her hair, the shape of her smile—that I could not capture in words. Her face "appears" in memory in the same form, from the same angle, in which I used to see her. This quasi-perceptual memory, then, is clearly similar to the experience of perceiving, and there is indeed a common element—the person herself whom I perceive in the one case and recall in the other. The experiences share the same *object*; the common element does not lie in any experiential state; on the contrary, it is qua experiences that they differ. In memory, I experience her as someone from the past, not actually present to my senses.

Similarly, we know that we can create new quasi-perceptual scenes in imagination, reorganizing sensory materials from past perception and experiencing them in more or less vivid images of things as they might be or might have been. As in perceptual memory, the experience of imagining an object is different from that of perceiving it—in imagination, one is aware of making it up. There is also, however, a partial similarity, and once again it is the result of the object as opposed to the mode of awareness. Of course what one imagines is not, except accidentally, an object he has actually perceived in the past. But the reason one imagines an object in a way that would be similar to a possible perception of the corresponding real object, is that the process of imagination makes use of materials retained from the past perception of real objects. Here again, therefore, the similarity to perception is a matter of the objects of awareness, not the mode of experiencing them. And there is no reason to posit a common experiential state.

In eidetic imagination, the image can become extremely vivid, the difference between the imaginary and the perceptual modes of awareness much harder to detect. In hallucinations, the capacity to distinguish them is apparently lost altogether. But this does not show that the experiential state involved in hallucination is identical to that in the corresponding perception. A hallucination is not the awareness of objects present to the senses; its qualitative content cannot be explained as the product of a present interaction between object and perceiver. It would have to be explained by analogy with (perhaps as a special form of) perceptual memory and imagination—as a reexperiencing, in a rearranged form, of sensory materials retained from previous perception. And once again the similarity to actual perception would be the result of the objects perceived in the one case, recalled and rearranged in the other; the difference would lie in the mode of experiencing them. Thus the best explanation of what happens in hallucination would be that the capacity for re-calling and rearranging perceptual experiences is set in operation by causes that prevent one from experiencing them *as* recalled or made up. But this is a distortion, an aberration. It does not mean that one is actually in the same state as when he perceives; it only means he cannot tell that he is not.

This approach to hallucinations is based on the realist view of awareness. Conversely, Firth's approach is based on a prior com-mitment to the representationalist model, and so cannot provide evidence for it. This becomes evident when he dismisses any ques-tions about the rarity of hallucinations, the fact that few have ex-perienced them, or their doubtful similarity to perceptions. Such questions, on the face of it, *would* be important if hallucinations are used to isolate a certain feature of perception ostensively. They do not matter, he claims, because we can always *imagine* what a hal-lucination is like, and we can image it having an exact phenomenal similarity to perception.[20] But how are we to imagine this? Ob-viously the idea is that we simply imagine our present experience occurring when no external object is present. But then the reference to hallucinations drops out. The belief in a "sensory constituent" conceived as a state of the subject rests on the mere assertion that perceptual experience can occur without its external object. It is not surprising in this regard—indeed, it is symbolic of the representa-tionalist approach—that the most commonly used example is not even a real hallucination, but the fictional case of Macbeth's dagger. Hallucinations serve only to dramatize a possibility already ac-cepted. In any case, there is no argument from hallucinations with-out a prior representationalist analysis of them; there is no argu-ment without circularity.

A final argument for the representationalist model is a form of the classical causal argument. The causal sequence in perception has usually been considered a one-way process, from object to recep-tors to cortex, with the conscious percept as the result. This in itself has often occasioned the claim that the same perceptual experience could occur so long as the last, intraneural stages occur, even if there

20. *Ibid.*, 380.

is no external object acting on the receptors.[21] The supposition is incomplete, because the receptors are not self-stimulating, but it might be expanded as follows. Suppose that some way were found to provide the same proximate stimulus at the receptors that is provided by ordinary objects, by means of a device that is utterly unlike them. Psychologists do this in a limited way with lights and mirrors, in the attempt to isolate stimulus variables, and we can imagine it carried further. The device would produce the same gradients of stimulus energy, the same patterns across the array, and the same variations that normally attend the actions of focusing, scanning, and moving.

The argument consists in the attempt to show that we are forced to use a representationalist model to interpret this hypothetical situation. In the first place, we could not argue, as in the case of hallucinations, that the resulting percept is radically nonperceptual, involving the recall of past perceptual material. The experience would result from actual, current stimulation by an environment acting on the senses. It is assumed, moreover, that the device would provide exactly the same proximate stimulation as do normal objects, so that the proximate cause would be the same. Therefore the effect must be the same. But in the hypothetical case, the effect cannot be an awareness of the experienced objects, in the sense of a real relation to external things, because those things are not there. At best, there is a state of the perceiver that is *experienced* as relational, that has the intentional character of a direction on an object. It is not, however, a real relation. But this effect is the same as in the normal case, since they have the same proximate cause. Therefore the normal percept is at best an experienced awareness of an object, but not a real relation to anything external.

Notice that this argument has the same basic pattern as the argument from hallucination. We are offered a reason for believing that the status of the object of direct awareness must be the same in the hypothetical and the normal case. Then, because it is assumed that we are not directly aware of an external object in the hypothetical case, we are asked to conclude that the same is true of normal perception. As I noted in regard to the argument from hallucination, however, we could just as well turn the argument around. Because

21. *Cf.* C. D. Broad, "Some Elementary Reflexions on Sense-Perception," in Swartz (ed.), *Perceiving, Sensing, and Knowing*, 39.

we are aware of external objects in normal perception, the same must be true of the hypothetical case. Logically, the argument brings us to a fork in the road, but does not tell us which way to go. The choice we make at this point will be determined by the model of awareness we bring to the situation.

In the hypothetical case, the external objects are the states or structures of the device producing the stimulation. If we accept a diaphanous model of awareness, we must deny that the perceiver is directly aware of those objects, because his experience clearly does not mirror or diaphanously represent them. In the realist model, however, we assume from the outset that perception is the awareness of external objects, but we make no assumption about how that awareness works. In particular, we must examine the facts of the particular case in order to apply the form-object distinction, *i.e.*, in order to distinguish the respects in which the way an object appears is functionally dependent on the object itself, from those respects in which it is functionally dependent on the way the perceptual system responds to stimulation provided by the object.[22] And we can follow this approach in the hypothetical no less than in any actual case of perceiving.

The subject in the hypothetical case would be perceiving in the same form in which we perceive, but that form would be his way of perceiving a world quite different from ours. The form-object relations would be different. Color, for example, might be the form in which he perceives some electrical state of the device. But if the reproduction of the proximate stimulus were as complete as imagined, he would be perceiving his world—the device. He would be responding selectively to its states and events, he would be discriminating them. Moreover, perception is not the product of a one-way causal process, as the argument tends to assume. It depends as well on active processes of moving, and of orienting and focusing the sense organs. If the subject's own activity did not result in experienced changes, things would take on a very different look.[23] Thus

22. Thus the pattern of causal relationships is relevant to determining the object of perceptual awareness, in distinguishing it from the form. But this does not imply a causal theory of perceptual objects, in the sense criticized earlier. As I will argue later, the entity perceived is that which is discriminated.

23. For examples, see James J. Gibson, "Perception as a Function of Stimulation," in Sigmund Koch (ed.), *Psychology: A Study of a Science* (6 vols.; New York, 1959, 1962), I, 483–84.

to reproduce the conditions of normal perception, the motor neurons mediating such actions must be wired to the device, so that they could alter its states in ways that in turn affect stimulation. This means that the subject could explore his world, sampling the stimulus information it provides. He would not only perceive his world but act in and on it. Of course his experience would not be similar to the objects he perceives, but then normal experience is not similar to its objects either. Perceptual awareness cannot be compared to its objects at all on the ground of similarity or dissimilarity.

Thus it does not follow from a description of the hypothetical case that the subject's experience would be only an internal, intentional relation to an object. Precisely because we know ahead of time that perceptual awareness is a real relation to objects not dependent on consciousness, we must say that what is perceived depends in part on what is there to be perceived, and on the way it interacts with our means of perception.

Of course we are assuming that the hypothetical case is one that endures over time—long enough for the subject to explore his world, long enough for it (and not the normal environment) to *be* his world. If we imagine the device switched on and off rapidly, so that stimulation is provided now by the ordinary sources, now by the device, then it is no longer clear that he is *aware* of the device-environment. But it is equally unclear that he would be aware of the ordinary environment when the device is off. It is unclear that his senses would be functioning any longer as means of cognition. The senses are natural systems, evolved to achieve a result in a specific environment. As with any other biological system, their function is integrated with the environment, and if the latter changes beyond a certain point, we may well be unable to say whether the senses are any longer performing their function.

The causal argument, then, is a final illustration of a more general truth. There are no local arguments for representationalism. No particular perceptual phenomenon in itself can establish the representationalist model (nor could it refute the model, for that matter). The phenomena require interpretation, and the principles of interpretation can be established only by reference to basic assumptions about cognition.

The representationalist theory of perception has often been described as representative realism; and though I have emphasized its difference from realism, the description is apt in one respect. Representationalism has usually been fueled by a realist impulse, a belief that reality exists independently of consciousness and is the ultimate object of knowledge. But this impulse has been too easily thrown by the phenomena of perceptual relativity and hallucinations, too quick to accept the Cartesian model as a means of interpreting them. As a result, it has been saddled with a host of problems generated by the model—as well as opening the door to skepticism and idealism.

This is why I have identified the model and its influence, and rejected it in every form. In particular, I have rejected the assumption that perception is constituted by an experiential state it shares with dreams, hallucination, imagination, and other experiences; and the consequence that perception must be defined by distinguishing it from them. This approach is appropriate if the mind is an inner theater, with various contents appearing before an inner eye. But if the mind is a faculty for grasping reality, if awareness by nature is a relation to what is outside the mind, then perception must be defined in quite a different way.

5

The Nature of
Perception

Perception by its nature is the awareness of external objects. This awareness is the function of a certain type of cognitive system, operating by means of the sense organs. Other systems produce other modes of experience—such as dreams and imagination—that are in certain respects similar to perceiving. But these are *other* systems, other modes of experience. To the extent that they rely on the perceptual apparatus, they are secondary and derivative phenomena. The same is true of hallucinations, even if they are phenomenologically indistinguishable from perceptions. Perception should not be defined, then, in terms of a genus that includes hallucinations and the like, as if these were phenomena on a par with perceiving. It should be defined as a type of awareness of external objects, to be contrasted with other types of awareness.

But what is required for a definition of a type of awareness? Consider a prior question—what do we need to contrast perception with? By taking it as the awareness of external physical objects, we are obviously contrasting it with introspection. We are also contrasting it with interoception, the sensory awareness of conditions internal to the body, as in hunger or pain. (In what follows, the term *external* will distinguish what is perceived from what is internal either to consciousness or to the perceiver's body.) The important task is to distinguish perception from sensation and from conceptual knowledge of external objects.

The differences among them do not lie along a single axis or dimension, but they can be reduced to two essential axes that will orient our search for a definition. These are the means and the object of awareness, the how and the what. Conceptual knowledge requires a conscious and voluntary *process* of concept formation, reasoning, and so on, whereas perception is direct, produced by a causal sequence that works automatically—a difference in the means by which awareness is attained. There is also a difference in the range of their objects. We are limited in perception to things present to the senses, but concepts allow us to relate them to things not present and to things that cannot be perceived at all. The distinction between perception and sensation is also drawn in terms of their objects, as we have seen. What we perceive are entities as wholes, as units possessing properties, not the properties themselves as units.

Perception should be defined, then, in terms of its means and its objects. And this is consistent with our basic premises that awareness is inherently and essentially relational, so that it cannot be described apart from its objects; and that it is a natural phenomenon with a specific identity, functioning by specific means. I would define perception as *the direct awareness of discriminated entities by means of patterns of energy absorption by sense receptors.*[1] Each element in this definition requires explanation and defense.

The Means of Perception

The key stage in the process of perception is the absorption of energy by the sense receptors. But sheer absorption is not enough. If the energy is completely undifferentiated, containing no gradients across the mosaic of receptors, it will be indistinguishable from the absence of stimulation. In one classic experiment, for example, a subject's eyes were covered with the two halves of a ping-pong ball, which were then bathed with diffuse colored light. There was no texture in his visual field, no means of judging depth, but only a colored fog—and the color quickly faded, replaced by the "brain gray" one experiences in total darkness. Color could be restored only

1. This definition is based on Robert Efron's, in "What is Perception?" *Boston Studies in the Philosophy of Science*, IV (1966–68), 147. I have substituted "discriminated entities" for "discriminated existents," for reasons that will become clear.

by introducing some contrast into the field. A gradient of stimulus energy is required—even for sensation. For perception, there must be a pattern of gradients. The character of the pattern, the minimum complexity needed for perception, can be specified only by psychology. As we have seen, there is a continuum from sensation to perception, and an exact border line can be drawn only by reference to the needs of psychological theory. But the term *pattern* conveys the general nature of the requirement. In vision, for example, there must be some texture in the optic array to allow the separation of a figure from a ground and to allow any determinate sense of depth.[2]

But of all the stages in the causal sequence, why should the definition make special mention of the proximate stimulus? Because it is the crucial nexus in the process. On the one hand, the range of what can be perceived is set by the nature of the energy to which sense receptors can respond. To be perceived at all, an object must be able to originate or (as in the case of vision) structure an array of energy at the receptors. And as we saw earlier, an attribute of such an object is perceptible only if there is some feature of the stimulus array that is specific to that attribute. On the other hand, the later, neurological stages of the process must be seen as ways in which the nervous system isolates and responds to these stimulus features. The opponent process theory of color vision, for example, would have no basis without the prior knowledge that the stimulus feature for color is wavelength, for opponent processes are wavelength analyzers. Thus James J. Gibson's project of isolating stimulus variables is a crucial first step in understanding the neurophysiology of perception. Without these variables, we would not know what to look for in the sensory pathways, or how to identify functionally what we found. The landmark work of D. H. Hubel and T. N. Wiesel, for example, was the discovery of "receptive fields" of cells in the visual pathways. They showed that the cells fired in response to certain patterns in the optic array.[3]

2. J. E. Hochberg, W. Triebel, and G. Seaman, "Color Adaptation Under Conditions of Homogeneous Visual Stimulation," *Journal of Experimental Psychology*, XLI (1951), 153–59. For a review of the factors involved in the optic array, see L. L. Avant, "Vision in the Ganzfeld," *Psychological Bulletin*, LXIV (1965), 246–58.

3. James J. Gibson, "Perception as a Function of Stimulation," in Sigmund Koch (ed.), *Psychology: A Study of a Science* (6 vols.; New York, 1959, 1962), I, 456–501; D. H. Hubel and T. N. Wiesel, "Brain Mechanisms of Vision," *Scientific American*, CCXLI (September, 1979), 150–62.

Why not include in the definition the fact that we must perceive objects in a specific form? The answer is that the fact *is* included. That we perceive by specific means entails that we perceive in a form. There is no possibility of a diaphanous awareness from which we need to distinguish perception. The form of perception is the experienced effect of the physical means of perceiving, which are the essential term in this relationship. The form in which we perceive an object's attribute is a consequence of the way the nervous system responds to the stimulus correlate of that attribute. This relationship is reflected in the fact that to identify any aspect of appearance *as* a form, one must show that it is causally dependent on the perceptual system. A complete account of the relationship would require an understanding of the neural processes involved. We can nevertheless establish some correlations between forms of perception and stimulus conditions, without knowing the neural link between them. We have a commonsense understanding that variations in the distance and orientation of the object give rise to variations in the form with which we perceive its size and shape. And classical psychophysics found correlations between certain sensory qualities and the dimensions of stimulus energy—between hue and wavelength, pitch and frequency, loudness and intensity.

These provide one way of measuring perceptual awareness. The awareness of any perceptible attribute has a finite limit of precision. Given two objects that differ in respect of such an attribute, the difference can be decreased to the point at which it can no longer be detected. The objects will still be physically different, but they will appear identical—they will be perceived in the same form. The smallest detectable difference is called the differential threshold for that attribute, and we can describe the perceptual awareness as more or less *specific* as the threshold is smaller or larger. In optimal conditions, for example, the differential threshold for color is about four nanometers on the spectrum. With color as with every attribute, however, the specificity of perception varies with changes in the conditions and is different at different points along the perceptible range of the attribute. Presumably these limits are set by the capacity of the sense organs and nervous system to resolve minute differences in the proximate stimulus. Such limits must exist for every relevant stimulus feature, although so far they have been established only for the simpler variables such as wavelength or sound frequency. Specificity is important because perceptual awareness is essentially discriminating, and the differential threshold measures one form of perceptual discrimination—the awareness of differences in the degree of perceived attributes.[4]

The causal process, however, does not exhaust what must be said under the heading of the means of perception, for it does not distinguish the perceptual from the conceptual awareness of external objects. I am aware of the package on the table in front of me, because I perceive it; I am aware that there is a package on the table downstairs, even though I do not see it, because I heard the delivery van arrive, and packages are always put on that table. In both cases, my awareness is the result of sensory stimulation, directly in the one case, indirectly in the other. This concept of directness isolates an essential feature of perceptual awareness, and the problem now is to formulate the concept more clearly. Conceptual knowledge is indirect because it is mediated. It involves an active, conscious process of integration. But what sort of mediation underlies the distinction we need to make? It cannot be simply that conceptual knowledge involves the exercise of definite means of cognition, for that would be true of perception as well. Nor can it be that conceptual knowledge involves conscious activity, as opposed to the automatic neural process that mediates perception, for conscious activity also plays an important role in perceptual awareness.

The normal adult human is not a tabula rasa. We bring to perception an enormous fund of background knowledge, and the act of perceiving is usually guided by the conscious purposes of expanding or applying that knowledge. Consider, for example, the role of attention. At any moment, the way in which one directs his attention affects what is perceived from among all the things that could be perceived, given present stimulation. It is doubtful that an act of attention is necessary for perceiving *every* object. Stimuli such as sudden chills, loud explosions, or noxious odors intrude themselves upon us quite apart from any conscious choice. But attention certainly can make the difference between perceiving or not perceiving an object—the classic examples being one's awareness of his clothes or of a low hum in the background. And the degree of at-

4. For more on the specificity of perception, see Efron, "What is Perception?," 137–73.

tention to an object has a marked effect on the character of one's perceptual awareness of it. Thus there are major differences in the scope, clarity, and specificity of awareness—that is, in *how much* of the object is perceived—along a continuum of attention from objects at the edge of the visual field, to pocket change fingered absentmindedly, to the road ahead while one is driving, to a pen one has found at last among the litter on the desk, to the face of another person in conversation, to the riveting sound of a scratching at one's door late at night.

Moreover, the history of what a person attends to affects what it is possible for him to perceive in a given situation. Attention is the major factor in perceptual learning. A person who is learning to taste wines, for example, is typically given two closely related wines, differing only in a single dimension, so that his attention will be drawn to that dimension and he will be sensitive to it the next time. Practicing perceptual attention allows him to register variables of the stimulus to which he was previously insensitive.[5] Similarly, a scientist and a layman may look at the same laboratory setup, and be subject to the same optical array, but the scientist will perceive much more than the layman will. The difference is not merely that the scientist feels more at home in the environment, or can identify conceptually what he sees; he *perceives* it differently. He is sensitive to finer differences in shapes and colors, and can discriminate perceptually—can isolate as units—the individual pieces of equipment that comprise what to the layman is a single complicated jumble. Thus the causal sequence set off by the proximate stimulus determines what can be perceived in any given conditions, but it does not necessarily determine what will be perceived. The conscious activity of the perceiver is also a factor.

This was one reason for the classical sensationalist view that perception as opposed to sensation is active. But the occurrence of conscious activity does not support sensationalism. For one thing, there is no difference in this regard between sensing and perceiving. I do not perceive my clothes unless I attend to them, but I have no sensations of them either, even though they are stimulating various receptors. Nor does it imply that the objects of perception are

5. *Cf.* Eleanor J. Gibson, *Principles of Perceptual Learning and Development* (Englewood Cliffs, N.J., 1969), esp. Chap. 7.

not given. The epistemological function of the concept of direct awareness is to locate the *given*, that which provides the basis for knowledge. The empiricist tradition followed Locke, and later Kant, in identifying the given with the passive element in experience, on the assumption that any conscious activity must be interpretive or constitutive.[6] The activity of consciousness, however, is not constitutive. And as we shall see, attention is to be distinguished from conceptual activities precisely on the ground that it is not interpretive. Nor, finally, does the presence of conscious activity imply that perceiving involves the use of concepts—another Kantian assumption. Animals and preconceptual children seem capable of degrees of attention, and even if an adult human cannot attend to an object without identifying it conceptually, there is no reason to equate the act of attention with the act of identification. On the contrary, we should stand the argument on its head. We cannot identify an object without some prior attention to it, so that the two cannot be equated. When I see a bird outside the window, I identify it as a bird automatically. But before I can do even this, something must draw my attention to that item in the visual field.

The sense in which perceptual awareness is direct, then, is not that it occurs passively. The concept of direct awareness must distinguish between the *types* of conscious activity involved in perception and conceptual thought. To understand this sense of directness, we should focus on the way in which perceptual objects are *given* while facts known conceptually are not. Consider a piece of inferential knowledge. What makes it indirect?

I know there is a package on the table downstairs, because I heard the delivery van, and I know that is where packages are always put. This knowledge is indirect, because my only cognitive access to the fact known is through other things I am aware of. I had first to identify a sound as the sound of a delivery van, which means that I had to relate it to other similar sounds I have heard in the past. Then, given that it was the sound of a delivery van, I had to employ my knowledge that packages are always left on the table—a piece of inductive knowledge that also depends on what I have perceived in the past. Unless I had heard the sound, therefore, and knew the relation between it and the presence of a package on the table, I could

6. *Cf.* D. W. Hamlyn, *The Psychology of Perception* (London, 1957), 51.

not have become aware of this latter fact. My knowledge of the fact depends on prior knowledge of its relations to other facts.[7]

The act of attention is different in this respect from the activity of inferring. We *are* normally led to attend to something because of some prior awareness. I focus on the feel of my clothes because I was just thinking about them; I turn to look behind me because I heard a sound there; the tree across the yard seems strange, so I look more closely at it. But in inferential knowledge, the content of the conclusion is determined by premises from which it is inferred, and the conclusion is only as reliable as the process by which it was reached. This is not true of the perceptual awareness to which attention leads. Some prior awareness may lead me to turn my attention in a certain direction, but *what* I will then become aware of depends solely on the stimulation available in that direction. Attention may determine how much I will extract from the stimulus, but it does not determine what I will extract. Nor does it matter *how*, by what particular process or from what prior awareness, my attention is attracted to the object; it is the object itself which directly determines what I will perceive. My awareness of that object is then as reliable as my senses, and it can give me knowledge of the object even if there was some error in that which first led me to turn toward the object. On closer examination, there may be nothing at all strange about the tree. Thus when one perceives an object, one's awareness of it does not depend on knowing its relation to other objects or facts. Attention is a ladder one can throw away. This is what constitutes the directness of perception.

This concept of direct awareness is obviously a realist one. It draws the distinction between direct and indirect within the range of our awareness of external objects. But of course the concept has a long history in the representationalist tradition, where it is defined so as to mark off the awareness of inner states from any awareness of external objects. The root idea behind this approach is that of a diaphanous type of awareness, a direct confrontation between mind and object that is not conditioned by any causal con-

7. Between the percept and inferential knowledge lies the perceptual judgment, the conceptual identification of what is directly perceived—*e.g.*, "This is a table." The acquisition of the concept involved ("table") depends on the awareness of patterns of similarity among objects. Hence the perceptual judgment is not a form of direct awareness; the entire conceptual level is indirect.

nection between them. This would mean we can be directly aware only of internal objects produced at the end of the causal chain in perception. But the concept of a diaphanous awareness is invalid, and we must reject the representationalist concept of direct awareness as well. The fact that we perceive the attributes of objects by means of stimulus features specific to them does not imply that we are aware of the attributes indirectly. The awareness of the attribute does not depend on any *awareness of* the stimulus feature or of the causal relation between them. Nor does the role of neural processes in isolating stimulus features make perception indirect, for there is no reason to construe these processes on the model of inference. Finally, the fact that we perceive the attributes of objects by means of a form does not imply that we are aware of the attributes indirectly. We are not perceptually aware of the form as opposed to the objective attribute, or of the relation between them. The form *is* the way we are directly aware of the attribute.

Some philosophers have also tried to define direct awareness in terms of the certainty of perceptual judgments. A subject is directly aware of a given object, they say, if he could not be mistaken in his beliefs about that object or in his belief that he is aware of that object.[8] The sense in which it is said that such a judgment could not be mistaken is that of infallibility or incorrigibility—a Cartesian concept to be examined later. But there is a local problem with the attempt to define direct awareness in terms of the certainty of judgments.

A judgment or assertion is about something. It predicates something of a subject and has the form "X is . . . " The thesis in question claims that we directly perceive X if we can make an infallible judgment that X is, for example, red or that we perceive that X is red. But what takes the place of the term X in the judgment? If it is an expression referring to an external object, then the judgment will not be of the sort intended. If it is an expression referring to an appearance, then the thesis will be incomplete without an analysis of appearances. In the realist view, an appearance is the fact of an object's appearing a certain way—which is the fact of the subject's perceiving it in a certain form—and is not an object that can have

8. See Norman Malcolm, "Direct Perception," in *Knowledge and Certainty* (Ithaca, 1963), 73–95, for a definition of this type. Malcolm cites a number of predecessors.

such properties as red. The thesis must then hypostatize appearances, on the model of Cartesian ideas, and treat the judgment as being about an idea or sense-datum. But for the judgment "This sense-datum is red" to be infallible, the presupposition that sense-data exist must be known with equal infallibility—that is, the sense-data theory must be infallible, a proposition that would come as a surprise to the theory's advocates no less than to its opponents. The problem here is that an explicit reference to the X in question, which assigns it to some category, will inevitably contain philosophical presuppositions that cannot by any stretch be called infallible.[9]

Nor can the problem be avoided by reducing the referring element in the judgment or assertion to a bare demonstrative. D. D. Todd has argued, for example, that judgments which *identify* what is perceived (as a physical object, sense-datum, afterimage) should be distinguished from judgments which merely *describe* it qualitatively. Examples of the latter would have the form "What I perceive is blue and star-shaped" or "*This* is blue and star-shaped."[10] Such a judgment would not identify the subject of the attributes, except as something present to awareness at a given time and place. But even this contains a bit of philosophical theory, as we can see by considering the color concept. Something is blue—what does this mean? If it means that something has the sensory quality blue as an intrinsic property, it makes a philosophical—and, in my view, untenable—assumption. If it means that something has the quality in the way physical objects do—*i.e.*, something is such that in these conditions I perceive it in this form—then it is not what the definition seeks. It is a judgment about a physical object. Moreover, if such judgments *could* avoid identifying the type of thing to which X belongs, they could not for that very reason serve to define a class of objects of direct perception.

9. This problem arises in Malcolm's formulation: "*A* directly perceives *x* if and only if *A*'s assertion that he perceives *x* could not be mistaken" (*ibid.*, 84). There is an additional problem with the case he discusses at greatest length, that of afterimages. I do not consider them objects of sight. When the eyes are open, an afterimage is merely an unusual form in which an external object is perceived. When the eyes are closed, it is a by-product of past visual stimulation and not a case of seeing anything. But quite apart from this, the judgment that something is an afterimage is easily mistaken. *Cf.* Fred Dretske, *Seeing and Knowing* (Chicago, 1969), 64.

10. D. D. Todd, "Direct Perception," *Philosophy and Phenomenological Research*, XXXV (1975), 352–62.

We cannot accept, therefore, any of the representationalist concepts of direct awareness. The concept describes our perceptual
awareness of external objects, and serves only to distinguish it from
conceptual knowledge about them. And with this, we have covered
the essential characteristics of the means of perceiving. They include a pattern of stimulus energy at the receptors, and they exclude the sort of conscious processing in which one thing is grasped
through its relations to other things. It remains, however, to discuss
the objects of perceptual awareness.

The Objects of Perception

The range of things that can be perceived is set by the capacities
of the sense receptors and the neural means for isolating stimulus
features. We have receptors sensitive to certain types of energy but
not others—to the energy of light but not of magnetic fields, to
gravity but not electrical charge. We can perceive only those entities
that originate or structure arrays of the relevant sorts of energy, and
only those attributes in virtue of which they do so. There does not
appear to be any single description of these objects. Nor is there any
further explanation, apart from the evolutionary development of the
sensory systems, of why they alone can act on the senses.

Within any given causal transaction between a particular object
and a perceptual system, there can be questions of detail about what
is the real object of perception. And the methods of answering them
are implicit in what has been said. Thus in perceiving any attribute,
we must distinguish between form and object, following the pattern in our discussion of color. The form depends on the way the
nervous system responds to a certain stimulus feature, and the object of awareness is that attribute of the external thing which is responsible for the stimulus feature.[11] In some cases, there is a legiti-
mate question about which stage in the causal chain, out of several
possible candidates, is the object. Coolness is the form in which we
perceive objective temperature, for example. But is the real object of
awareness in this case the heat-energy level of the physical object,
or the rate at which it conducts heat away from the skin, or the low-

11. Causality, though relevant in this way to determining which attribute is the
object of perceptual awareness, does not determine the object in the sense of what
is discriminated.

ered energy state it produces in the skin itself? The method for an-swering such a question is to determine whether a subject can de-tect variations in each attribute while the others are held constant.

But these issues and methods are concerned chiefly with the perceptual awareness of attributes, and thus do not suffice to dis-tinguish perception from sensation. Nor does the general realist principle that we are directly aware of external phenomena, for the principle is true of sensory as well as perceptual awareness. The dif-ference lies in the fact that perception, as opposed to sensation, in-volves the discrimination of entities. Not only are we aware of ex-ternal things that are in fact entities; we perceive them as such. Not only do we discriminate their attributes; we discriminate *them*, in the sense of isolating them as units against a background. This form of discrimination, involving the awareness of entities as such, is the defining characteristic of perception in respect of its objects—the entity is the proper object of perceptual awareness.

The thesis in question should not be taken to mean that per-ceptual experience consists in a set of snapshots, each one a single percept of a single entity. Perception is an ongoing process of mon-itoring the environment and of searching for specific bits of infor-mation, actively seeking stimulation that will answer prior ques-tions. This search is directed as much toward the qualitative nature of entities present to the senses as toward the presence or absence of the entities themselves. At any moment, the focus of attention may be on a specific attribute and not on the entity as such that has it. Nevertheless, the world we monitor and explore is, for us, a world of entities. Entities provide the structure within which we move cognitively, and this structure is present to awareness in some form even when we do not attend to it. We may focus on attributes, re-lationships, or actions, but we are aware of them *as* attributes, re-lationships, and actions of entities. Our experience would be quite different if our activities of exploration took place at the level of sen-sation, if our normal context lacked the structural features provided by the awareness of entities.[12]

Nor should the thesis be taken to mean that the awareness of entities is uniformly clear and discriminating. At any moment, a vast

12. Thus the definition would be misleading if offered as an equivalence for the locution "S sees x," as Dretske does, in *Seeing and Knowing*, 20.

context surrounds objects at the focus of attention. This perceptual penumbra serves as the ground against which we perceive. We are aware of this ground, but more or less dimly, and it shades off into something approaching a sensational form of awareness in which the features of entities as such are lost. In vision, there is a physiological gradation from the fovea outward across the retina, so that shape perception becomes poorer away from the center of the visual field and figures cannot be distinguished clearly from their ground. And in all the senses, attention can have the same effect. I may be looking directly at the conductor, but if my mind is on the music I may hardly see him, may hardly discriminate him from the background. There is a similar continuum even for objects attended to. A medium-sized object a few feet away in good illumination stands out clearly as an entity to my sight. A speck on the horizon, or a little bump in the wood I am sanding, does not stand out so clearly, no matter how hard I concentrate on it. A sound or odor may be so vague that we cannot get much beyond a sensational form of awareness of them. Nevertheless, it is the entitative character of what we perceive that defines this continuum. To understand that character, we will consider examples in which it is perceived most clearly.

Discrimination in the most general sense means simply the awareness of difference, and in this sense it is involved in any form of awareness. Even a sensation requires some contrast within the field of qualities; as I noted above, a completely undifferentiated stimulus array produces no sensory awareness. At the other end of the cognitive scale, conceptual knowledge involves some predication of an attribute. This has meaning only because the attribute predicated is understood by contrast with other attributes. If it is said that something is X, it is always reasonable to ask, X—as opposed to what? Perception is defined, then, by the *type* of discrimination involved. We can distinguish it from conceptual knowledge along one axis. Perception is direct, it does not require the cognitive integration of prior knowledge. The important problem is to distinguish it from sensation, and this is a matter of the objects discriminated.

As a preliminary statement, we can say that the units of perceptual discrimination are groups of qualities, a constellation of qualities jointly differentiated from their background. An old shirt is draped across the back of a chair. In perceiving it, I discriminate the shirt as a unit from the chair, the floor, and the other things forming its background. What does this mean? The various regions of color that comprise the shirt are perceived as "going together." Even though there is a patch of brown on the edge of the shirt that is closer in color to the chair than to any other color in the shirt, even though there is a sharper color contrast between that patch and the other parts of the shirt than there is on the other side between that patch and the chair, that patch of color is still perceived as a part of the shirt, as going together with the other colors to make up a single unit. This way of formulating the holistic character of perception was employed by the Gestalt theorists, who went on to formulate principles determining what goes together in this sense—principles such as proximity, simplicity, good continuation.[13] And these may be important in color integration, in discriminating objects with variegated surfaces from similarly variegated backgrounds. But there is a philosophical problem with the formulation if we take it as a general description of the ways qualities are integrated in perception.

The problem is that we have in effect started by taking the awareness of the qualities for granted, and then noticed that in perception certain qualities in the field go together and others do not. We are then led to ask Hume's question, What is it that binds the qualities together? And we are more or less forced to Hume's answer: nothing—that is, nothing that is given perceptually. On this approach, Hume was right that we have "no [perceptual] idea of substance, distinct from that of a collection of particular qualities."[14] We see the colors of the shirt, its shape and texture, but we do not see any metaphysical substrate—any bare particular or prime matter—that underlies and holds them together. We are then faced, it seems, with a choice between the historical alternatives. We can follow Hume and say that our perception of qualities as going together is guided by past experience of what qualities have usually appeared in conjunction with each other. Or we can follow Kant and say that the perceiver imposes an organizing structure—a category of substance—on the sensory manifold, so that he experiences

13. See Julian Hochberg, "Perception I. Color and Shape," in J. W. Kling and L. A. Riggs (eds.), *Experimental Psychology* (3rd ed.; New York, 1972), 432–37, for a summary of these principles.
14. David Hume, *A Treatise of Human Nature*, ed. Ernest C. Mossner (Baltimore, 1969), Book I, Pt. 1, Chap. VI.

qualities as going together because he himself has joined them. In either view, the qualities alone are given, and in themselves they are unrelated. What makes certain ones go together as qualities of a single entity is something contributed by the perceiver. Neither is a *realist* account of the discrimination of entities.

It would be fruitless to argue in reply that we *do* perceive some mysterious relation between the qualities and an equally mysterious "something I know not what" that underlies them. We perceive no such thing. The proper reply is that the issue has been set up invalidly. We cannot take the awareness of the individual qualities for granted and then ask what holds them together. That assumes the thesis of sensationalism. Indeed, Hume's question has the matter backwards. We begin with the awareness of a whole nature, a thing standing out from its background. The isolation of individual qualities does not come first; it is a more sophisticated and derivative ability, the result of our capacity to focus selectively on aspects of what is already perceived. To look at an object and wonder why this shape is connected with this color (or with any color), and this color with this texture, is a highly conceptual approach, one that presupposes a great deal of prior activity of analysis. If I hold a yellow rubber ball in my hand and examine it, the question is not how or why the various qualities I perceive go together. The question is how I come to separate them. The color and the shape are not related externally. It is this yellow surface, the yellowness itself, that stretches around to form a sphere, and the sphere is nothing but the yellow standing out against the background. When I squeeze it I become aware of its softness and resilience, and this is information about the very spherical shape I am holding. When I drop it and let it bounce, it is a single item that moves. There is no cause for wonder here at what metaphysical choreography allows the qualities to move in formation. There is only a yellow, resilient sphere moving and making a noise when it hits. It is not surprising, therefore, that if we ask what holds the qualities together, the question seems puzzling, or that if we take the question seriously, the only possible answer seems to be an activity on our own part. For it was we ourselves who took the qualities apart in the first place.

It is nevertheless possible to describe those aspects in what we perceive that are essential to perceptual discrimination. In doing so, we can justify the principle that the entity is the proper object of perception, because those aspects correspond to the traditional conception of a substance or entity. To begin with, we perceive attributes, relations, and actions *as* attributes, relations, and actions of things. The gray color to my right is the color of the coffee cup, the grainy texture I feel is the texture of the desk. In the figure-ground experience, a contour is perceived as one-sided, as an attribute of the figure and not the ground. Experientially, as Wolfgang Köhler put it, "the reality of a form depends upon the existence of a definite whole which, when segregated as such, *has* that real form."[15] This should not be taken to mean that we perceive the attributes as units and then perceive some relation they bear to another unit, the entity. The entity is nothing but the qualitative nature before us, taken as a unit. But when we focus selectively on one particular aspect of it, we never lose entirely the context of the whole. The attribute (or relation or action) is experienced as an aspect of a unitary whole.

We can see the centrality of this feature of perception when we notice the disorienting effect of its absence. A common experience while driving at night is to lose momentarily any sense of the layout of the road ahead. I round a bend, and suddenly I cannot tell how the road continues beyond the range of my headlights. A dark mass looms ahead. Is it merely the empty sky one sees when the road ahead dips down, or is it a hillside? And if so, which way does the road go around it? Two red lights appear on the left. Are they the taillights of a single car, or reflectors marking the edge of the road? What is disorienting about this experience is precisely that one has no sense of what features belong to what objects, so that the scene ahead has an unsettling lack of structure. A more extreme case is provided by the possibility of camouflage. The goal of camouflaging an object is to make the internal borders of its surface more prominent than its border with the environment of ground and trees. When camouflage is successful, the object is not seen, even though all of its facing surface may be stimulating the receptors of the observer. The object as such is not seen because the colors are not seen as features of that object. This is what it means to say that the thing is not differentiated from its background.

There is another manifestation of the fact that we perceive things as subjects of attributes. I noted above that perception is normally

15. Wolfgang Köhler, *Gestalt Psychology* (New York, 1929), 200.

an active process. *What* is perceived is given directly by the objects, but the perceiver chooses his objects through the activities of looking, listening, touching. Perceptual awareness normally results from the action of perceptual exploration, and the action is not restricted to adult, conceptual perceivers—animals and babies engage in it ceaselessly. But exploration is not random activity; it is not the pursuit of new stimulation for the sake of novelty. It is guided by the awareness that additional stimulation of a specific sort is available, that there is more information to be had about something. This awareness is provided by—it presupposes—the awareness of objects as entities, as subjects of attributes. In discriminating a figure from a ground, we experience the contour not merely as border between two visible regions but as a border between the visible and the invisible facets of the figural object. The contour is experienced as an edge, and there is depth at the edge. Implicit in this is the awareness that one could look around the edge and see the other side, or reach out and grasp it from behind. It is something that could be explored. There is nothing analogous at the level of sensations. In a sensation of red or warmth, or of a particular pitch or taste, the qualities are self-contained; as objects of sensations, they do not point beyond themselves toward anything else.

In the visual case of the figure-ground discrimination, the possibility of exploration is provided by the one-sidedness of the contour, the fact that it is experienced as a feature of the figure, not the ground. This is an instance of the general point that perceptual exploration presupposes the awareness of things as subjects of their attributes. Because one experiences the qualitative content of perception as a nature, as *the* nature of a thing, one is set to explore that nature further. Because the perceived attributes are experienced as attributes of a thing, one realizes that the thing has other attributes not perceived at present, features available from different standpoints. In perceiving things as entities, we are aware of a structural feature of the world which guides our perceptual exploration, and without which we would not know where or how to look. Conversely, when a film maker shoots an object in a tight close-up, or out of focus, so that it cannot be discriminated as an entity, the effect is a peculiar feeling of passivity, a contemplative mood in which exploration is abandoned.

We perceive entities, then, because what is perceived is experienced as a subject of its attributes. But another element in the traditional concept of entities is that they are subjects of change—they can alter their attributes and remain the same thing—and this too is reflected in perception. We perceive change over time, especially motion, and in doing so, we are aware of it not as a replacement of one total state by another but as a change in the one unitary thing discriminated over that time. When an outfielder tracks the moving ball, he is aware of it as a single object changing its position relative to him, not as a series of atomistic states replacing each other, as in an animated cartoon. When the acid turns the litmus paper red, it is a change in color of that particular piece of paper, not the replacement of one constellation of qualities by another. Perceptually, these two features of entities are related. The ability to detect motion is extremely sensitive, and it is apparently the most important basis for the ability to pick out entities from the background. A bird that is invisible in the bush, even though nothing hides its contours, is seen as soon as it moves. Marius von Senden noted the same relationship in the experience of the newly resighted patient: from motion he "gets his first clue that a specific meaning attaches to each of the various colour-patches belonging to the sensory order. He for the first time guesses *what* he is supposed to see; . . . this being provided, in most cases, by the patch itself as it moves and thereby stands out from the rest."[16]

I have abstracted these two features that characterize the discrimination of entities from the special case of perceiving solid physical objects, which are paradigmatic cases of entities. But of course we also perceive many nonsolid things, and since we perceive them too as subjects of attributes and of change, it is appropriate to broaden the concept of entity. Consider the extreme case of hearing, in which we never perceive entities in the narrow sense at all. What we hear are sounds, but we hear them as particulars, discriminated from the background of other sounds. The complicated wave train arriving at the ear is analyzed into its components. The qualitative features of sounds—their pitch, loudness, duration, pattern—are experienced as attributes of particular items in the auditory context. And we experience modulations of sound as changes in a single item discriminated over time. The whistle of the teakettle

16. Marius von Senden, *Space and Sight*, trans. Peter Heath (London, 1960), 136.

grows louder. It is precisely because we perceive this as a change in a single sound that we can infer something about the temperature of the water. We orient ourselves toward a sound, and determine its direction, by turning the head and noticing how the sound changes. Because we experience this as a change in a single sound, we can determine its direction. And we could not understand speech unless we heard the modulations forming separate phonemes as changes in a single wave train discriminated as a unit.

The necessity, for perception, of discrimination in this sense allows us to decide an issue that arises for hearing in particular, although it applies to any sense modality that involves a medium. Does the fact that we hear sounds mean that we hear the sounding object or the wave train it causes? To answer this, we need to ask what is being discriminated from what. The answer is that we can hear both, in different conditions. Consider the difference between hearing footsteps and hearing a symphony. I am at my desk in an office; a phone is ringing, typewriters are clacking, a drill is at work in the street outside, and footsteps are approaching my desk. I discriminate the last from other *events*, from the actions of other objects in my environment, not from other noises considered merely as wave trains. I experience each footstep as having a definite distance from me, definite enough for me to tell that each one is closer than the one before, whereas the wave train has only a direction. And I experience the footsteps as something I could learn more about by turning to watch, since I can see events as well as hear them. I do not hear the foot or the person as such, since I do not discriminate either from the background of other solid objects, as I could by vision; but I hear the footstep as a physical event, discriminated temporally. In the case of music, by contrast, I do hear it as a wave train, a pattern of sound in the narrow sense. I discriminate each melody and phrase from other melodies and phrases. I could not find out more about the music by watching the events that produce it. In fact, the visual awareness is distracting. What I hear, then, is not a set of events at the lips and fingers of the musicians, but the wave train itself they produce.

Some sounds can be heard in either way, depending on the perceptual ability of the hearer and on the conditions of perception. For example, we normally hear speech the way we hear music, as a wave train. The units of perception are the variations which consti-

tute phonemes or words; we discriminate each one from other patterns in the aural array. But a voice teacher is able, by training and
attention, to hear speech as an event in the vocal apparatus—he
might hear a certain sound, not as the letter *r*, but as the event of
the palate arching improperly. Or consider the case of a sound one
may hear while driving in traffic. It begins as an amorphous grind-
ing noise, with no particular location or direction, and it fills the auditory sphere. I may wonder if it is coming from my car, but this is
an abstract question based on past experience; I have no perceptual
sense of it as coming from anywhere. Gradually, however, as another car passes, the sphere elongates in the forward direction, until I hear it as an event at the tailpipe I see dragging on the pavement.[17]

Thus it is not true, as some have argued, that we always hear a
sound in the sense of a wave train. David Sanford claims, for example, that a sound is the primary object of hearing, in the sense
that whatever else we hear, we hear by means of hearing a sound.[18]
If *sound* is to be taken in a certain general sense, then we do always
hear sounds—in the way we always see sights or dance dances. But
if it means specifically a wave train, the claim is false. Sometimes the
wave train as such is discriminated. Sometimes, however, what is
discriminated is the event producing the wave train. In the latter
case, we no more hear wave trains than we see light (in the object
mode of visual perception). The question of what is heard can be
settled only by determining what is discriminated. This was the basis for the earlier claim that although we normally see physical objects that reflect light, there are modes of color vision (the film and
illumination modes) in which we see the light itself. And similar
considerations apply to the other modality that employs a medium—smell.

The awareness of an odor comes closest, of all the modalities,
to a sensory form of awareness, but the features which constitute
perceptual discrimination can be discerned here as well. We expe-

17. Hearing it as an event in this way might well not occur without seeing it.
This does not prevent the experience from being a direct auditory perception of the
event. There is intermodal as well as intramodal integration, and if it is automatic,
the result is a direct perception.

18. David Sanford, "The Primary Objects of Perception," *Mind*, LXXXV
(1976), 194.

rience an odor simply as the presence of a certain qualitative content. But we experience this content as a unit possessing various qualitative dimensions, isolated as a unit from other smells, subject to change over time, coming from a certain direction, and having a nature we could learn more about by inhaling more strongly or changing position. But what is it we are perceiving? In most cases, we perceive the state of the medium, the gas or particle suspension. The question is whether we ever discriminate the object as such that emits it. Although it seems doubtful that we can do this, perhaps the element of smell in tasting food would qualify as an example. But other species, with more highly developed olfactory senses, can smell objects. A bloodhound on the scent certainly appears to experience the scent as a physical trail, and its contours seem to stand out as clearly for him as a white line would for us.

The question, What is discriminated? also gives us a way to decide what is seen when light from an object follows an unusual path through the medium to the eye, a set of issues raised especially by Roderick Firth. In mirror reflections, for example, we see the objects themselves because they are discriminated from their backgrounds just as they are when seen normally; the left-right reversal does not affect this. A better test of the criterion is a translucent medium such as a frosted-glass window. If the distortion of the glass is small enough that the contours of objects can be seen through it, and there is some sense of depth, then we see the objects: they can be discriminated from their background. But if the distortion eliminates texture gradients and the other stimulus variables for depth, then we do not see the objects. We see the window itself, and the objects behind it are experienced merely as a play of colors across its surface. It is worth noting here that a causal theory of perceptual objects has no resources for such a distinction. The exact point at which the irregularity in the causal chain is enough to preclude the perception of an object cannot be specified apart from the presence or absence of discrimination, which is therefore the real criterion.[19]

19. Roderick Firth, "The Men Themselves," in Hector-Neri Castaneda (ed.), *Intentionality, Minds, and Perception* (Detroit, 1967), 357–82. Alvin Goldman, in the most sophisticated statement of the causal theory, adds that S must discriminate O in order for O to be an object. The requirement is an extra qualification on the causal condition. But this discrimination is not itself defined in terms of causality. Goldman says only that "something in S's percept represents its distinctness," without explaining this representational capacity ("Perceptual Objects," *Synthese*, XXXV [1977], 280).

Watching television provides another interesting case. On the one hand, it is natural to classify television with representational objects such as paintings. The latter are perceived as representing other objects, but *what* is perceived—what is discriminated—is the representational object itself, not what is represented. On the other hand, television is similar to such things as microscopes or a blind man's stick, which extend direct perception to things that otherwise could not be perceived. There is no continuous path of light from object to eye in television, but in live television at least, there is a nearly continuous and contemporaneous causal chain that preserves the crucial features of the optical array. There is a vivid sense of depth, and motions can be followed as they occur. Because of the distance between the perceiver and what is televised, however, one has no sense of being able to discover anything more by active exploration, except about the television set itself. The experience is passive in a way that the ordinary perception of objects is not. This case therefore sits on the border line, for it possesses some features of direct perceptual discrimination but lacks others.[20]

In summary, we have seen that to perceive is to be aware of a world of particulars. They are discriminated from the background of other particulars, they possess definite natures that are given as the qualitative content of perception, and they are subject to change over time. I describe this fact by saying that the entity is the proper object of perception. This does not mean we cannot perceive attributes, relationships, or actions. Rather, we perceive them as features of things; we perceive them in terms of the structural framework I have outlined. The only major exception is the sense of hearing, through which we perceive individuated events. But the type of discrimination involved in hearing is analogous to that in the other senses, so that the concept of an entity may be extended to hearing as well. Moreover, auditory perception is subordinated to the senses of vision and touch: we locate the events we hear in terms of the spatial framework of solid objects we can see and touch.[21]

20. *Cf.* also Maurice Charlesworth, "Sense-Impressions: A New Model," *Mind*, LXXXVIII (1979), 24–44.

21. Peter Strawson claims, in *Individuals* (London, 1959), 64–66, that a subject capable only of hearing would have no awareness of space whatever. However, the temporal relation between the onset of a noise at the two ears (or the phase difference for a continuous sound) provides a purely auditory basis for the experience of the sound's direction.

To say that we perceive entities as such does not mean that we consciously relate individual qualities to some new item—the entity as such—that is given as a distinct item to perception but not sensation. We perceive by means of the same stimulus arrays that in other conditions might give rise to isolated sensations. But there is a level of perceptual integration in the nervous system's response to the array, and by means of it we are aware of a level of organization in the world perceived. And as this integration is automatic, the awareness which results is direct. The substantive or entitative features we perceive are given in the same way that the qualitative content is given. In none of the examples illustrating these features is there any reason for us to think that the awareness of them results from the prior awareness of anything else. But the objections to this realist theory of perceptual objects are directed against just this point, and they fall into two groups. One consists of arguments to the effect that concepts are necessary for grasping these features of what is perceived; the other attempts to show that the perception of a thing's parts is more direct than the perception of the whole.

Before we can pursue the first group of objections, a point of terminology needs clarification. In describing the proper objects of perception, I have used a number of abstract, philosophical concepts—substance and entity, attribute, change. But this does not by itself imply that the perceiver himself must employ these concepts to grasp the features they designate. We are aware of certain things directly, nonconceptually, but in order to describe them, *we* must put them into language. A perceptual form of awareness cannot be communicated directly. What one is aware of must first be identified conceptually, so that it can be expressed in words. Description and communication are linguistic activities. But if the constraints which these goals set on theorists of perception were taken as constraints on the perceiver, we would be forced to deny that he is aware of *anything* nonconceptually, since every feature of what is perceived, even the sensory qualities, is necessarily *described* in terms of abstract concepts.

For the same reason, we should not be misled by the "S perceives that . . ." construction. It is often assumed that this designates a conceptual, propositional form of perception, in contrast to "S perceives X," which stands for direct perceiving. There is no reason, however, to assume that this grammatical distinction corresponds exactly to the distinction in types of awareness, apart from the belief that the structure of language diaphanously mirrors the structure of what it describes. It is true that we would not normally describe a person as having seen, for example, that the X-ray tube was in the lab, unless we thought he possessed the concepts for X-ray tubes and laboratories and had actually used them in identifying what he saw. But exceptions to this rule abound. Given the thesis that we perceive attributes not as isolated units but as attributes of entities, it would be more accurate to say a person perceives that something is red than to say he perceives red. The propositional form "S is P" emphasizes the entity-attribute connection, and is thus well suited to a context in which we are emphasizing the perceptual awareness of the connection. No conclusion about the nature of that awareness can be drawn merely from the form of words used to describe it.[22]

As for the objection itself, the claim is that the awareness of entities as such—as subjects of attributes and of change—requires concepts. The only real argument for the claim has been connected inseparably with sensationalism, and I have already taken issue with it. The claim assumes that the given is that in respect of which we are passive, and that only discrete qualitative contents are given passively. The problem, then, is to explain how the qualities are related, and since no relation is perceived in the objects themselves, the inference is that it must be imposed by the perceiver. But as Kant argued, the substance-attribute relation is a logical category, bound up with our judgmental, *conceptual* thinking. Therefore our awareness of it must be conceptual. In more contemporary terms, the thesis is that the substance-attribute relation is a feature of our conceptual framework. This relation is not a product of sensory stimulation, but a structure we bring to stimulation in order to organize the sensory flux. In either case, the crucial assumption is that the relation is not a feature of the objects themselves, and cannot be directly perceived. It can then be argued plausibly that since the structure is imposed, the most likely method of imposition is through concepts. But apart from this assumption, the claim has no basis. And the assumption itself is based on the thesis of sensationalism. Once we

22. Thus it is futile to attempt to define "S perceives that x is P," as many have done. The statement form is used to convey various different pieces of information.

have rejected this thesis, we can trust our common sense of the matter, which is that the perception of things as things is given directly, in the same way the perception of their attributes is.

What has just been argued in the abstract can be seen more concretely, in regard to specific claims in the Kantian mold. It has been said, for example, that what counts as an entity in a given context depends on what substantive or sortal concept we have in mind. As I walk around a house, whether I see one entity, or four, or many hundreds, depends on whether we are counting houses, walls, or individual bricks. Thus a perceiver cannot be said to have perceived an entity unless he has a concept of which the thing in question is an instance. But this commits the fallacy I warned against at the outset. It is true that we might not describe a person as having seen, for example, an X-ray tube, unless he possessed an understanding of what an X-ray tube is; the statement might be misleading. But this does not mean that he cannot actually perceive the thing we know to be an X-ray tube, cannot pick it out from its background. And with the house, the structure itself, the walls, and the bricks are all in fact entities—they possess attributes and can act as units—even though we do not treat them all as entities in the same act of attention. If we attend to the wall as the unit, the brickwork is seen as a series of divisions internal to the entity. Thus the focus of attention does not create entities where none in fact are. We attend selectively to certain features that are there in fact, and they determine what it is possible to perceive. We could not integrate the redness of a brick with the size of the wall and the shape of the house, treating them as features of a single entity.

Moreover, the act of attention does not depend on a prior conceptual understanding of the things attended to. This may be true in *certain* cases. It is not likely that a person looking at a car engine for the first time would spontaneously pick out the carburetor, unless he knew ahead of time what to look for. And in the special case of speech perception, it may well be that the ability to pick out individual words from the optical or auditory array depends on, or develops along with, the understanding of what the words mean (a point developed further in Chapter 7). But this is not true generally. In the normal case, there are patterns in the stimulus array that are specific to the real entities around us, and allow us to discriminate them directly. The denial of this depends on some form of the thesis of sensationalism.

But let us pursue for a moment the physiological basis for the perception of entities. In vision, the optical array provides information about contours and depth; in hearing, there are patterns in the abruptness of onset and offset, as well as patterns of pitch and overtone, and variations among these; the other senses are less well understood, but presumably there are parallel structures in the proximate stimulus. These allow us to pick out units from a background. But how, it may be asked, could the physical stimulation of receptors give us the abstract, metaphysical relation between entity and attribute, or between the entity and its changes?[23] The answer is that we do not perceive the abstract relation. We perceive concrete entities as unified natures, attending to specific qualities and changes without losing the contextual awareness that these are aspects *of* the unified natures. We must beware again of looking for a glue to bind what we ourselves have separated. We notice similarities between perceived objects, and we form concepts to identify the respects in which they are similar. As a result we have concepts of individual attributes considered apart from the things which possess them. To use these concepts in grasping *facts*, or stating them in language, we must therefore use a subject-predicate structure to reunite what has been distinguished in thought. And we make this explicit by recognizing that an attribute must always be an attribute of some subject. But this subject-attribute relation holds between items that have been separated conceptually. We do not perceive the relation as such, because we do not perceive any separation between the elements related. The basis for conceptual awareness is there in perception, because we can focus selectively on aspects of what we perceive; conceptualization is our way of reducing the information so available to a manageable order. But we do not *perceive* these aspects as separate units whose relation to the unified wholes of which they are aspects must be given *in addition to* the qualitative content of perception.[24]

As for the first set of objections, then, we perceive things as entities directly, without requiring either specific concepts for the par-

23. This appears to be the essence of Hamlyn's objection to Gestalt theory, in *Psychology of Perception*, Chap. 4.
24. *Cf.* Anthony Quinton, *The Nature of Things* (London, 1973), 26.

ticular types of thing perceived, or the abstract concepts we use to describe entities as such. The second group of objections concerns the holistic character of perception, the fact that we perceive entities as wholes. The objections claim that in some sense we perceive the parts of entities directly, and are at best indirectly aware of the whole object. In vision, for example (and the objection is stated almost exclusively in terms of vision), we always see objects from a specific direction, and can therefore see only those sides that reflect light in that direction; the backside and inside of an object are hidden. There is no question about this fact, and it implies that the perception of a thing as a whole does not involve an awareness of the whole of it— front and back, inside and out, through and through. But the objection goes further. Because of this fact, it is said, we do not perceive the entity as such directly. There have been two arguments for this conclusion.

G. E. Moore argued that when one looks at an inkstand, he is certainly not directly aware of the inkstand itself, the three-dimensional entity holding the ink. At most, he is directly aware of an entity, or item of some sort, corresponding to the facing surfaces of the inkstand. Moore did not state his reason for this view, but his hesitation over soap bubbles suggests what that reason is. To see an object directly, he assumes, we must see all of it; it must not contain any sides, parts, or aspects hidden from view. From this it would follow that we do not perceive the inkstand itself directly. Moore claimed that we know the latter only by description, as a thing which bears a unique relation to the item we directly see. Moore was understandably puzzled about what this relation could be.[25]

But there is no reason to accept Moore's principle of direct awareness, and there is good reason to reject it. Taken literally, the principle that an object of direct awareness must contain nothing that is not perceived would imply that direct awareness must be a form of omniscience. This quest for omniscience is the silent partner in the classical Cartesian quest for an infallible type of knowledge, and we should reject it for the same reason. It seeks a form of cognition that is free from conditions, that is not subject to any limitation placed on it by the means of cognition. Nor is there any such object in real-

25. G. E. Moore, "Some Judgments of Perception," in Robert Swartz (ed.), *Perceiving, Sensing, and Knowing* (Garden City, N.Y., 1965), 8–17.

ity as Moore describes—an expanse of color, or a surface without depth. If it is two-dimensional, it does not exist as such. A two-dimensional surface is a mathematical abstraction, and we certainly do not perceive abstractions. But if it is a real surface, it is a three-dimensional layer, possessing an inside and a backside which are no more perceived than are the corresponding parts of the entity itself. A special mental entity must therefore be invented to satisfy Moore's description, and thus his principle leads inexorably to representationalism.

The same applies to David Sanford's slightly different version of Moore's argument. Sanford argues that a color expanse is the primary object of vision, because the color expanse that is the qualitative content of our perception of an entity could be present even if the entity itself were not, and we would be unable to distinguish the two cases. But a color expanse is not an existing thing; it is an abstraction from existing things. To become a real object, it must be given a third dimension, and therefore unperceived aspects. But suppose the argument were that a virtual image or hologram of an object might be indistinguishable from the object, and the color expanse as a visual object were defined as what the image has in common with the real entity.[26] The possibility of such images only means that two quite different things can look identical; it does not mean that they must share some constituent. In one case, we perceive a physical existent of one kind, a solid, tangible entity; in the other case, we perceive a different sort of physical existent, a light phenomenon. The fact that the two might be indistinguishable is irrelevant. What is directly perceived depends on what is actually there.

A second argument has been offered by Frank Jackson, who claims that we are directly aware of the facing surfaces of objects— or a color expanse corresponding to them—not of the object as a whole, because we perceive the object in virtue of the expanse, but not vice versa. That is, we would not see the object (in these conditions) unless we saw the expanse, but we could see the expanse alone without seeing the object of which it is a part. Thus an object of immediate or direct visual awareness is one not seen in virtue of our seeing anything else. In the first place, however, this definition

26. Sanford, "Primary Objects," 196. He seems to have these suppositions in mind when he refers to "a physically existent coloured expanse which was not a surface."

of directness depends on Moore's. The facing surfaces are seen in virtue of our seeing the regions of color that comprise them, just as the whole object is seen in virtue of our seeing the facing surfaces. Jackson must therefore distinguish the relations between the perception of the whole and the perception of the facing surface, and between a part and the whole of the facing surface itself. But the only difference is that the whole in the first case, but not the second, includes parts not seen. Moore's criterion of directness is therefore implicit in Jackson's.[27]

More important, however, there is no such asymmetry as he asserts between the awareness of the entity as a whole and the awareness of the facing surface. It is true that from a given angle, we see the entity as such because we see the facing surfaces. But it is also true that we see the latter as we do because we discriminate the entity as a whole. Color constancy depends to some extent on the discrimination of the entity that has the colored surface. It depends on seeing the surface as having a certain depth and a certain angle of orientation to other surfaces, and as standing out from the background of other objects. If the surface were seen through a reduction screen that allowed only light from that surface to pass through, so that the subject were reduced to the awareness of a color expanse, the perceived color could change radically. In short, we perceive entities because we are perceptually aware of certain of their perceptible attributes. But the awareness of any such attribute is affected by the perceptual context, and the discrimination of entities as such forms the essential structure of that context.

The second set of objections, then, like the first, is directed against the features that essentially characterize perception, and may therefore be seen as an expression of sensationalism. They also illustrate a broader point. Human cognition has various levels or stages, formed by the integration of material available at the preceding level. Each type of integration makes possible the awareness of a new type of structure in reality that could not be grasped without it. The formation of abstract concepts, for example, allows us to recognize the existence of types, or patterns of similarities in things, whereas at the perceptual level we can only see particular similarities between particular things. Again, induction acquaints us with

27. Frank Jackson, *Perception* (Cambridge, England, 1977), 19.

lawful behavior, action required by aspects of an agent's identity that are shared with other entities. Without inductive inference, we can only observe the particular way an individual object acts on a specific occasion, taking every such action as a basic and unanalyzable fact.

In each case, the cognitive integration provides an awareness of a structure into which the facts known at the preintegrative level fit, giving us a deeper understanding of these facts. But the awareness of the structure also orients us toward the possibility of other facts of the same type, ones exhibiting the same structure. To form the concept of man is to grasp the existence of a type that may have instances other than those we know already, so that we approach strangers with a prior understanding of their needs and capacities and of the sort of action appropriate toward them. To recognize that the glass not only broke but had to break because it is glass, is to recognize the existence of a causal law that can guide our future encounters with glass. Cognitive integration thus alerts us to the existence of other, as yet unknown facts of a given type, and it provides a goal for active inquiry, so that we need not wait passively on reality to reveal itself.

Each form of integration, however, "goes beyond the evidence" in a sense—when the evidence is understood solely in terms of the previous level. There is therefore a philosophical temptation to explain away the integration. Thus the nominalist claims that a concept is nothing but a set of particulars, a tool of convenience that yields no further cognitive riches. Again, Hume argued that causal laws are merely conjunctions of the particular facts known prior to induction. They do not take us beyond those facts or give us any genuine reason for expecting other facts of the same type. In each case, the claim is that the integration does not acquaint us with anything beyond what was already known before; it does not give us the awareness of a real structure. And the argument is that no claim to possess such an awareness could be justified—where the only admissible form of justification is appeal to the facts known preintegratively. But we should resist that temptation. Every form of integration is justified precisely by the fact that it reveals a new level of structure in reality. Of course this structure cannot be understood, or the acceptance of it justified, by a preintegrative level of awareness. That is what makes it a higher-order structure.[28]

Perception is the first such stage of integration, and it gives us the awareness of entities as units of existence, identity, and change. The integration is not performed consciously, as is the case with concepts and inductive laws, so in a strict sense it cannot be described as an integration of a prior level of awareness—the integration of sensations. The mode of integration not being conscious, the material integrated cannot be taken as states of awareness. But perception does result from the neurological integration of sensory input which, were it left unintegrated, would produce sensations. The consequence at the conscious level is that a qualitative content that might, in part, have been experienced in the form of isolated sensations is experienced instead as the awareness of entities possessing qualitative identities.

Sensationalism is motivated by the same basic approach as nominalism or Hume's analysis of induction. The features that characterize perception qua perception, that give us the awareness of entities qua entities, are not given in any form at the level of sensations. These features are given by perceptual integration itself. The sensation of an isolated quality will not reveal that it is a quality of an entity, or that the entity has other qualities as well, available from other perspectives, through active exploration. So to claim that these facts are given directly must seem an intolerable paradox to those who assume that only the sensational level is given.

But they *are* given. I have pointed to experiences in which the entitative features stand out most clearly and can be seen to be given as directly as the qualitative content. And I have answered the claims that these experiences should be mistrusted, that the features must really be the product of imposing categories on sensory data or of making sophisticated subconscious inferences. Perception is a distinctive form of cognition, not a blend of sensations and concepts. As the awareness of entities, it reveals the structure in which the qualities exist that are available to isolated sensations. And in pro-

---

28. We do need a philosophical account of the structure, and of the way cognitive integration reveals it, including a reason for believing that it *is* a new and nonreducible structure. The account necessary for types and laws would be quite different from the one provided here for perception.

viding this structure, every percept points toward its own expansion, directing exploration toward a fuller awareness of the identity of what is perceived, allowing us to escape the passivity of sensation.

It is because perception is a distinct form of cognition that I have taken some pains in this chapter to define it. The definition incorporates three distinguishing features: perception occurs in response to patterned stimulation of sense receptors, it is a mode of direct awareness, and it is the awareness of entities as such. These traits underlie and explain the other features of perception. Taken together, moreover, they capture and systematize our judgments about what is and what is not an instance of perceiving, without disguising the fact that there are borderline cases along each of the dimensions.

The definition completes our inquiry into perception. I have dealt with the major issues that arise within each of the two perspectives we have on perception—the internal, phenomenological perspective we have as subjects of perceptual awareness, and the external perspective we have on the physiological bases of perceiving. I have also dealt with the epistemological question of how the two perspectives should be integrated. But there is another set of epistemological questions concerning the role perception plays in grounding our conceptual knowledge about physical objects. These questions will be addressed in Part II.

Part II

Perceptual Knowledge

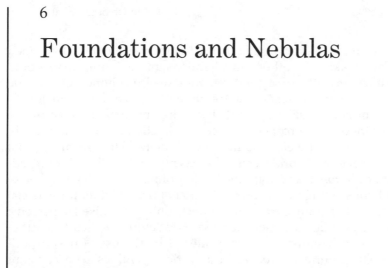

6

Foundations and Nebulas

It is a truism that questions of epistemology have dominated philosophy since the Renaissance, as questions of metaphysics and
ethics did before. It is a truism, but it is true nonetheless, and it is
the chief reason why perception has been such an important topic.
Scholars have come to it for other reasons, but perception has drawn
most of its audience from epistemologists interested in the bases of
human knowledge. Perception was seen as a type of cognitive contact with reality that could ground the abstractions we employ and
the propositions we assert, our knowledge of past and future, causes
and universals, things seen and things unseen. Epistemologists have
asked whether perception can give us such a ground. Are the senses trustworthy? Can they yield any certainty? Do they provide
enough information to support the rest of the structure? How do they
support our conceptual knowledge? At the most basic level, these
questions can be asked concerning such judgments as that the thing
before me is a desk, that it is brown, wooden, hard—items of
knowledge that seem, in everyday life, to be read off directly from
perceptual experience, that seem merely to identify in conceptual
form the directly observable aspects of the things we perceive. Following tradition, we may call these perceptual judgments, and the
traditional questions concerning them are, Can they be justified with
any certainty by perception? And if so, how?

If we could simply build on the theory of perception developed in Part I, taking no other considerations into account, there would be either very little to say of this matter, or else volumes. On the one hand, answers to most of the traditional concerns about the justification of perceptual judgments have already been provided by the realist theory of perception. Since we directly perceive external objects and some of their attributes, there is no need to construct a proof that the external world exists. There is no need for the elaborate edifice of inference and hypothesis that philosophers have spent so much time trying to construct. We do not need to infer the external causes of experience from their effects on us, because we perceive those causes directly, not their effects. We do not need to synthesize our sensations—by innate rules or by the use of past experience—to ground our belief in a world of entities with constant properties, because these are given. The perceptual judgment, indeed, is merely the conceptual identification of what is given.

For the same reason, however, a full discussion and validation of this point would take us far afield, since it would require a theory of concepts and conceptual knowledge. We would need to consider the process of concept formation, its sources in perceptual awareness and its bases in reality, picking our way across the tangled problem of universals. This would take us into questions about the relation between concepts and language, the role of concepts in storing and organizing knowledge, the nature of justification and evidence. And we would need to consider what has been said on these matters by cognitive psychologists as well as philosophers. To undertake such a project merely for the sake of explaining perceptual judgments would be to let a very small tail wag an enormous dog. It is, in any case, beyond the scope of this work.

Yet it would be misleading to outline the obvious consequences of the realist theory of perception—and leave it at that. The issues of perceptual knowledge have been debated extensively in twentieth-century philosophy, and the theory I will propose does not fit neatly into any of the categories taken for granted in the debate. In particular, the theory does not fit neatly on either side of the contemporary conflict between foundational and coherence theories of justification.

This latter issue arises over the structure of knowledge. It is obvious that some of our knowledge, indeed most of it, is acquired and validated by inference from prior knowledge. But what about this prior knowledge? If we follow the inferences upstream, will we arrive at a form of knowledge that is not based on inference? Is there *basic* knowledge, in the sense of judgments we can make without any inference, without any support at all from other knowledge? Foundationalists believe that there is. They hold that basic knowledge is *necessary* for any other kind, because if inferential knowledge did not rest ultimately on noninferential, there would be nothing to tie the first sort to reality. An inference is only as reliable as its premises, and were there no ultimate premises, we would have no way of deciding on the truth of any others. Foundationalists also believe that basic knowledge is *possible*—that there are judgments which can be justified without inference, facts that can be known without prior (conceptual) knowledge of other facts.

Anti-foundational or coherence theories, on the other hand, hold that basic knowledge is neither necessary nor possible. It is not possible because a judgment can be justified only in the context of a vast network of background knowledge; the real unit of justification is the context or network itself. But it is not necessary, either, since the standard of justification is precisely the coherence between a given belief and its context. Thus we have two quite different pictures of human knowledge (and the issue has often been debated in terms of these pictures). One side speaks of knowledge as a building each floor of which rests on the one below, with the structure ultimately resting on a foundation that is in direct contact with reality—or as a tree with perceptual roots to which every branch can ultimately be traced. The other side speaks of nebulas and clouds, of webs and ships at sea, and in general of anything that floats, anything that hangs together by internal connections and not the external force of gravity.

But to state the issue this way is to put it in highly formal terms, to abstract from the real substance of the conflict. The issue is really a labyrinth that epistemologists have entered for at least three different types of reasons. First, although foundationalism and the coherence theory are pictures of knowledge as a whole, the debate between them has centered largely on perceptual knowledge. For it is in perception, if anywhere, that basic knowledge is to be found. And so the various local issues concerning perceptual justification have assumed a global importance. These issues will be covered in the next chapter.

Second, the debate has been an attempt to integrate two basic features of conceptual knowledge, its contextual and its hierarchical nature. Foundationalists have stressed the latter, trying to make good on the insight that there is an order in knowledge, that we must start with some sort of cognitive contact with reality and build upon it hierarchically. In the process, however, they have often suggested that each brick in the edifice is a self-contained entity. And coherence theorists have objected, rightly, that all knowledge is contextual. As knowers, we face nature with a vast system of beliefs which must be kept integrated, and no belief, however closely tied it may be to sensory input, has a special immunity from this fact. Coherence theorists have normally accepted their opponents' assumption that hierarchy and context are incompatible, and have merely chosen the other side. The chief goal of a theory of knowledge should be to integrate them, but this would require precisely the full-blown theory of conceptual knowledge that is beyond our scope. I can only indicate as we proceed the direction I think such a theory should take.

At the most fundamental level, finally, there is a conflict between two global conceptions of the relation between the body of our knowledge and the world known. The exponents of foundationalism in contemporary philosophy have defended it from the standpoint of what I will call Cartesian empiricism, which incorporates a representationalist view of knowledge. The coherence theory, on the other hand, has been fostered not only by the first and second considerations mentioned above but by an underlying form of idealism. It is crucial to identify the effects of these models on the issues of perceptual knowledge, in order to clear the way for a realist view.

Cartesian Empiricism and Its Critics

Cartesian empiricism integrates Descartes' view of the nature and structure of knowledge with the empiricist thesis about its source. With Descartes, it accepts the prior certainty of consciousness. Although an independent world is the ultimate object of knowledge and standard of truth, knowledge of it must be based on a foundation of prior knowledge of our own conscious states, which can be known infallibly. Unlike Descartes, it maintains that the conscious states in question must be those involved in perceptual experience, not innate ideas about logic, mathematics, and the like. Thus, as a type of empiricism, it holds that perception is the source of our knowledge of reality; as a type of Cartesianism, it holds that the perceptual judgment about external objects cannot be basic, but must itself be derived from antecedent knowledge about experience.

The result is a view familiar from the works of the classical British empiricists and of such twentieth-century writers as Bertrand Russell, A. J. Ayer, C. I. Lewis, and Roderick Chisholm.[1] The perceptual judgment is seen as the product of an inference from premises expressing knowledge of experiential states. Since my interest is in the pattern itself, and the idea that perceptual judgments require an inferential justification, I will not explore the various ways that view has been exemplified. I will focus instead on the essential theses of Cartesian empiricism and its essential motives. There are two of each. The first thesis is that the foundations of knowledge must be phenomenal. They consist in knowledge of experiential states, conceived as states of the subject that could occur in the absence of the external object. The second thesis is that the foundations must be infallible and thus immune from any doubt, revision, or qualification. Correspondingly, the motives behind these claims are the representationalist theory of perception that most empiricists have accepted, and the Cartesian desire to answer the skeptic, to validate our knowledge of the world in the face of the skeptical belief that it might all be illusory. Each claim is supported, directly or indirectly, by each of these motives.

For the representationalist theory of perception, we have seen, what is given is only the experiential state itself—we are directly aware of its representational content, but not the external object it represents. Thus for the Cartesian empiricist, the perceptual basis of knowledge must be the conceptualization of that experiential content. We cannot be aware of an external object until we have identified the experiential state as something that implies the pres-

1. Ayer and Lewis were phenomenalists, but I include them because their phenomenalism is better seen as a variant on Cartesian empiricism than as a form of idealism. Both would oppose the sort of idealism discussed later in the chapter.

ence of an external object. As Russell put it, "In order to know anything at all about the table, we must know truths connecting it with
things with which we have acquaintance"—the circle of our acquaintance, for Russell, being restricted to sense-data. Alterna-
tively, for the adverbial theories, the basic knowledge would be that
one is in a certain adverbial state, for example, "appeared to redly."[2]
In either case, basic knowledge must be phenomenal; it must be
knowledge about appearances.

So much is fairly clear. But it should be noted that the converse
is also true. The claim that phenomenal knowledge is epistemologically prior to the perceptual judgment presupposes a representationalist view of appearances. It has been argued that the claim does
not depend on any theory of perception, that it follows merely from
an asymmetry in the logic of justification. One can justifiably believe something about appearances without being justified in a belief about external objects, but not vice versa. Any justification for a
belief about an object would entail some justification for a belief about
how it appears.[3] But this asymmetry is suggested with the adult
perceiver in mind—one whose background knowledge of the world
and of appearances allows him to note how something looks before
he knows how it (really) is. And for this reason, the asymmetry could
not support a claim of epistemological priority until we explain how
this perceiver came by his background knowledge. If we approach
this from a realist theory of perception, it will be clear that the asymmetry runs in the other direction.

I have argued that an appearance is a relationship between an
object and a subject. To form a judgment about the way an object

2. Bertrand Russell, *The Problems of Philosophy* (1912; rpr. Oxford, 1959), 47. *Cf.*
John L. Pollock, *Knowledge and Justification* (Princeton, 1974), Chap. 3. Chisholm's view,
in *Theory of Knowledge* (2nd ed.; Englewood Cliffs, N.J., 1977), is slightly different.
The proposition that I am appeared to redly, he would say, is known noninferentially, but it is not the premise by which I justify a belief about an external object (that
it is *F*). According to his Epistemic Principles B and C, that belief is justified by the
belief that I am perceiving the object to be *F*. Chisholm's reluctance to rely here on
propositions about appearing stems from a problem he finds in empiricism. See his
Perceiving (Ithaca, 1957), 69–75. In any case, the fact of being appeared to is presumably relevant to the belief that I am perceiving something to be *F*.

3. *Cf.* Michael Slote, *Reason and Scepticism* (London, 1970), 21–23; and Roderick
Chisholm, "Russell on the Foundations of Empirical Knowledge," in P. A. Schilpp
(ed.), *The Philosophy of Bertrand Russell* (Chicago, 1944), 419–44.

appears—about the form in which we perceive it—is to judge concerning the product of an interaction. But the nature of this interaction is not given to the subject. He cannot *perceptually* discriminate the intrinsic attribute of the object from the form in which he perceives it. The distinction is available only at the conceptual level. To have the concept of an appearance or a form, the subject must have at least some grounds for isolating the aspect of what he experiences that is relative to him. He must have noted cases of variation in his perception of the same object or cases of anomalies such as the bent stick in water. Even so, the variation will mean nothing to him unless he already knows that he is perceiving a single object through the series of appearances and that the object is not itself changing. Similarly, the way the stick looks in water will mean nothing unless he knows that it really is straight. Hence any explicit judgment about appearances presupposes some knowledge of external objects, and so the latter sort of knowledge is prior to the former. Before he has made this distinction between form and object, the child would express his judgments by saying "This is red (straight, a stick)," and *this* must be taken as referring to the object of his perceptual awareness—for realism, the external object. Only if he is directly aware of an experiential state could such a judgment, formed prior to any explicit concept of appearances, be taken to be *about* appearances. To claim that phenomenal knowledge is epistemologically prior is therefore to presuppose a form of representationalism for perception.

In any case, it is clear that the representationalist element in the traditional empiricist's view of perception forces him to regard the foundations of knowledge as phenomenal. It also encourages the idea that this knowledge is infallible. After all, the arguments for representationalism normally turn on the diaphanous model of awareness. They are so many ways of showing that the perceptual faculty is not a perfect mirror of nature. And the experiential states are introduced precisely as inner objects of diaphanous awareness. Appearances themselves do not appear but are confronted directly. There is no causal process that intervenes between the state and our awareness of it. What, then, could go wrong? What source of error is left? But the *Cartesian* empiricist's desire to answer the skeptic gives him an independent reason for believing that the foundations of knowledge must be infallible, and this establishes a connection running in the other direction, from the infallibility to the phenomenality of basic knowledge.

As we saw earlier, Descartes took the skeptic's challenge seriously only because he had already accepted the representationalist model, which allows that all our experience might occur in the absence of an external world. There is thus only one source for Cartesian empiricism—the model itself. But the issue of skepticism generates a logic of its own concerning the bases of knowledge. The skeptic typically argues that because it is possible for us to err, it is possible that we are in error with regard to any judgment we form; hence we can be certain of nothing. Descartes accepts the skeptic's criterion of certainty and is therefore compelled to look for a type of knowledge that is not fallible. Ideally, this foundation would have the form of an assertion whose truth is guaranteed by the very fact of asserting it—the type of which the *cogito* is the most notable instance. But the empiricists thought they had the same feature in phenomenal knowledge.

In fact, not even the *cogito* is infallible in the sense required by the skeptic's criterion.[4] (This is a problem with the criterion, not an argument for skepticism.) But phenomenal beliefs lack even the self-referential feature of the *cogito* that gives the latter its appearance of infallibility. Why, then, were these beliefs classed with the *cogito*? The answer lies partly in the diaphanous model, as just indicated. But it also lies partly in the sensory atomism of the sensationalist tradition. Consider the curious concept of incorrigibility, often used interchangeably with infallibility. *Incorrigible* literally means uncorrectable and is normally applied to the irremediably wicked. Its use in regard to propositions that are supposed to have reached the very pinnacle of cognitive success can be explained as follows. The phenomenal judgment is regarded as something that merely registers the presence of an experiential state, regarded in turn as a sensory atom, bearing no intrinsic relation to other states, much less to external objects. The judgment has, therefore, no implications requiring further verification beyond the existence of the state. It is free from any danger of being corrected, revised, or qualified by knowl-

4. Even if one adopts a noninferential view of the *cogito*, according to which its certainty comes from our grasping that the act of saying "I am conscious" guarantees the truth of the statement, it still takes a process of thought to grasp that point, and the process could in principle err.

edge acquired later; it is an isolated piece of knowledge, outside any cognitive context. Thus C. I. Lewis said of his "expressive statements," so called because their function is solely to express what is immediately given, that they can be verified completely and decisively because they imply nothing beyond the content of the experience.[5]

In any case, the Cartesian empiricist's project of showing how knowledge of an external world can be inferred from knowledge about states of consciousness has fallen into well-deserved disrepute. If the attempt is actually to derive the existence of an external world as a conclusion without presupposing it in any way, the project is doomed by the fact that the data do not support the conclusion. Neither induction nor deduction can bridge the gap created by the assumption that experiential states could exist in the absence of any external source.[6] If, on the other hand, the attempt is merely to describe how in fact we do come to believe in external objects, and come to believe about them what we do, it is manifestly inaccurate. Although twentieth-century versions of Cartesian empiricism have been more sophisticated than their eighteenth century antecedents, they encounter the same problems that undercut the latter. Nor is there any need to construct such inferences. Having rejected the representationalist theory of perception, and the legitimacy of the skeptic's claim, we do not need to assume that the bases of knowledge must be either phenomenal or incorrigible.

On these and other grounds, Cartesian empiricism has been criticized heavily in recent years. But its major rival has been a type of epistemological idealism. Since knowledge cannot be erected on a foundation of incorrigible propositions about experiential states, some philosophers infer that it cannot have and does not need any foundation whatever. Since our ordinary conceptual scheme, with its belief in an external, public world, cannot be justified by a diaphanous awareness of inner states, some infer that it cannot have and does not need any support whatever from a nonconceptual form

5. C. I. Lewis, *Analysis of Knowledge and Valuation* (La Salle, Ill., 1946), 180. Incorrigibility is a curious property not least because if the given has no connection with other facts, so that phenomenal statements have no implications, it is a mystery how they could serve as the inferential bases of knowledge. *Cf.* Hans Reichenbach, "Are Phenomenal Reports Absolutely Certain?" *Philosophical Review*, LXI (1952), 147–59.

6. *Cf.* Frederick L. Will, *Induction and Justification* (Ithaca, 1974), Chap. 3.

of awareness. This alternative view—put forward by Wittgenstein, Wilfrid Sellars, W. V. Quine, Richard Rorty, and others—holds that questions of justification, evidence, and truth arise only within our conceptual scheme and cannot be raised about the scheme itself. The scheme is a social product, instilled in us chiefly through the process of learning a language. Objectivity consists not in any relation of correspondence between our judgments and the world independent of them, but rather in relations of coherence among our judgments. The standards of coherence and of objectivity generally are set by the scheme itself. Once again, a Cartesian model of knowledge is to be replaced with a Kantian one.

There are differences among the philosophers mentioned above. There are also major differences between them and Kant—or the classical nineteenth-century Idealists, with whom they are often compared—and it would be well to note these differences at the outset. The contemporary writers have adopted materialist or behaviorist views of mind, in contrast to the metaphysical idealism which held that the stuff of reality is mental. Indeed, the attack on Cartesian dualism is typically offered—especially by Wittgenstein—as an integral part of the attack on Cartesian epistemology. As an *object* of scientific knowledge, then, man is seen as a physical organism in a physical environment. The result is that the units of epistemological analysis are not the ideas, judgments, or conscious states of which the Idealists spoke, but pieces of linguistic behavior—utterances, assertions, statements.

Another point of difference is less essential but more intrusive. Their attack on foundationalist epistemologies, in which they deny the possibility of any pure statement of the given, is frequently offered as an anti-Kantian thesis. Kant's theory of knowledge posited two distinct faculties of cognition, with distinct functions—the sensibility, which intuits; and the intellect, which conceptualizes. This suggests the possibility of judgments which do nothing more than formulate intuitions and, at the other extreme, of judgments which formulate relations among concepts, with no empirical content. This picture has a structural similarity to Cartesian foundationalism, and indeed C. I. Lewis' version of the latter was explicitly modeled on Kant. The contrast between Kant and the coherence theory, however, is not essential. There is a strain in Kant's philosophy which leads him to deny that there could be any pure intuitive, preconceptual awareness. In any case, it is irrelevant whether the coherence theory as such is Kantian. The point is that the coherence theory depends on the "Copernican Revolution," the reinterpretation of objectivity that Kant originated.[7]

As I argued in Chapter 1, this view of objectivity defines epistemological idealism. Insofar as man is not merely an object but also the *subject* of scientific or indeed of any knowledge, insofar as he is the utterer of sentences that have meaning, truth, or logical relationships and are not simple physical noises and marks, the new idealists place man in the same epistemological position that Kant did. They assert or imply that the objects of knowledge qua objects are in some sense constituted by the means employed in knowing them; and that the standards of objectivity must be defined by reference to this constitutive activity.

The sense in which these theories claim that the objects of knowledge are constituted is not that of the Kantian mind synthesizing nature from the manifold of sensations, or the absolute spirit objectifying itself. They claim, rather, that the objects our statements refer to, the universe our discourse describes, cannot be understood epistemologically except by reference to the linguistic apparatus we employ in speaking of it. The sort of dependence involved is best seen as an extension of C. S. Peirce's definition of truth and reality: "The opinion which is fated to be ultimately agreed to by all who investigate, is what we mean by the truth, and the object represented in this opinion is the real. . . . Reality is independent, not necessarily of thought in general, but only of what you or I or any finite number of men may think about it. . . . But the reality of that which is real does depend on the real fact that investigation is destined to lead . . . to a belief in it." Contemporary idealists may

---

7. See Richard Rorty, "Strawson's Objectivity Argument," *Review of Metaphysics*, XXIV (1970), 207–44, and "The World Well Lost," *Journal of Philosophy*, LXIX (1972), 649–65; and C. I. Lewis, *Mind and the World Order* (1929; rpr. New York, 1956). Kant's categories are fixed and necessary, and for this reason Rorty classifies him with Locke and Descartes (and presumably Plato and Aristotle) as an absolutist—one who believes in a "permanent, neutral framework for inquiry"—despite the fact that Kant believes the framework is imposed by us, not by the world (Richard Rorty, *Philosophy and the Mirror of Nature* [Princeton, 1979], 8ff.). In classifying Rorty *et al.* with Kant, on the other hand, I am taking this last (idealist) point as essential to Kant, and ignoring the difference between his absolutism and the contemporary writers' relativism.

not share Peirce's confidence that the process of inquiry will necessarily lead to a unitary result, one agreed upon by all inquirers.
But they share Peirce's view that the concept of reality—"the reality
of that which is real"—can only mean that which is required by our
theories, particularly by the referential apparatus they employ. In
Quine's phrase, to be is to be the value of a variable. At any rate,
consciousness, in the form of our theories, is the primary term in
this relationship. The world is the framework of objects in terms of
which we pursue our investigations. But this only means it is the set
of things posited by theories not in question at the moment.[8]

Nor is it surprising to find this idealist thesis supported by idealist arguments. Thus Quine has argued that reference is "inscrutable" because we cannot describe what our terms refer to without
using those terms. We cannot step out from behind our language to
achieve a diaphanous view of the reality beyond. We can only as-
cend to a metalanguage and claim that term a in language L refers
to x's. But this only means an equivalence of reference as between
languages, between a in L and x in the metalanguage. The reference
of x in turn could be given only by appeal to yet another language.
There is no way to establish the relation between any term and items
outside language altogether. As Quine said, "Specifying the universe of a theory makes sense only relative to some background theory."[9] The argument is exactly parallel to the classical idealist argument that we could not know the real objects to which
representationalists say our ideas correspond, because we could
know those objects only by means of other ideas.

If the objects of knowledge are determined in this way by reference to our theories, then it would be vacuous to define the truth
of a theory by its correspondence to those objects. This correspondence would be guaranteed by the very definition of the objects and
thus would not select among competing theories.[10] Can truth then

8. C. S. Peirce, *Collected Papers*, ed. Charles Hartshorne and Paul Weiss (6 vols.;
Cambridge, Mass., 1931–35), 5.407–408; W. V. Quine, "On What There Is," in *From
a Logical Point of View* (New York, 1961), 13. *Cf.* Rorty, "World Well Lost," 663; and
Hilary Putnam, *Reason, Truth and History* (Cambridge, England, 1981), 52.
9. W. V. Quine, *Ontological Relativity* (New York, 1969), 54–55.
10. Thus linguistic idealists have no quarrel with, but likewise do not feel
threatened by, the Tarskian type of correspondence—"Snow is white" is true if and
only if snow is white.

be defined as correspondence to objects altogether independent of inquiry? Only at the cost of making truth unascertainable. Taking the belief in independent objects as the essence of "metaphysical realism," Hilary Putnam argues that "the most important consequence of metaphysical realism is that *truth* is supposed to be *radically non-epistemic*—we might be 'brains in a vat' and so the theory that is 'ideal' from the point of view of operational utility, inner beauty and elegance, 'plausibility', simplicity, 'conservatism', etc., *might be false*. 'Verified' (in any operational sense) does not imply 'true', on the metaphysical realist picture, even in the ideal limit." Given his assumption of the primacy of consciousness, Putnam is right—he is merely presenting in modern dress what Kant grasped about Hume. If one assumes with the Cartesians that we could generate the entire array of cognitive contents (in this case, theories), and perform on them all the cognitive operations of testing and justification, without any contact with reality independent of us, then the epistemological standard of truth as correspondence to such a reality is fruitless. The alternative is then to define truth, with John Dewey, as the "warranted assertibility" of a statement, established by its coherence within the network of other statements. It must, at any rate, be defined by reference to the inquirer or to the process of inquiry. In Quine's words, "Where it makes sense to apply 'true' is to a sentence couched in the terms of a given theory and seen from within the theory, complete with its posited reality."[11]

The issues of truth and the procedures of verification bring us to the second essential element in idealism: the claim that our epistemological standards of objectivity must be defined by reference to the constitutive activity by which we know. The view of truth to which linguistic idealists are committed requires a prior concept of verification or justification. Canons of justification cannot therefore be validated as ways of arriving at true conclusions. What, then, is their basis? At this point, we must consider a distinction which Rorty has argued is implicit in all the writers.[12] In order to combine a ma-

11. Hilary Putnam, "Realism and Reason," *Proceedings and Addresses of the American Philosophical Association*, L (1977), 485. The verificationist element in Putnam's address is discussed at length by William Alston, in "Yes, Virginia, There is a Real World," *Proceedings and Addresses of the American Philosophical Association*, LII (1979), 779–808. W. V. Quine, *Word and Object* (Cambridge, Mass., 1960), 24.

12. On this distinction, see especially Rorty, *Philosophy and the Mirror of Nature*, 140–42 and Chap. 4.

terialist metaphysics with an idealist epistemology, they distinguish between the causal and the justificatory conditions for knowledge. Causally, our knowledge depends on the impact of the environment, the response of the senses, and the workings of the nervous system. The result is best seen as a piece of linguistic behavior, and the whole sequence is the province of the natural scientist. Questions of justification, meaning, knowledge, and truth, on the other hand, arise only when our utterances are seen as actions within a social practice governed by rules.

The practice is what constitutes the cognitive domain. An utterance is distinguished from a physical event only insofar as it is a way of participating in the practice, and it can be evaluated cognitively—as meaningful, justified, true—only by reference to the rules legislated by the practice. The rules themselves, like the Kantian rules of synthesis, have no basis in reality beyond the fact that the practice does legislate them. As David Pears puts it, speaking of Wittgenstein's later philosophy: "Outside human thought and speech there are no independent, objective points of support, and meaning and necessity are preserved only in the linguistic practices which embody them. . . . There is, for example, no independent objective basis which will justify logical inference, and the only possible justification of it is that this is how people think and speak. . . . Each [mode of human thought] is accepted on its own terms, and justified by its own internal standards." Rorty has aptly characterized this view as "epistemological behaviorism": "Explaining rationality and epistemic authority by reference to what society lets us say, rather than the latter by the former, is the essence of what I shall call 'epistemological behaviorism.' . . . For the Quine-Sellars approach to epistemology, to say that truth and knowledge can only be judged by the standards of the inquirers of our own day . . . is merely to say that nothing counts as justification unless by reference to what we already accept, and that there is no way to get outside our beliefs and our language so as to find some test other than coherence."[13] These rules of justification are thus social, mutable, and pragmatic, unlike the fixed Kantian categories. But both assume the primacy of consciousness in setting epistemological standards.

13. David Pears, *Ludwig Wittgenstein* (New York, 1970), 179, 183, 184; Rorty, *Philosophy and the Mirror of Nature*, 174–78. See also Wilfrid Sellars, "Philosophy and the Scientific Image of Man," in *Science, Perception and Reality* (London, 1963), 39–40.

Of all these writers, Wilfrid Sellars has gone furthest in applying the neo-idealist model to perceptual knowledge. Sellars relies
throughout on the distinction between causal and justificatory conditions for knowledge. The connection between external objects and
our perceptual statements, in his view, is a matter of causality. We
are conditioned to make certain statements at the stimulus of the
relevant objects. The causal chain involved may or may not include
sense impressions, of the sort that Cartesian empiricists accepted.
This can only be determined by scientists in the attempt to explain
the connection. But he rejects the attempt by certain linguistic
Cartesians, such as A. J. Ayer, to show that there is some special
justificatory relationship between the statement and an experiential
state. Ayer claimed that a phenomenal statement requires only that
the subject choose the right word to apply to the state, the choice
being determined by "a meaning rule of the language," a rule of the
word-thing type. Sellars points out the circularity in this. In order
to know that such a rule—of the form "Red objects are to be called
'red'"—applies to the case at hand, one would have to know that
the object is red. That is, one must have acquired the knowledge that
was to be explained. His conclusion is that the rules for justifying a
statement are exclusively of the word-word type.[14]

When a language learner has been conditioned to utter "This is
red" in the presence of a red object, he does not yet *know* that it is
red; his utterance is no different in principle from the similar sound
made by a parrot. A human speaker, however, follows rules in
making his utterance, and Sellars claims that the stage of following
rules is reached only when connections have been established among
the conditioned responses, and not merely between individual responses and their stimuli. The speaker must be able to say, not
merely that this is red, but that it is not blue or green. His responses
must be modified in the appropriate ways by input from other
speakers. And he must have made the same utterance often enough
in the past to recognize his spontaneous utterance now as a reliable
indicator of the presence of a red object. "The coming to see something as red [*i.e.*, to know that it is red] is the culmination of a complicated process which is the slow building up of a multi-dimen-

14. A. J. Ayer, "Basic Propositions," in *Philosophical Essays* (London, 1954), 120;
Sellars, "Some Reflections on Language Games," in *Science, Perception and Reality*, 333.

sional pattern of linguistic responses (by verbal expressions to things, by verbal expressions to verbal expressions, by meta-linguistic expressions to object-language expressions, etc.) the fruition of which as conceptual occurs when all these dimensions come into play."[15]

What justifies a perceptual statement, then, what establishes its place in the cognitive order and makes it a piece of knowledge as opposed to a mere conditioned response, is the pattern of its relationships within a coherent network of other statements. There is no foundation that could be known independently of what it founds, no piecemeal learning of facts. In Wittgenstein's words: "When we first begin to believe anything, what we believe is not a single proposition, it is a whole system of propositions. (Light dawns gradually over the whole.)" But Wittgenstein's metaphor, though it captures the gradual process by which a child becomes a human knower, is misleading if it suggests that the process is a dawning of some new sort of consciousness in the child's mind. As Rorty makes clear in expounding the point, learning a language brings about no such inner change: "All that its acquisition does is to let us enter a community whose members exchange justifications of assertions, and other actions, with one another. . . . What has happened is a shift in a person's relations with others, not a shift inside the person which now *suits* him to enter such new relations."[16]

This idealist model of knowledge has brought out problems implicit in Cartesian empiricism, especially the linguistic forms adopted in this century, just as Kant's system drew out the implications of Descartes' philosophy. The linguistic version of idealism is also subject to the same problems of self-stultification that beset the Kantian version. On the one hand, the claim that our knowledge consists in conditioned verbal responses, justified and made true by their place in the conceptual framework of our society, is not itself offered as a conditioned response, made true in this way. In assert-

15. Sellars, "Some Reflections on Language Games," "Empiricism and the Philosophy of Mind," and "Phenomenalism," all in *Science, Perception and Reality*, 321, 339, 167–69, 90 (quotation).

16. Ludwig Wittgenstein, *On Certainty*, ed. G. E. M. Anscombe and G. H. von Wright, trans. Denis Paul and G. E. M. Anscombe (1969; rpr. New York, 1972), sec. 141. See also Will, *Induction and Justification*, 213–14. Rorty, *Philosophy and the Mirror of Nature*, 185, 187.

ing their thesis, Wittgenstein, Sellars *et al.* put themselves forward as cognitive subjects who are free to weigh the merits of the thesis and who have adopted it because they have grasped a fact their opponents have overlooked. That fact has to do with conceptual schemes and people as real objects in the world. They have therefore stepped out from the confines of their own thesis about assertions, to assert a thesis based on an insight into the real nature of these objects. Quine argues that reference is inscrutable, for example, without evincing any doubt whether the thesis is really *about* language—about real languages, as they are independently of his claim. The thesis in question is inconsistent, then, because what it asserts is not compatible with the assertion of it.

Second, the thesis is incompatible with the knowledge used to explain and defend it. We saw that Kant relies on a theory of syntheses carried out by the noumenal self to explain in what sense the objects of knowledge depend on the subject, and to justify his claim that they do so depend. Similarly, linguistic idealists rely on a theory of human beings as objects of scientific knowledge, including theories of how language is learned and social practices inculcated, to explain in what sense the objects of knowledge and the truth of propositions depend on our conceptual scheme, and to justify their claim that they do so depend. The problem for Kant was that by his own thesis the noumenal self must remain unknown, precluding any knowledge of its synthesizing activities. The problem for his heirs is rather the opposite. The psychological theories by which Sellars would explain how we are conditioned to accept a practice of justification are themselves elements within our conceptual scheme. As causal theories, they describe a dependence among items within the scheme, but not a dependence of the scheme as such on anything. But in the absence of the latter sort of dependence, the causal theories must be taken to describe reality—they are made true by the way things are, not by our practices and conventions. Similarly, Rorty argues that our knowledge can be fully explained by historians of knowledge, with no such thing as "the relation of knowledge to reality" left over to be understood.[17] But we need to ask whether these historians really know the historical reality. Is their knowledge to be accounted for by the fact that they have grasped

17. Rorty, *Philosophy and the Mirror of Nature*, 178.

what actually happened? Or will future historians explain why our historians came to believe what they did about why we believe as we do? And what about the knowledge of those future historians?

The problem may be clarified in terms of another Kantian distinction. In rejecting the Cartesian tradition, Kant argued that the physical world is as well known to us as the inner world of experience. But both are phenomenal, as objects of inner and outer sense. The noumenal objects—the thing-in-itself and the self-in-itself—are equally unknown. Thus Kant described himself as a phenomenal realist but a transcendental idealist. The linguistic idealists are in the same position.[18] In rejecting Cartesian empiricism, they are denying that knowledge of experiential states has any epistemological priority over knowledge of nature. Indeed, they typically argue for the opposite type of priority, as in Wittgenstein's argument against private languages. But their idealism prevents them from saying that our knowledge of either nature or the self is knowledge of things as they are independently of our knowledge about them. And this creates a dilemma.

Some of these writers have said that although truth (at least in the ordinary sense), justification, and the like are relative to conceptual schemes, there is nevertheless some sense in which our conceptual scheme is preferable to that of our predecessors, and in which that of our successors will be preferable to our own—that is, conceptual schemes progress in the direction of greater adequacy to reality. Sellars, for example, has employed the early Wittgenstein's concept of truth as picturing to this end: the ideal limit of inquiry is a conceptual scheme in which assertions are true by the internal standards of the scheme, but also in which the basic singular (atomic) statements of microphysics *picture* microphysical objects. The problem is that this is a nonintentional relation: "Picturing is a complex matter-of-factual relation and, as such, belongs in quite a different box from the concepts of denotation and truth." (This is necessarily so, since all the intentional, cognitive relations to an object have been made relative to conceptual schemes.) But then Rorty argues, rightly, that any such matter-of-factual relation must fall within some theory of the world and must therefore be relative to it. Once accept the

18. *Cf.* Hilary Putnam's distinction between internal and external perspectives (*Reason, Truth and History*, Chap. 3) and between internal and external realism ("Realism and Reason").

theses of transcendental idealism, in other words, and there is no way to sneak around them to achieve some sort of realism, however limited. The same may be said of the attempt to give an *evolutionary* account of how beliefs, scientific theories, or conceptual schemes are selected for survival value and must therefore progress in the direction of greater adequacy to reality. If the meaning, the reference, and the truth of our present theories—that is, their intentional features—do not relate them to reality, then evolution cannot provide the missing link between subject and object, as it is itself one of our theories.[19]

Yet if there is no way for idealists to step outside our theories of the world to see their connection with the world itself, as Rorty argues, there is for the same reason no way to step outside and see their relation to a transcendental knower. And without this, one cannot claim that our standards of justification depend on us in any meaningful way. Rorty argues that we have the standards we do, not because we have grasped some feature of reality that requires them—not because they can be grounded in fact—but because we acquire them by being inducted into a social practice. Our possession of these standards, then, can be fully explained by historians describing the social evolution of the standards and by psychologists describing how the individual within a culture acquires them. These scientific descriptions are of course themselves offered within our conceptual framework and are therefore subject to the idealist theses about knowledge. Suppose, then, that historians and psychologists do not adopt the sorts of theories Rorty ascribes to them. Suppose that the historians come to believe that the only way to explain the genesis of a belief or practice is the discovery of certain facts. Suppose that psychologists come to believe that the child's cognitive growth can be understood only in terms of his awareness of the environment. (Some psychologists, for example, have described the child's acquisition of a language, not in terms of classical conditioning, but in terms of a process by which he matches the words he hears from his elders to his own prelinguistic awareness of objects

19. Wilfrid Sellars, *Science and Metaphysics* (London, 1968), 136; Rorty, *Philosophy and the Mirror of Nature*, 295–99. *Cf.* D. T. Campbell, "Evolutionary Epistemology," in P. A. Schilpp (ed.), *The Philosophy of Karl Popper* (La Salle, Ill., 1974), 413–63; and Peter Skagestad, "Taking Evolution Seriously: Critical Comments on D. T. Campbell's Evolutionary Epistemology," *Monist*, LXI (1978), 611–21.

and their patterns of resemblance.)[20] By idealist principles, the
adoption of such theories would mean that the objects of which they
speak—knowers in contact with an independent reality—actually
exist. But the theories themselves imply that the child or the society
is not entering into self-contained, self-justifying practices, as epistemological behaviorism claims, but into practices grounded in what
each grasps of reality. The idealist theses would then imply that the
idealist theses are false. Epistemological behaviorism thus requires
some *transcendental* psychology of just the sort which makes Kant's
theory inconsistent. If the science of our day cannot support a transcendental realism, in other words, the psychology of our day cannot support transcendental idealism.[21]

   These dialectical arguments are only so many ways of expressing the insight which underlies the primacy of existence: that the "It
is" must accompany all my assertions; that consciousness is radically dependent on reality for its contents, conceptual as well as perceptual; that the function of cognition is to identify what exists independently of it. But it is easier to grasp this point in the abstract,
and to see why idealism cannot be right, than to work out the details of an adequate theory of knowledge. Indeed, this is why idealism flourishes. Any simpleminded realist theory which treats our
knowledge as a mirror of reality is easily shown to be false; conceptual thought is no more diaphanous than perception is. We must take
account of the specific and fallible means by which cognition occurs, thus allowing for the relativity of the *form* in which we know
objects and for the possibility of error. Otherwise, epistemology will
swing back and forth between the unintegrated truths that our
knowledge is of a world independent of us, but that much depends
on us.

   It is thus not surprising that the arguments of the linguistic idealists consist almost exclusively in pointing out the inadequacies of
Cartesian empiricism, which is taken as the only way to retain the
idea of an independent world as the basis and standard of knowl-

   20. See Katherine Nelson *et al.*, "Early Lexicons: What Do They Mean?" *Child
Development*, XLIX (1978), 960–68; and Jeremy Anglin, *Word, Object, and Conceptual
Development* (New York, 1977), esp. Chap. 1.
   21. For a fuller discussion of this sort of problem, see Bernard Williams, "Wittgenstein and Idealism," in Godfrey Vesey (ed.), *Understanding Wittgenstein* (New York,
1974), 76–95.

edge. The Cartesians tried to show how a form of direct awareness—capable of registering particulars and abstracting common
properties—mediates between the world and our conceptual
scheme; the failure of Cartesianism has been taken to mean that no
such mediation is possible. This mistakenly equates a general thesis
with one particular formulation of it. The Cartesians are not the only
trustees of the realist principle they have mismanaged so badly. That
principle should be separated from the other premises which make
Cartesianism unworkable. Although I have done this, in detail, for
perception itself, the same cannot be accomplished here for conceptual knowledge. I can, however, give some indication of how perception fulfills the mediating role sought by Cartesians.

Nonpropositional Justification

I will argue in the next chapter that the conceptual identification of perceived objects as being of certain types, or possessing certain properties, is based directly on the perception of the objects
themselves. The connection is not one of inference or of any step in
thought from one fact to another. It is merely the articulation of what
is perceived, the transition from a perceptual to a conceptual awareness of the same fact. In the language of justification, the perceptual
judgment is justified by the perceptual awareness itself. This may
seem an obvious corollary of the view that we directly perceive external objects. But it contradicts an assumption frequently made by
epistemologists in this century. In arguing that perceptual awareness is direct, I distinguished it from conceptual awareness, and part
of what this means is that it is not propositional in form, it involves
no predication of a subject. But it is typically assumed that justification occurs only at the level of propositional knowledge, that what
justifies a judgment or assertion must be another judgment or assertion in accordance with the logic of propositions. For the sake of
brevity, we can call this the propositional theory of justification. It
is normally treated as self-evident, and rarely discussed as such, but
examples abound of its influence on theories of perceptual knowledge. And it is obviously incompatible with my view that perception itself is a source of justification. It will be worth our while,
therefore, to examine the role of the premise in the foundationalism
debate, and the motivation for adopting it.

Its effect on Cartesian empiricism is to provide further support for the idea that the bases of knowledge must be both phenomenal and infallible. Its relation to the first feature is evident in a comment by Bruce Aune: "If there is to be a fundamental basis of empirical knowledge—something by which the truth of ordinary claims is to be defended—this basis must be propositional in character: it must be the kind of thing that can have a place in an argument. . . . If, accordingly, the true basis of knowledge is regarded as phenomenal, it can at best consist of propositions about immediate experience." The propositional theory thus provides another basis for a representationalist theory of knowledge, independently of the Cartesian motives discussed earlier. Perception can play a role in the justification of beliefs about the world only by way of beliefs *about* perceptual experience, from which knowledge of external objects must be inferred. Aune assumes the propositional theory explicitly, but it is also implicit in attempts to find the justification for perceptual judgments by asking what we would say in response to the question, How do you know? Any answer to this request for justification would itself have to be a statement. The consequence is the same, as a passage from Chisholm's *Theory of Knowledge* indicates: "As we emphasized earlier, the appearance of a physical object— the way of being appeared to which the object as stimulus serves to cause—plays a fundamental role in the context of *justification*. If I ask myself Socratically what my justification is for thinking that it is a *tree* that I see, and if I continue my self-examination in the way we attempted to describe in Chapter 2, I will reach a point at which I will justify my claim about the tree by appeal to a proposition about the way in which I am appeared to."[22]

The propositional theory also adds another motive for requiring that the basis of knowledge must be infallible or incorrigible. The logic of this effect can be seen in Keith Lehrer's assumption that there is an exhaustive dichotomy between a coherence theory and a theory of *self-justified* beliefs: "The coherence theory might well be renamed the *relation* theory, for the fundamental conception is that some *relation* between beliefs is what determines whether or not a belief is justified. Consequently, the notion of self-justification must

22. Bruce Aune, *Knowledge, Mind, and Nature* (New York, 1967), 32; Chisholm, *Theory of Knowledge* (1966), 97.

be explicated in such a way that self-justified beliefs are ones that are justified because of some *intrinsic feature* of the belief rather than because of some relation of those beliefs to others."[23] A belief that is not justified inferentially by its relations to other beliefs might, on the face of it, be justified by its relation to something other than a belief, such as a nonpropositional form of awareness. But the propositional theory—implicit in Lehrer's assumption that the only relation which can justify is a relation to other beliefs—eliminates this possibility. The choice is therefore narrowed. On the one side is a coherence theory; on the other, a theory which holds that basic, noninferential knowledge is self-justifying. Self-justification in turn means that the mere acceptance of a proposition is a reason for accepting it. And for this to be even remotely plausible, the proposition must express some streak of cognitive infallibility, so that the question of further justification does not arise.

This connection is evident in attempts by foundationalists themselves to explain how phenomenal beliefs can be self-justifying. They are supposed to be justified in some way by the experiential states they are about.[24] This would mean, as Carl Hempel noted, that "to describe the evidence in question would simply mean to repeat the experiential statement itself," and the statement is therefore self-justifying. But notice the peculiarity here. The fact which makes a judgment true does not in itself ordinarily justify the judgment; the latter is justified by whatever puts one in a position to know the fact. The color of the chair does not justify my judgment that it is red unless I *see* the chair and its color. But if we extend this requirement, the phenomenal judgment would have to be justified by some prior awareness of or attention to an experiential state. This would involve a form of nonpropositional justification and would raise the question of how we come to identify conceptually the state we are aware of. To avoid this, foundationalists have described experiential states as "self-presenting." These states guarantee their own conceptual identification, without the need for any fallible process of recognition. Phenomenal judgments are thus at once self-justifying and infallible.[25]

23. Keith Lehrer, "The Knowledge Cycle," *Nous*, XI (1977), 18.
24. *Cf.* Lewis, *Analysis of Knowledge and Valuation*, 254.
25. Carl Hempel, "Some Theses on Empirical Certainty," *Review of Metaphysics*, V (1952), 621. *Cf.* Chisholm, *Theory of Knowledge* (2nd ed.), 20–33.

We can understand this concept of "self-presenting" states as a response by Cartesian empiricists to a dilemma caused by the propositional theory of justification. The noninferential foundations of knowledge must be justified by perception in some way, but cannot really be justified *by perception*. As Anthony Quinton notes: "Philosophers have sought to evade this dilemma by recourse to the Janus-faced notion of experience. The fact that we cannot, it seems, have an experience without somehow being conscious or aware of it has seemed to provide foundation stones for the edifice of knowledge which are at once statements, capable of standing in logical relations to the rest of the structure, and parts . . . of the extra-linguistic world, self-describing entities."[26] The passage brings out a deep-seated ambiguity about the nature of perception and of cognition that underlies the propositional theory. The view that knowledge must have a foundation derives from the realist principle that the ultimate object of our knowledge is an independent world. The idea of foundations raises the question of the basic point of contact between subject and object, between our knowledge and the world known. And the ambiguity occurs in the drawing of this line. On the one hand, perception is located on the side of the subject, as our basic experience of the world. In this respect, perception is taken to be a cognitive occurrence, capable of justifying beliefs. This is implicit in the very thesis of empiricism, which directs us to our perceptions—as opposed to our emotions or desires—as a basis of knowledge.[27] The assumption must be that perceiving, unlike feeling or desiring, is a form of awareness, capable of justifying our judgments by putting us in a position to know the facts they affirm.

On the other hand, philosophers who have taken the "linguistic turn" typically see our knowledge of the world as a system of statements, identifying in this way the cognitive with the linguistic order. From this perspective, perception falls on the side of the object, since it is part of the "extra-linguistic world." The point has been reinforced by the fate of Cartesian ideas in the twentieth century. Descartes viewed ideas both as states of the subject and as objects of inner awareness. Twentieth-century philosophers have not been

26. Anthony Quinton, "The Problem of Perception," in Robert Swartz (ed.), *Perceiving, Sensing, and Knowing* (Garden City, N.Y., 1965), 503.

27. Anthony Quinton, "The Foundations of Knowledge," in Alan Montefiore and Bernard Williams (eds.), *British Analytical Philosophy* (London, 1966), 84.

insensitive to the difficulties of combining these features. Moreover, although they have shared the Cartesian motives for wanting
to speak of representations, they have resisted the notion of an inner perceiver *looking at* representations.[28] Thus twentieth-century
representationalism typically sees perception, not as the awareness
of experiential states, but simply as the occurrence of the states as
natural effects of natural causes. And if so, perception must be noncognitive and hence incapable in itself of justifying statements. Thus
Wittgenstein asked: "How can a *proposition* follow from sense-
impressions?"[29] The concept of justification requires that what justifies a statement be something in the cognitive realm. A noncognitive fact may be the object of knowledge, but cannot itself serve
to justify. Hence if the cognitive realm is exhausted by the conceptual or linguistic level, there is no alternative to the propositional
theory of justification. Only a statement will be able to justify another statement. And if there is a noninferential foundation of
knowledge, it can only consist in statements with a special sort of
internal justification.

The propositional theory, then, is an expression of the two
complementary ideas that all cognition is linguistic and that perception is a noncognitive occurrence. In Cartesian empiricism, as I
noted, these ideas have an ambiguous status. They are held implicitly and are joined to the older and contradictory idea that perception is a form of cognition, that it involves a preconceptual and diaphanous awareness of the effects of external objects on the senses.
This older idea is suppressed by the new ones, but its effects are retained; and the result is the "Janus-faced notion of experience." Experience is taken to consist in noncognitive states, but these states
are assumed to lie at an especially permeable location on the border
between our knowledge and the extralinguistic world. Unlike other
natural facts, the states present themselves, they describe them-

28. A good example of what they have wanted to avoid is provided by J. R.
Smythies, "The Problems of Perception," *British Journal for the Philosophy of Science*,
XI (1960–61), 228: "There is no reason why *perception* should not require an elaborate
physiological apparatus . . . yet *sensing*—the immediate prehension of sense-data
available to introspection—should require none. It may merely be the property or
activity of the Pure Ego."

29. Ludwig Wittgenstein, *Philosophical Investigations*, trans. G. E. M. Anscombe (New York, 1953), Pt. I, sec. 486.

selves, they *are* their own descriptions. Contemporary idealists, on the other hand, eliminate the ambiguity by rejecting the older idea altogether. They accept as clear-cut articles of faith the theses that all cognition is linguistic and that perception is a noncognitive occurrence. The theses are implicit, for example, in Sellars' statement of "psychological nominalism": "all awareness of *sorts, resemblances, facts*, etc., in short, all awareness of abstract entities—indeed, all awareness even of particulars—is a linguistic affair."[30]

Something like this view plays a major role in the case for a coherence theory of justification. Consider Laurence Bonjour's argument against the epistemology of the given, against the idea that certain basic judgments can be justified by a direct, nonpropositional, "intuitive" form of awareness such as perception. The appeal to the given assumes that such an awareness can justify a judgment because it is cognitive, but that it does not itself require justification precisely because it is given, because there is nothing volitional about it. When I open my eyes and see a chair, I do not choose the content of my awareness—I do not choose to see a chair with four legs and crimson upholstery instead of a Mack truck with sixteen wheels and steel-gray sides. It is given and can therefore serve as the basis for the judgment that this is a chair. But Bonjour objects: "It seems clear on reflection that these two aspects cannot be separated, that it is one and the same feature of a cognitive state, viz. its assertive content, which both enables it to confer justification on other states and also requires that it be justified itself. If this is right, then it does no good to introduce semi-cognitive states [*i.e.*, intuitive awareness] in an attempt to justify basic beliefs, since to whatever extent such a state is capable of conferring justification, it will to that very same extent require justification." The feature of a cognitive state which allows it to justify and which itself requires justification is described as its "assertive content" or as "the cognitive thesis that-p."[31] Thus the argument assumes that only something with a propositional content can justify a belief, or that to be a cognitive state in the first place, an experience must have a propositional content.

30. Sellars, "Empiricism and the Philosophy of Mind," 160.

31. Laurence Bonjour, "Can Empirical Knowledge Have a Foundation?" *American Philosophical Quarterly*, XV (1978), 12.

But what support do idealists offer for psychological nominalism? It is almost entirely negative, consisting in an attack on the Cartesian idea of a diaphanous awareness underlying our statements. Gilbert Ryle, Wittgenstein, and others criticized the basic Cartesian model of an inner theater, with an inner observer diaphanously observing an array of mental contents. Wittgenstein and Sellars in particular also attacked the idea that concept acquisition or language learning could be explained in terms of any such awareness of inner states. But whatever the merits of these arguments, they certainly do not by themselves support the theses. It is possible to reject the diaphanous model, as I have, and yet retain the idea that perception is a nonconceptual form of awareness. Hence the diaphanous and the linguistic models of awareness are false alternatives, and an argument against the one will not support the other.

Can anything more be said in favor of psychological nominalism? Rorty argues that if we are not talking about propositional knowledge, the only sense we can give to the concept of awareness (having rejected the diaphanous grasp of inner contents) is a discriminative response to stimuli. But this is a noncognitive capacity that perceivers share with computers, amoebas, photoelectric cells, record changers, and the like.[32] Rorty's argument amounts to a rhetorical question—what else could nonlinguistic awareness be?—and given what has gone before, we can answer it. Any effect whatever is a discriminative response to stimuli, in the sense of a differential reaction to them: that is what a causal relation *is*. In that sense, the perceptual awareness of an object is a discriminative response to it, but the awareness has a distinctive nature that distinguishes it from other effects of other causes. The whole of Part I is a description of this nature.

In short, there is no independent basis for the linguistic model of awareness. Yet the model is not an arbitrary hypothesis. It is an integral part of linguistic idealism, of a piece with the dichotomy between causal and justificatory conditions of knowledge, the coherence theory, and the other tenets outlined above. And like the others, it has Kantian antecedents. Kant rejected the possibility that an unsynthesized manifold of sensations could contain any conscious-

32. Rorty, *Philosophy and the Mirror of Nature*, 182ff.

ness of objects. He rejected the notion of Cartesian ideas, which are both contents and the awareness of that content. His reason for this is connected with the "Copernican Revolution." The Cartesian tradition had analyzed the knowledge of an object into two components—a relation between the object and a mental representation of it, and the direct awareness of that representation. As we have seen, Kant rejected the first element of the analysis, on the grounds that the external object becomes unknowable and hence otiose as a standard of objectivity. What makes the state a representation of an object is the network of its relations to other states.

Kant objects on similar grounds to the second element in the analysis. The Cartesian starts with a picture of a knower facing a world of objects, his awareness of them a real relation between him and external objects. In response to the problems of relativity and error, he simply reproduces that same picture inside consciousness. There is a mental spectator facing a manifold of mental contents. But then his awareness of the contents becomes a mysterious, diaphanous phenomenon, and not a real relation at all, since the awareness is not really distinct from the contents. Here, too, Kant rejects the picture and redefines the awareness of objects in terms of the same organization of representations that defines objectivity. Thus the syntheses according to concepts which constitute objects of knowledge out of the manifold are also necessary to constitute the consciousness of objects. And just as objectivity is not a real relation between subject and object, neither is awareness; both are simply ways of describing what is really a single stratum, the manifold itself. This yields a synthetic view of awareness, in opposition to what idealists have always derided as a "spectator" or "mental-eye" view. All awareness depends on a precognitive synthesis, and this implies that all awareness must be judgmental, that intuitions without concepts must be blind (noncognitive), because the synthesis proceeds in accordance with conceptual principles or rules whose conscious expression is propositional. It also implies that there could be no such thing as a single judgment standing alone as an isolated cognition, because the synthesis that constitutes the judgment as a cognitive phenomenon also embeds it in a network of other judgments. As Norman Kemp Smith noted, this synthetic view is the real basis for the coherence theory of knowledge.[33]

33. "Spectator" view is John Dewey's term, in *The Quest for Certainty* (1929; rpr.

The twentieth-century debate exhibits a similar dialectic, the same melodic line in a different key. The contemporary analogue of Kant's "conscious relation to an object" is the intentional idiom we use to describe cognitive phenomena—meaning, reference, truth, and the like. Each of these applies to cognitive vehicles that are of or about something. The attempts by representationalists to ground these relations at the perceptual level—to give analyses of them in terms of sense-data—relied on the diaphanous awareness of inner contents, which was attacked by Wittgenstein and Sellars, as by Kant before them. How, then, do we account for intentionality? Since the attempt to ground it perceptually in a quasi-real relation between subject and object had failed, it was not likely that any such relation would appear at the conceptual level. Instead, it is to be defined functionally. For a subject to believe, or mean, or refer to something is for him to be in a certain state to which a content can be ascribed. And content can be ascribed only in virtue of the role that state plays in the rule-bound pattern of behavior, especially verbal behavior, in which the subject engages. Thus just as objectivity is not a real relation between our knowledge and an independent world, neither are our intentional states; both are merely ways of describing or evaluating what in fact is a single stratum (the series of our natural states) in terms of our social practices. In this way, we can understand the point of Sellars' remark that "in characterizing an episode or a state as that of *knowing*, we are not giving an empirical description of that episode or state; we are placing it in the logical space of reasons, of justifying and being able to justify what one says."[34]

The result is something analogous to Kant's synthetic view of awareness. The only real sense we can give to awareness—as a relation to an object and not merely as a differential reaction to stimuli—is in terms of these intentional relations, which must be "synthesized" in the process of language acquisition. Thus the process, as described by Wittgenstein or Sellars, is analogous to Kant's theory of synthesis and yields the same epistemological consequences. Just as Kant saw his categories as rules for synthesizing judgments, they see language acquisition as a process of mastering rules for us-

New York, 1960), 23; "mental-eye" view is Sellars' term, in "Some Reflections on Language Games," 335; Norman Kemp Smith, *A Commentary to Kant's 'Critique of Pure Reason'* (2nd ed.; New York, 1962), xxxvi–xlv.

34. Sellars, "Empiricism and the Philosophy of Mind," 169.

ing words, constructing sentences, making assertions in a social context. The rules have a substantive content. They can be expressed propositionally as a framework of beliefs about the world which are adopted in the course of learning a language, just as Kant's categories can be expressed as synthetic a priori truths about nature.[35] Thus there could be no such thing as a single statement standing alone as an isolated cognition, since the intentional features it has as an intelligent utterance—the features that distinguish it from the noise made by a parrot—are the synthetic result of a process which also embeds it in a context of other statements, all of them interrelated by the substantive framework. And of course there could be no foundational level of awareness prior to or "below" the linguistic and judgmental because it could have no intentional features. In particular, the sensory experience that follows on the stimulation of sense organs is at best a *causal* factor in the production of statements, not a source of cognitive justification for them.[36]

In this way, the analogy with Kant's synthetic model helps tie together many of the themes in linguistic idealism. But the modern version, no less than Kant's, is a reaction against a prior Cartesian model that created the problems the synthetic view is introduced to solve. It has no argument against the realist view of cognition I have offered, once we distinguish the "spectator" view of awareness from the diaphanous model to which it has normally been joined. Perceptual awareness is not diaphanous, nor is it the awareness of inner contents. But it is not a synthetic product, as the idealists claim. It is not reducible to the occurrence of representations with intentional content (the "vertical" issue of Chapters 3 and 4), but is a real relation between the perceiver and the external objects he perceives. Nor is it the product of a synthesis of sensations by means of concepts, subconscious inferences, or hypotheses (the "horizontal" issue of Chapters 2 and 5). We are thus justified in rejecting the synthetic model of awareness and, with it, the idea that perception is noncognitive. As the discrimination of entities, as the awareness of them and their attributes, it is thoroughly cognitive. And so we can also dispense with the propositional theory of justification. As

35. This is a recurrent theme in Wittgenstein's *On Certainty*. See especially secs. 95–105, 151–52, 162.

36. *Cf.* Rorty, "Strawson's Objectivity Argument," 241–42; and Sellars, "Phenomenalism," 90–91.

the primary form in which we are aware of the physical environment, perception itself is what justifies our conceptual identifications of the objects in that environment. It provides a mode of nonpropositional, noninferential justification.

7

Perceptual Judgments

Most theories of perception have not drawn any clear distinction between the percept and the perceptual judgment. Indeed, they could not, for they have held that a judgmental element is precisely what distinguishes perception from sensation. If perception is the awareness of external objects, not merely of experiential states, representationalist theories have held that that is because experiential states are interpreted as signs of external objects—interpretation being the work of judgment. If perception is the awareness of integrated wholes, with properties that are constant through changes in the conditions of perception, sensationalist theories have held that that is because the object is constructed from the fluctuating data at the receptors—construction being the work of judgments that mediate inferences or impose categories. My argument against both views has as much bearing on the perceptual judgment as on perception itself. The realist theory of perception does not require that the judgment serve as a kind of epistemological glue, binding sensations together or putting us in touch with reality. We are free to distinguish the judgment from the percept and to consider the former on its own terms.

The perceptual judgment is the conceptual identification of what is perceived. Transforming our perceptual awareness of the world into conceptual form, it gives us a way to retain and communicate what we perceive and to express the evidence of the senses in a way that can bring it to bear on abstract conclusions. My approach to the perceptual judgment is centered on this fact; my goal is to understand the link it creates between the perceptual and the conceptual awareness of objects. This nexus was not irrelevant for the traditional theories. Even if the basic level of propositional knowledge were beliefs about inner representations, for example, the beliefs would still involve the conceptual recognition of the representations as being of certain types, and this raises questions about the nature of recognition. But this fact received little attention—partly because of the motives for regarding sensory states as "self-describing," and partly because of the larger problem of getting from the sensory state to entities in the external world. For realism, on the other hand, the nature of recognition is the *only* epistemological issue concerning perceptual judgments, and there is much to be said about it that finds no place in the traditional theories.

It is not a small issue, and in the absence of a complete account of concept formation and conceptual thinking, I cannot address all of it. I can only outline the connection, showing the various ways in which the cognitive content of perceptual awareness serves to ground the cognitive content of the perceptual judgment, and then indicate some of the implications for traditional questions about our knowledge of the external world. I will follow the tradition, however, in discussing these matters in a somewhat artificial context. We are concerned with a type of knowledge whose justification is noninferential, knowledge that is based directly—in a sense of directness that will require explanation—on perception. But my examples will be judgments of a sort that are rarely made explicit, such judgments as that this is a desk, that it is brown, hard, etc. These identifications are normally automatic for an adult; explicit judgments are made only in regard to less routine or obvious matters. No one would bother with the conscious judgment that the surface of the puddle exhibits a familiar pattern of ripples; we go straight to the conclusion that it is raining. Indeed, far more sophisticated judgments are often made in a way that is experienced psychologically as direct. When a person arrives at a party, for example, he may "directly observe" that the host has expensive taste in furniture, that the music was not intended for dancing, that something is going on between the couple in the corner.

These latter judgments obviously rest on a body of experience which includes much more than the particular experiences that occasion them. In this respect, they differ in degree from the judgments concerning the desk. But I would deny that there is a difference in kind. In particular, I would reject the Cartesian empiricist's claim that certain judgments are specially justified by perceptual experience in the sense that they do nothing more than formulate the content of a single experience. As I will argue later, any judgment "goes beyond" what is given, by assimilating it to abstract types and attributes, and we are aware of these abstractions only through the integration of other perceptual data. In this respect, there is no difference in kind between the simpler and the more sophisticated judgments mentioned above. The differences among them lie along a continuum defined by the complexity of the conceptual apparatus brought into play. This does not mean that anti-foundationalists are right in seeing conceptual knowledge as a self-contained structure that cannot be fully anchored in perception. It does mean that the only defensible sort of foundationalism will be a temporal, developmental thesis: that every element in the conceptual knowledge which informs an adult's perceptual judgments can be traced back to perceptual sources.

I concentrate on the simpler judgments, then, not because they represent a special class but because they exhibit in simpler form the link between perceptual awareness and conceptual recognition. My main concern, in any case, is with the nature of that link, with the ways in which perceptual awareness provides a cognitive ground for the perceptual judgment. The next section will deal with the relation between the discrimination of entities and the referential component of the judgment. The two sections following will examine the relation between the perceptual awareness of attributes and the predicative element in the judgment, considering certain general issues about concepts and then the specific issues pertaining to concepts for sensory qualities. In the last section, I will discuss the evidence for holding that perception is affected by emotional and cognitive influences in a way that would undercut its ability to provide objective evidence for perceptual judgments.

Perception and Reference

A perceptual judgment is a belief about a particular object present to the senses. Its linguistic expression would be a singular statement, with a singular referring term that picks out something in the world as the subject of predication. Questions of justification normally concern the predicative element of the judgment. Why do we believe that x is P (and not R)? But a similar question might also be raised about the subject. Why do we believe it is x (and not y) that is P? And the answer is that x is perceptually discriminated. Thus the first principle of perceptual justification is that for a judgment to be justified by perception, the person must perceptually discriminate the object he takes to be an instance of the concept predicated.

The general reason for this principle is obvious. A perceptual judgment is justified by the way an object appears to a perceiver. Because the thing before him looks a certain way, he can identify it as a tree, as green, and so on. The appearance will not justify predicating these attributes of any object at random, however, but only of the particular item that appears, and only if it is picked out *as* a particular item. Thus I might "see" a camouflaged soldier in the sense that his facing surfaces are parts of my field of view, but I am not in a position to form a judgment about him. Nor would the appearance of the field justify such a judgment, unless I can isolate the soldier as a figure against the ground. If I cannot isolate *him*, but only the various patches of color that in fact are parts of his clothing, then I can form justified judgments only about those patches. This is one reason why it is important that what we discriminate in vision is the entity itself, not merely its facing surface. If the latter were true, then Moore would be right in denying that any perceptual judgment about the object itself could be based directly on perceptual awareness.[1]

At one level, it can be argued that the principle will automatically be satisfied, since perceptual contact with an object establishes that object as the referent of the judgment. If I am watching a bird fly across a field, the most natural expression of the judgment I form about it would be "That is a hawk." The statement exhausts the conceptual content of the judgment, yet the same statement might express a judgment about a different bird, in a different field, by someone else. What makes these judgments *about* different things is not their conceptual content, but rather the fact that he and I are perceiving different birds. This is simply a way of noting that the

1. G. E. Moore, "Some Judgments of Perception," in Robert Swartz (ed.), *Perceiving, Sensing, and Knowing* (Garden City, N.Y., 1965), 8–17.

reference of the demonstrative *that* is determined by my perceptual focus; it is a linguistic expression of that focus. There could therefore be no failure of correspondence between the object of perception and the object of the belief.

There are of course other singular referring expressions, such as names or definite descriptions, and unlike demonstratives, these can refer to objects independently of the particular context of the statements in which they are employed.[2] Suppose, then, that I am looking over the people in the room, and form the judgment that the man with the martini is tall. It is natural to assume, with Russell, that the phrase "the man with the martini" refers to the man I am looking at because that man satisfies the description. But now suppose that the man I see has water in his glass while another man behind me has a martini. Is my judgment about the latter and not the former? Clearly not. In Keith Donnellan's terms, the definite description is being used referentially, to describe what I have picked out independently of the description; it is not being used attributively, to make a statement about whatever uniquely satisfies the description.[3] I am, in effect, making two statements—"This is a man with a martini" and "He is tall." In both, perception determines the referent of the subject term.

The same distinction could be applied to names, and so we can say that even if a perceptual judgment employs a referring expression other than a demonstrative, the expression is used referentially. If the expression is being used attributively, then the judgment is asserted as true of whatever object satisfies the description, whether or not it is present. The judgment would not be a perceptual judgment, based on the way present objects look. It could not be a perceptual judgment until I grasp that *this* (an object I perceive) is the object that satisfies the description. Consequently, there is a necessary correspondence between what a person perceives and

2. This is not to say that such expressions can refer independently of perception altogether. It might be argued, for example, that names acquire their reference through some initial perceptual contact (by someone) with the object. *Cf.* Jaegwon Kim, "Perception and Reference Without Causality," *Journal of Philosophy*, LXXIV (1977), 606–20.

3. Keith Donnellan, "Reference and Definite Descriptions," *Philosophical Review*, LXXV (1966), 281–304. See also Leonard Linsky, *Referring* (London, 1967), 116.

what his perceptual judgment is about, and to that extent our first principle will automatically be satisfied.[4]

Although discrimination is necessary for justification, the perceiver need not discriminate an object before he entertains any thought about what predicates might be ascribed to it. Perceptual exploration is a directed process, and the temporal order is often reversed. In searching for a pencil, one explores the environment with a certain type of object in mind, and one is set to discriminate objects of that type. In situations of minimal clarity, such as a landscape at twilight, one may employ background conceptual knowledge about typical items to "try out" various ways of seeing the visual field as an organized layout of entities. "Suppose that were a tree trunk—no, that can't be right, there are no branches above it. . . . Then what if it is the edge of a rock; this would have to be the other edge." And in learning new concepts such as architectural terms, one may need explicit guidance in picking out just that portion of the world that is an instance of the concept. In all these cases, however, the perceptual discrimination of an object has a certain *epistemological* priority to any judgment that results (as it must if it is to be a necessary justifying condition). The conceptual content of the judgment-to-be may aid in picking out the object, but it does not constitute the object as a unit. That is a perceptual function. Nor has one actually made a definite judgment—"Here is a pencil," "That is a rock," "This is a cornice"—until the object has been discriminated. If the conceptually guided search for an object were enough to constitute perceptual discrimination, then the search could never fail.

Perceptual discrimination is not a unitary phenomenon. It admits of degrees. It involves the awareness of different sorts of structures in the different sense modalities. There are borderline cases. So it is not always easy to apply our principle of justification. But the difficulty provides yet another confirmation of the principle, for the same factors that are relevant in determining what (if anything) has been discriminated, are relevant in determining what (if anything) the corresponding perceptual judgment is about. It will be helpful to consider cases.

4. Tyler Burge makes essentially the same point, in "Belief *De Re*," *Journal of Philosophy*, LXXIV (1977), 348–49.

I have argued that to perceive a thing as a whole, one does not have to perceive the whole of it—front, back, and inside. Nor does one have to perceive the whole of a thing to be justified in forming a judgment about it. I can identify the creature across the room as a cat, even though most of its body is hidden by a chair. The subject of my judgment is of course the whole animal, not merely that portion of it reflecting light to my eyes—if the judgment were about the latter "entity," it would be false. But neither am I discriminating just that portion. The visible border between cat and chair is experienced as an edge of the chair, not of the cat; I experience the cat as extending beyond that accidental limit to my vision; I do not discriminate the portion I see from the portion that extends beyond. On the other hand, one might see all of a figure 4 in an embedded-figures test, in the sense of seeing every line, without discriminating the numeral as a unit. In this case, we would not be justified in taking anything to be a 4. There is no general principle governing how much of an object must be perceived in order to discriminate it. That depends on the object, the context, and the perceptual skills of the perceiver. But in any specific case, a reason for thinking an object has not been discriminated would be a reason for thinking that a perceptual judgment about it is unjustified.

Consider a more extreme case of occlusion. A hunter is looking across a valley and sees a patch of brown amid the undergrowth on the facing hillside. Could he not judge that it is a deer, even though he sees no part of the deer's contour and hence does not discriminate the deer as such? There seems a clear divergence here between what is discriminated (the patch) and what the judgment is about (the deer). But then we must ask, How *is* it possible for the judgment to be about the deer? Two answers seem plausible, and both eliminate the problem. First, the hunter clearly would not be in a position to recognize what he sees as a deer unless he sees the brown patch as lying behind the plane of the bushes, not in front of them. If so, he will experience the brown patch as extending beyond the contours he sees. We might then say that the hunter is after all discriminating the deer as an indefinitely extended object. More likely, his experience as a hunter is leading him through an implicit inference—that shade of brown is a color that deer have, but not bushes or earth, so there must be a deer there. In this case, the judgment is not a *perceptual* judgment but the conclusion of an inference, and so it is not a counterexample to the principle.

In hearing, as I have noted, we never discriminate entities in the sense of solid physical objects; we discriminate events in the physical environment. Yet we often form judgments about objects on the basis of the sounds they make. "What's that noise?" "It's only the pipes in the wall." The problem this may seem to pose for our principle is easily solved. The statement is clearly an abbreviated form of the judgment "That is the banging of pipes in the wall." It illustrates an important feature, however, of our concepts for sounds. Except for the areas of music and speech, terms that classify sounds as such are notoriously vague—bangs, screeches, roars, clamors. To eliminate this vagueness, we specify the sound by the type of object making it: the banging of pipes, the rushing sound of tires on wet pavement, the screech of a parrot (quite different, respectively, from the bang of a gong, the rushing noise of the wind, the screech of brakes). These are predicates describing what we discriminate in hearing, but judgments involving them have direct implications about the nature of the objects in the environment. Since it is typically the latter which concern us, we often do not make explicit the perceptual judgment about the sound itself.

Suppose that I test the water in the tub and judge that it is warm. What is that judgment about? It is about the water in the tub, even though I have tactual experience only of a medium surrounding my hand, with no sense of its edges. But the judgment *is* about the body of water as a whole, only because I can *see* it as a whole—vision picks out the object, touch informs me of its nature. The example illustrates another feature we have already noted about perceptual discrimination: the integration of sensory input may include integration among the sense modalities. There is no reason, therefore, why one modality cannot pick out the object about which one judges while another modality provides the justification for predicating of it what one does.

But suppose that I cannot see the water. I am groping in a cave and plunge my hand into something that feels wet and cool. Is my judgment *about* the definitely shaped pool of water that I have in fact touched? In one sense it is, for that is what is there. But I am not in a cognitive position to form a judgment about that pool as a unit; I have no sense of it. There is still perceptual discrimination involved. I feel on my skin the border between air and water; I feel the varying resistance of the water as I swish my hand back and forth. But I do not discriminate the pool as such, only an indefinite region of the water, and my judgment is about the water in an equally indefinite way. The same is true of smelling an odor or feeling a breeze—or perceiving liquids and gases in general. Some discrimination is necessary to pick out the object from its perceptual background, but the object is typically perceived as extending indefinitely, and any judgment about it has a correspondingly indefinite reference.

So far, I have dealt chiefly with judgments involving concepts of natural kinds. But we also identify the qualities of things and the materials they are made of. In this regard, we need to recall the distinction between discrete and continuous qualities. For the most part, primary qualities are discrete. It is the whole apple that is round, not the parts; the apple is the indivisible subject of its shape. But concepts for many qualities, especially the secondary ones, as well as concepts of materials, pick out continuous features of things. Part of a red surface is itself red, a wooden thing is wooden through and through. Our principle of justification holds that one must perceptually discriminate the item that is judged to be an instance of the concept predicated. This principle has the same implication for the discrete qualities that it has for natural kinds—one must discriminate the entity that has the quality. But a part of an entity is as much an instance of a *continuous* quality as is the entity as a whole. What does the principle entail in this case, and can it be defended?

As we have seen, the structural features involved in the discrimination of entities are always present in normal perception, even if one is not attending to them. The awareness of qualities, even continuous ones, is always set in the context of the awareness of entities. In judging that a patch of the wall is yellow, one is discriminating the patch—if the patch is different in color from the surrounding wall. Even if it is the same color, one is still discriminating the wall. To have a genuine test of the principle, we need to look at awareness on the level of sensations. In peripheral vision, for example, one can detect the motion of objects too far out in the visual field to allow judgments of their shape, contour, or distance.[5] It does

5. See R. L. Gregory, *Eye and Brain* (New York, 1966), 91.

not seem in this case that any perceptual discrimination has occurred, but judgments of motion are still reliable and thus presumably justified.

It would be possible to argue that if the type of discrimination which remains in this situation is not genuinely perceptual, then the judgment involved need not be considered a *perceptual* judgment, and thus the case would be irrelevant for our principle. But it is more reasonable to modify the principle in such a way as to include this as a limiting case. We should say that to be justified in a perceptual judgment, the person must discriminate whatever his judgment is about. In peripheral vision and similar cases, the judgment may be about an amorphous something, discriminable at the subperceptual level. In the normal case, when the judgment is about a definite entity, *perceptual* discrimination will be necessary to pick it out, and the thrust of the principle will be preserved. (What I have said here of degenerate cases of discrimination has been said of a normal perceiver whose experience is not limited to this level of awareness. It is not clear that someone who was so limited could have formed the concepts involved in qualitative judgments—certainly not if concept-formation requires the detection of similarities and differences among the entities possessing a quality.)

Before turning to the other principles of justification, we should consider one final issue, an argument from hallucinations. To discriminate an object is to be aware of it. Thus veridical perception is a necessary condition for the justification of a perceptual judgment. Yet it has seemed to many philosophers that nonveridical experiences also have the power to justify beliefs. Illusions are cases in which an object actually is discriminated—the problem is one of identifying it correctly—and will be discussed later. In hallucination, however, no real object is discriminated at all. If hallucinations have the power to justify perceptual judgments, then, it seems that our principle is false.

It is not clear, to begin with, that a hallucination does occur in a justificatory context. Consider dreams, which are often joined with hallucinations when the objection is stated. Dreaming is by nature a noncognitive activity, in which the subject is detached from any perceptual contact with reality and not in control of his mental processes. There is no way an issue of justification could arise, because he is not doing anything that calls for justification. Similarly, hal-

lucinations occur through inner causes that radically disrupt cognitive functioning. It is not clear how much control a hallucinator
has over his judgment, his reason, his ability to weigh evidence objectively. When one's faculties are not operating normally, questions about the justifiable use of them are moot.

But let us assume for argument's sake that a hallucination *could*
justify a perceptual judgment about an external object (the object
corresponding to the content of the hallucination). This would still
not contradict our principle, unless one added the assumption that
the hallucination would justify the judgment in the same way, for
the same reason, that a percept could. This is the assumption I reject, as it is based on the representationalist view that percepts and
hallucinations are two species of the same genus, defined in terms
of experiential states. If a hallucination could justify, it would be in
virtue of its internal, phenomenal similarity to an actual percept. It
is then assumed that that in respect of which the two experiences
are similar—the phenomenal character, the qualitative content—
must be that in virtue of which both justify the judgment. This does
not follow. The reason for thinking that a hallucination might justify is not its qualitative content per se; otherwise, imagination could
also justify. The reason is that a hallucination is like an actual percept having that qualitative content. But the reason for thinking that
the percept could justify a judgment is not that *it* is like a possible
hallucination. There is an obvious asymmetry here. If there is such
a thing as hallucinatory justification, it is parasitic on the existence
of perceptual justification. The latter must therefore be understood
on its own terms, and our principle stands as a condition of it.

Perception and Predication

The perceptual judgment is more than an act of reference. It is
a way of identifying a perceived object. In cognitive terms, it is the
recognition of the object as possessing an attribute or belonging to
a type. In logical terms, it involves a predicative as well as a referential element. From either perspective, it is a *conceptual* form of
awareness, having a propositional structure.

Thus the perceptual judgment is distinct from more primitive
types of recognition. Children learn to recognize an object, when it
reappears after being hidden, long before they begin to acquire lan-

guage. More important, there is preconceptual awareness of qualitative recurrence, in adults as well as children. H. H. Price illustrated the point with the shape of a blackberry bush. One can
recognize the shape immediately, even though he has no concept
for that particular shape, could not begin to describe it in words, and
cannot think of it determinately in its absence. In the same way, a
nuance in the style of a piece of music, an elusive flavor in a food,
an expression on another's face, can all "ring a bell" long before one
can identify what they remind one of, or name the abstract feature
that caused the bell to ring. For this reason, psychologists often distinguish between familiarity and identification as aspects of recognition.[6]

By contrast, the perceptual judgment is conceptual. It identifies
the object as an instance of an abstract feature that is grasped as such
in conceptual form; it classifies the object on the basis of similarities
that have been explicitly isolated and named. It is a propositional
form of knowledge. But it differs from other propositional conclusions in that the predication involved is immediate. When a doctor
diagnoses a patient, he typically relies on various symptoms as criteria, the symptoms themselves being recognized conceptually, in
propositional form. The diagnosis could therefore be expressed as
an inference in the logic of propositions. S has symptoms X and Y;
only those with disease Z exhibit these symptoms together; therefore S has Z. Similar inferences could be formulated for many of the
conclusions we reach in everyday life, even though the reasoning is
typically carried out automatically. In each case, however, if we followed the reasoning upstream, we would come to direct observations that are not the product of inference, even implicitly. There are
some symptoms that a doctor can recognize immediately. There are
cases in which the recognition of an object is not mediated by the
use of criteria, and the recognition is experienced with the same
sense of immediate familiarity that characterizes preconceptual recognition.

Thus although the justification of criterial recognition can be
understood in terms of inference, the justification of immediate rec-

6. For a summary of the evidence on "object permanence," see Eleanor J. Gibson, *Principles of Perceptual Learning and Development* (Englewood Cliffs, N.J., 1969),
384–88. H. H. Price, *Thinking and Experience* (1953; rpr. London, 1969), 53–54. See
A. L. Glass, K. J. Holyoak, and J. L. Santa, *Cognition* (Reading, Mass., 1979), 59–63.

ognition cannot. The problem is to explain how the nonpropositional perceptual awareness of the object justifies the propositional recognition of it. More specifically, having found that a judgment is not justified unless one has perceptually discriminated the object to which the judgment refers, we must go on to ask which of the entity's attributes one must perceive—and how one must perceive them—in order for the predicative element of the judgment to be justified. What are the perceptual conditions for being justified in assigning what one sees to the class subsumed by a concept?

Foundationalists in the tradition of Cartesian empiricism implicitly accepted a simple theory of recognition. The identification of a thing as an instance of a type was regarded as criterial. The concept for a kind being equated, by definition, with a list of criterial features, the recognition of a kind presupposed recognition of those features.[7] The features themselves, however, are recognized directly and automatically. It is simply a matter of labeling an attribute one is directly aware of, in a way that requires no further explanation. The theory was thus a natural counterpart to the sensationalist element in the sense-data theory—each sense-datum or experiential state was regarded as the awareness of an individual quality. Here indeed is the source of what Anthony Quinton called the "Janus-faced notion of experience" (as experiential state and as item of conceptual knowledge). If one fails to distinguish between the sensory awareness of a determinate quality and the conceptual recognition of an attribute, one will hardly see the need to explain the relation between them. The traditional theory was also another source for the assumption that beliefs about experiential states are incorrigible. Conversely, the most powerful argument against the doctrine of incorrigibility, by J. L. Austin and others, was that even a phenomenal judgment would involve some conceptualization of the phenomenal state and would thus commit one to some (corrigible) claim about its similarity to other phenomenal states.[8]

It should be emphasized that the objection here is not that the use of a word, such as *red*, to describe what one sees presupposes that one is correctly using the word—a fact not given in a sensation of red. As C. I. Lewis argued:

7. *Cf.* Price, *Thinking and Experience*, 44ff.
8. Anthony Quinton, "The Problem of Perception," in Swartz (ed.), *Perceiving, Sensing, and Knowing*, 503; J. L. Austin, "Other Minds," in Anthony Flew (ed.), *Logic and Language, 2nd Series* (Oxford, 1953), 136–37.

It is essential to remember that in the statement or formulation of what is given . . . one uses language to *convey* this content, but what is *asserted* is what the language is intended to convey, not the correctness of the language used. If, for example, one say, "I see a red round something," one assumes but does *not* assert, "The words 'red' and 'round' correctly apply to something now given." The last is not a given fact of present experience but a generalization from past experience indicating the customary use of English words. But one does not have to know English in order to see red.[9]

Lewis is certainly right that what a statement asserts is the judgment or belief it expresses, not the semantic conditions in virtue of which it can express just that content. What he overlooks is that the statement "This is red" does not directly express the seeing red, but the judging that this is red. What is seen is assimilated to the concept of a certain *type* of object.

The traditional theory failed to recognize, in other words, that any concept, even a concept for a "simple quality" like a color, is abstract and therefore subsumes a range of qualitatively discriminable instances. What we perceive, however, are the individual, determinate qualities of particular objects. Hence we do not literally see the abstract features we predicate, and some account is required of the relation between the two. To recognize an object as red is to recognize it as possessing the same quality as other red objects one has perceived. But given the existence of other shades of red, the object is at best *similar* to most of the other red things one has seen. The same object will also be similar to shades of orange and purple at the border line with red, and it will be similar to other objects in respect of other attributes. The recognition of it as red therefore involves the isolation of a relevant dimension of similarity; a sense of the necessary degree of similarity along that dimension; and a capacity to ignore the perceptible differences that remain within that range of similar shades. These cognitive capacities are preconditions for the perceptual judgment.[10]

In a certain type of aphasia, for example, those capacities are apparently lost. In a case described by Kurt Goldstein, an aphasic

9. C. I. Lewis, *Analysis of Knowledge and Valuation* (La Salle, Ill., 1946), 183. See also Roderick Chisholm, *Theory of Knowledge* (2nd ed.; Englewood Cliffs, N.J., 1977), 33.

10. I have discussed these matters further in "A Theory of Abstraction," *Cognition and Brain Theory*, VII (1984), 329–57.

woman was unable to sort skeins of colored yarn by grouping together the reds, the greens, the blues. She was not color-blind and
was able to match identical or nearly identical shades, but she could
not detect the similarities among perceptibly different shades of the
same color. After repeated experiments she did begin sorting in the
manner requested. When asked how she did it, she replied that in
order to please her doctors she had remembered which skeins they
had called red, green, blue. She denied emphatically that the shades
were similar in themselves, that they had anything in common other
than being called red by her doctors.[11] She was, in effect, a patho-
logical nominalist. It is clear that she lacked an ability to make perceptual judgments about color in the way a normal subject can, and
that her perceptual judgments could not have been justified in the
way a normal subject's could. Yet nothing in the traditional theory
gives even a hint as to the nature of the capacity she lacked.

Once we recognize, moreover, that the link between percept and
perceptual judgment is mediated by various capacities to isolate
similarities and ignore differences, there is no longer any a priori
reason to believe that the recognition of attributes is prior to the recognition of kinds. It may well be easier in some cases to pick out
clusters of similarities than to isolate the individual dimensions of
similarity that comprise them. A cat, for example, is identified partly
by shape, but we have no concept for a cat's specific shape, and we
could describe the shape only by reference to the concept "cat." It
is relevant, too, that children typically learn words for certain kinds
of objects before they learn words for the criterial attributes.[12]

It is clear, in any case, that a complete account of immediate
recognition would require something more than is offered by traditional theories. That which must be perceived, in order to justify
the predication of a concept, must be present as part of the qualitative content of perception. It must also be discriminated from other
aspects of the qualitative content—just as the object itself must be
discriminated if it is to be the subject of a justified judgment. The
discrimination of entities I have described at length. What would be
necessary for a description of the qualitative discrimination? 1) In

11. Kurt Goldstein, *Language and Language Disturbances* (New York, 1948), 267–
69.
12. Eleanor Rosch, "Principles of Categorization," in Eleanor Rosch and Barbara Lloyd (eds.), *Cognition and Categorization* (Hillsdale, N.J., 1978), 28–48.

order to know *what* must be discriminated, we would need to know what it is in the object that makes it an instance of the relevant attribute or type. We would need a theory of universals. 2) In order to know *how* it is discriminated, we would need to know how dimensions of similarity are isolated and retained as concepts, and how those dimensions are then used to isolate qualitative aspects of a perceived object. We would need a theory of concepts. And these questions would have to be addressed together, since any analysis of similarity will have implications for both. But they are beyond our scope here, and in this respect, as I have said all along, my theory of perceptual justification is incomplete. It is worth looking a little further into the matter, however, in order to see what sorts of epistemological issues are left hanging.

One traditional goal of perceptual epistemology was to distinguish between observational and nonobservational predicates by determining whether the instances of a concept could be recognized perceptually. Even if such a distinction can be drawn, however, it will not suffice as a criterion for deciding whether a given judgment can be justified by perception. Wrens, for example, are the sort of thing which can be recognized perceptually, yet most people who possess the concept of a wren *cannot* recognize one by sight, in the way a bird watcher can. The difference between the ordinary perceiver and the bird watcher clearly has an epistemological consequence. The latter would be justified in judging that a certain bird he sees is a wren; the former would not. The difference exists, not because they possess different concepts, but because they possess the same concept in different ways. It would be necessary, then, to formulate a criterion for the *way* in which one must possess a concept if perception alone is to be a sufficient ground for predicating it.

Ordinarily, we would describe the difference between the ordinary perceiver and the bird watcher simply by saying that the latter can tell a wren by sight. But that would give us a circular criterion. Ordinarily, too, the bird watcher will have more extensive conceptual knowledge about the features that distinguish wrens from other birds. But an ordinary perceiver might acquire exactly the same conceptual knowledge of features by reading a field guide, yet still be unable to recognize a wren perceptually. What prevents him from doing so is that he cannot tell by eye just how small and plump the body must be, or just how sharp the bill. This is what the bird watcher *can* do, and to express the nature of his ability in the form of a principle, we would need to know how relevant dimensions of similarity and difference are picked out at the perceptual level. We would need, in other words, answers to questions (1) and (2) above.[13]

Another, more important issue concerns the content of what is predicated in a perceptual judgment. Anyone who has the concept of a car knows that cars are man-made objects, that they have engines, that they run on gasoline, that their purpose is transportation, and so forth. It would be possible to see all this knowledge as part of the content of the concept and thereby predicated of an object that one recognizes as a car. Thus to judge that a thing is a car is at the same time to judge that it is a man-made object, that it has an engine, etc. On the other hand, one might regard the latter as distinct judgments, arrived at inferentially from the premises that this is a car and that all cars are man-made objects, that all cars have engines, etc. Is there any epistemological difference between these positions?

Apparently there is not. One might favor one view over the other on psychological grounds, depending on whether one sees concepts on the model of file folders containing knowledge about their referents, or on the model of nodes in a network of propositions. One might also favor one view over the other on logical grounds, depending on one's view as to the relative priority of concepts and propositions. But in either case, a judgment that this is a car commits one to the truth of the propositions that it is man-made, has an engine, etc. In one case the commitment is direct; in the other case, the commitment exists because if the conclusion of a valid deductive inference is false, at least one of the premises must be false. Thus, in either case, any doubt as to whether the object is man-made, has an engine, etc., would undercut one's justification for judging that it is a car.

But I have spoken as if the content of the concept is all of a piece, and the major tradition in the theory of concepts has denied this assumption. To focus the issue here, we can contrast two views about

13. Despite the tendency among contemporary philosophers to regard such questions as exclusively psychological, I believe they have philosophical dimensions that psychology alone cannot address. See David Kelley and Janet Krueger, "The Psychology of Abstraction," *Journal for the Theory of Social Behavior*, XIV (1984), 43–67.

the cognitive content of concepts. The traditional view, accepted by most Cartesian empiricists, is that concepts are constituted in some sense by the definitions we give them. Each concept then has an intension or meaning determined by the definition, and statements expressing that meaning are analytic. In virtue of its meaning, a concept will subsume a class of objects in the world; those objects may have properties in common other than those which define the concept; and universal statements identifying those properties, as well as statements identifying the idiosyncratic qualities of individual instances, are synthetic. An opposing view would be that the cognitive content of concepts is determined by the objective kinds of things they pick out in the world. Instances of a given kind possess an open-ended number of properties in common. At a given stage of knowledge, we define the concept by reference to the most essential common properties, i.e., those which explain the greatest number of others. But the definition does not constitute the concept or give it its content; the content is determined by the nature of the things we have grouped together; a growth in knowledge may lead us to revise the definition without thereby changing the concept or its content. There would thus be no distinction between analytic and synthetic truth. The defining properties would have to be discovered in the same way as any other property. For convenience, we may refer to these as the construction and the discovery theories, respectively.[14]

Of course they are not so much theories as archetypes or skeletons of theories. But the distinction as I have drawn it is enough to raise an epistemological issue about perceptual recognition. Any theory of recognition must deal with the fact that among the things we know about the referents of any concept, some will be imperceivable facts, or at least facts not perceived on a given occasion on which the concept is predicated. The purpose or function of a car is

14. For a representative construction theory, see Lewis, *Analysis of Knowledge and Valuation*, Book II. A discovery theory of concepts is developed by Ayn Rand, in *Introduction to Objectivist Epistemology* (New York, 1979), esp. Chaps. 1–2, 5, 7. A discovery theory is also implicit in the views of Saul Kripke and Hilary Putnam on the semantics of natural-kind terms. See Saul Kripke, *Naming and Necessity* (Cambridge, Mass., 1980); and Stephen Schwartz (ed.), *Naming, Necessity, and Natural Kinds* (Ithaca, 1977), esp. Schwartz' "Introduction," 13–41, and Putnam's "Is Semantics Possible?" and "Meaning and Reference," 102–18, 119–32.

not a perceivable fact, and the engine is not actually perceived on most occasions. The question then arises, How can the perceptual awareness of an object justify a judgment about it, if the judgment commits one to the existence of facts that are not perceived?

The construction theory would suggest one answer to the question. It could say that in predicating a concept of an object, one is predicating only the defining features for that concept. Those are the only features whose presence in the object one is committing oneself to. We can then define a class of observation predicates as those whose defining features are all perceptible. A judgment involving an observation predicate could thus be justified conclusively by perception; all other judgments will require inductive support. The result is a kind of structural foundationalism, in which an adult's knowledge can be represented as a structure resting on a foundation of judgments involving only observation predicates.[15]

On the discovery theory, by contrast, this sort of foundationalism would be impossible. In denying that there is any epistemological difference between defining and nondefining features of a kind of object, it eliminates any ground for saying that a judgment predicates of an object only some of the features known to be characteristic of that kind of thing. Even in the case of concepts for attributes (as we will see shortly), an adult's knowledge will include such matters as the causes and effects of an object's possessing that attribute, or methods of measuring the attribute. Thus there is no concept that can be predicated without committing oneself to the existence of facts not perceived. There are no observation predicates in the sense defined by the construction theory. This does not necessarily create any epistemological problem in justifying the judgment. Whatever inductive evidence one has that things of kind K have property P will serve equally to cover one's commitment to the implication that this K has P. But it does mean that all of an adult's perceptual judgments rest in part on inductive knowledge already acquired. More broadly, it means that foundationalism can be true only in a temporal or genetic sense. Each step in the growth of

15. In Cartesian empiricism, of course, the construction theory was joined to a representationalist theory of perception. Hence the only observation predicates were those describing experiential states. In principle, however, the theory of concepts could be detached from the theory of perception, allowing for a construction theory of basic judgments about physical objects.

knowledge may be supported by perception, but the knowledge so acquired is integrated into one's concepts in such a way that the recognition of a new object as an instance of a concept involves a judgment which goes beyond what is perceived on that occasion.

The discovery model of concepts would still allow for a kind of rough distinction between concepts which do and concepts which do not allow for immediate recognition. One necessary condition is that the instances be perceptible entities; otherwise, they could not serve as subjects of perceptual judgments. Thus "electron" is not an observation predicate, not even in a Wilson chamber, since what one perceptually discriminates there is not the electron itself but the bubbles in the medium. Another necessary condition is that the instances of the kind in question share some perceptible properties. Some functional concepts, such as "carburetor," may have instances that are discriminable, but share no perceptible properties, since many different sorts of objects could serve the function of a carburetor. Beyond these necessary conditions, however, there is a continuum of concepts whose instances are more or less recognizable by perception, depending on how reliably the perceptible properties they share are connected to the properties essential to the kind in question.[16] The visible shape and size of a cat, for example, are strongly connected to the features biologists consider essential—it would violate biological law for an animal to have the genes of a cat and the shape of a goldfish. On the other hand, the perceptible USDA stamp which makes prime beef recognizable by sight in the supermarket is connected in a fairly tenuous way with the properties that make a piece of meat prime. The countless dimensions of inductive evidence which define this continuum would make any sharp distinction between observational and nonobservational predicates arbitrary. But they would also make the distinction unnecessary. No epistemological question would turn on the distinction because all the epistemological work would be done by the inductive evidence in a given case.

The choice between a construction and a discovery model of concepts, then, will make some difference in the type of perceptual

16. A discovery model does not commit one to a theory of intrinsic essentialism; essentiality may be relative to the current state of knowledge. *Cf.* Rand, *Introduction to Objectivist Epistemology*, 68–69; and Irving Copi, "Essence and Accident," in Schwartz (ed.), *Naming, Necessity, and Natural Kinds*, 176–91.

epistemology one pursues. How does one make the choice? Once again, a full theory of concepts and universals would be required. But there is a certain correspondence between epistemological realism and the discovery model, insofar as the latter holds that the content of a concept is determined by the nature of the things it subsumes. There is a parallel correspondence between representationalism and the construction model, insofar as the latter holds that concepts have an inner content determined by us (by consciousness) and an outer content determined by what is there in the world. This would give us a reason for leaning toward the discovery model, and I have adopted that model as a basis for my analysis of sensory concepts.

Concepts of Sensory Qualities

There is no reason to assume that the conceptual recognition of particular qualities is epistemologically prior to the recognition of objects as instances of kinds. But of course we do form judgments about sensory qualities. And because questions about form and object, and about the effects of our perceptual apparatus on our perceptual awareness, arise in connection with the awareness of qualities, perceptual judgments about qualities raise certain questions that are not directly relevant to judgments about kinds. The intrinsic attribute we are aware of in the object is distinct from the sensory form by means of which we are aware of it, the form being the aspect of the qualitative content of perception which results from an interaction between the external object and the perceiver. The first question, then, is whether concepts for sensory qualities designate the intrinsic attributes or the forms in which we perceive them. In this regard, we also need to ask how concepts of appearance relate to concepts for the qualities. I have also argued that in different conditions of perception, the same intrinsic attribute could be perceived in different forms. What role, then, does knowledge of the conditions play in the justification of perceptual judgments about sensory qualities?

The answer to the first question, in brief, is that it poses a false alternative. The discovery view of concepts will give us a way to show that even though concepts of red, square, hard, and the like, are concepts of qualities, not kinds, there is a broader sense in which they pick out kinds of objects in the world; and that the concept serves to integrate our expanding knowledge about the distinction between form and object. We can distinguish three stages in the development of such concepts: the naïve level, on which one has no knowledge of illusions or perceptual relativity, no concept of appearances; the commonsense level, defined by the possession of just that knowledge; and the scientific level, which incorporates knowledge about the causal mechanisms of perception. These are stages in the development of a single concept, which picks out a stable kind of object in the world.

A perceiver looking at any object is aware of a certain qualitative content. He has no perceptual way to isolate the aspects of that content which depend on him (or on the conditions of perception) from the aspects which depend solely on the nature of the object. What he perceives is an attribute-in-a-form, a unitary qualitative content experienced as wholly external, as the identity of the object he discriminates. It is only with the aid of background knowledge that he can isolate the relational aspects of that identity, and the naïve level is defined by the absence of such knowledge. Hence any qualitative concept formed at this level will not be a concept of the attribute as opposed to the variable form in which it is perceived, nor will it be a concept of the form as opposed to the attribute. At this stage, the subject lacks the information necessary for making that distinction. He is grouping together objects which he takes to be similar independently of him, but in fact he is grouping together objects which appear similar to him. Thus, taking a color concept as our example, we have a choice. We might say that the subject has acquired an early form of the concept "red." He implicitly takes anything which looks red to be red, but will later learn that this is a mistake and will reclassify certain objects under a new concept formed for that purpose—the concept "looks red." Or we might say that the subject has acquired an early form of the concept "looks red." He takes this to be a property which objects have independently of him, but will later learn that this is a mistake and will form a new concept ("red") for the property that objects do have independently of him.

Roderick Firth has argued for the second alternative: "In fact at this stage the child says 'red' just in those circumstances in which we, as adults, could truthfully say 'looks red to me now,' so that it would not be unreasonable to assert that the child is using 'red' to express a primitive form of the concept 'looks red.' " [17] The passage suggests two arguments for the conclusion, and neither is sound. The first is that the child's concept is coextensive with the later concept "looks red" and therefore should be identified with it. But the two are not coextensive. Given the mechanisms of color constancy, there are objects which a child will not call red, even though adults, capable of adopting a reductive focus, would recognize that those objects do look red. The second argument is criteriological. The child's implicit criterion for predicating "red" is whether an object looks red to him; therefore his concept is that of looking red. But this is a verificationist form of the representationalist pattern of argument: we are aware of A by means of or in virtue of B; therefore we are directly aware of B, not A. I rejected this argument as a way of deciding what we really perceive, and there is no more reason to accept it in the context of concept formation.

There are positive reasons as well for preferring the first interpretation. The naïve subject forms his concept of red by grouping together those objects which look similar to him in respect of color. Since he has no clue that any of these similarities depend on the way objects interact with his senses, he will take it for granted that the similarities exist independently of him. And by and large, he will be right. The product of each object's interaction with his senses is the form in which he is aware of an intrinsic attribute of the object. He is grouping together objects which he perceives in similar forms, but because he rarely sees objects in abnormal conditions, most of the objects will be similar in intrinsic attribute—they will possess the same reflectance properties. In this respect, he has indeed isolated a class of objects whose similarities exist independently of him. He is likely to misclassify objects that he perceives in abnormal situations, and he will have to reclassify them later, just as whales were first classified as fish and then had to be reclassified. But on the discovery theory of concepts, neither the fact of reclassification nor the increment in knowledge that makes it necessary implies that a new concept has been formed.

The commonsense level is achieved when one learns about the

17. Roderick Firth, "Coherence, Certainty, and Epistemic Priority," *Journal of Philosophy*, LXI (1964), 547.

sorts of perceptual relativity that are common knowledge—those revealed by a reductive focus on the perceptual field and those experienced in illusions. The scientific level involves knowledge of the deeper sort of relativity revealed by science. There is no sharp distinction here. As we saw earlier, there is a hierarchy of levels of relativity. But there are two broad differences between the commonsense and the scientific levels in terms of their effects on a concept of a sensory quality.

First, the commonsense level will require some reclassification of objects in terms of the concept; the scientific level will require none. The sorts of relativity discovered at the commonsense level involve variations in dimensions of the qualitative content of perception as a result of variations in specific conditions of perception. The refraction of light in water will make a straight stick look bent; prior exposure to the cold will make a room seem unusually warm. Because of variations in such conditions, objects that are similar (or different) in intrinsic attribute will not always appear similar (or different). Since the concept of a sensory quality is a concept of objects that are similar independently of us, we need to take this sort of perceptual relativity into account when we classify objects on the basis of perception. What further effect will scientific knowledge have on the way we classify objects? In the case of primary qualities, it will have none whatever. The sorts of relativity discovered at the commonsense level are the only sorts of relativity that affect the perception of primary qualities. Once we have abstracted the shape of the stick from the effects of perspective, refraction, and other such conditions we have isolated the intrinsic attribute, and science adds nothing essential to that knowledge.

In the case of secondary qualities, however, science does seem to tell us something new, by revealing that the sensory *qualia* themselves—sensory redness, warmth, and so on—are relational properties, and the intrinsic attributes are certain microscopic features of objects. But this does not affect our commonsense-level classifications of objects on the basis of color. Once we have abstracted from the effects of unusual lighting or prior exposure to bright lights, we have isolated a class of objects that in fact share the same intrinsic attribute, even if we have not isolated the attribute itself from the sensory form in which we perceive it. Science tells us something further about this class, just as it tells us something further about dogs when it discovers the underlying biological features they have in common. In neither case, however, does science necessitate a re-classification of objects under the concept.

Second, the sort of perceptual relativity discovered at the com-monsense level is important for the perceptual judgment, as we shall see. But the deeper sort of relativity that science reveals in the case of the secondary qualities is essentially irrelevant to the perceptual judgment. Precisely because it abstracts the microscopic attribute from the qualitative form in which we perceive it, the scientific con-cept of that attribute is not one that can be predicated immediately on the basis of perception. What is predicated on the basis of per-ception is a concept—"red," "warm," "sweet"—which does not distinguish the intrinsic attribute from the form. The concept des-ignates a class of objects which share a common intrinsic attribute and which (in normal conditions) are perceived in the same form. There is, however, one minor consequence of scientific knowledge for the perceptual judgment. In the case of the primary qualities, perception can justify quantitative as well as qualitative judgments. If one has learned a system of measurement, one can judge by sight that an object is about twelve inches long or is moving at thirty miles an hour. There is no analogous, cardinal method of measuring sen-sory *qualia* like red or warmth, and until scientists discovered the in-trinsic attributes, the only sorts of quantitative judgment possible were ordinal ones—this is warmer than that, a deeper red, etc. But the cardinal measurements of the intrinsic attributes, once known, can be used in perceptual judgments—the room is about seventy degrees, that spot of light is a red of about 600 nanometers on the spectrum.

Finally, the distinction between the commonsense and the sci-entific levels gives us a way to settle questions about the relative pri-ority of concepts for sensory qualities and concepts of appearance. At the commonsense level, the former are necessarily prior. Con-cepts of appearance are formed when one notices that certain ob-jects are similar to F objects in a way that F objects are similar to each other, but background knowledge tells one that the similarity exists because of something other than the objects themselves. The stick that looks bent in water is similar to actually bent sticks in a way that is perceptually indistinguishable from the way bent sticks are sim-ilar to each other; but one knows that immersion in water cannot bend a previously straight stick. The beige living-room curtains look similar, at sunset, to the rust-colored curtains in the dining room, but one knows that the setting of the sun would not actually change the color of curtains. Thus the concept of appearing *F* is formed in order to classify objects which are similar to *F*'s in a way that is perceptually indistinguishable from the way *F*'s are similar to each other, but which cannot be classified as *F*'s because they are not similar to *F*'s in that respect independently of the perceiver or the conditions of perception. Once we have formed the concept of appearing *F*, we can of course recognize that objects which are *F* also (in normal conditions) appear *F*. But we would not form a separate concept of appearing *F* unless we had first noticed the "illusory" objects. Hence the concept of appearing *F* is dependent on the concept of *F*. The order could not be reversed at the commonsense level—we could not understand red (or square) objects as those which look red (look square) in normal conditions—for the reasons stated earlier in reply to Firth. In the case of secondary qualities, however, the scientific level allows us to distinguish the intrinsic attribute from the qualitative form that is common to the perception of objects having the attribute and to the perception of those that merely appear similar. At that point, we typically refer to the intrinsic attribute in dispositional terms, as that feature of objects in virtue of which, in normal conditions, they are perceived in that form. This would be a kind of description of *F*'s in terms of appearing *F*.[18]

To formulate criteria for the justification of perceptual judgments about sensory qualities, we need to look more closely at the sorts of perceptual relativity discovered at the commonsense level. As cases of immediate recognition, such judgments would be subject to whatever general principles of recognition would be formulated in accordance with the discussion in the preceding section. But

18. This distinction of levels gives us an answer to a problem raised by Robert Swartz in "Color Concepts and Dispositions," *Synthese*, XVII (1967), 202–22. We can often explain why a thing looks red by noting that it *is* red. This is a genuine explanation, since it rules out any abnormality in the conditions. Yet in a dispositional analysis of color terms, it becomes "This object looks red to me in these conditions because it is the sort of object that looks red to me in these conditions." The answer is that at the commonsense level, where the explanation makes sense, the concept "red" is not to be analyzed dispositionally. That analysis is possible only at the scientific level, and if the explanation were offered at that level, it would indeed be vacuous.

as judgments that identify instances of sensory qualities, they must also take account of the facts about perceptual relativity that require us to distinguish being F from appearing F.

It is important to emphasize at the outset that that distinction exists only for a conceptual level of cognition. Perception is the awareness of an external object in a form determined by the inter-action between the object and the senses. There could be no form-less perception, in which an intrinsic attribute is diaphanously re-vealed to us. That would be perception by magic, without any causal process. For the same reason, there are as many possible forms in which a given attribute can be perceived as there are possible com-binations of sensory mechanisms and conditions of perception. Any mechanism, under any condition of perception, that allows us to discriminate the attribute allows us to perceive it. There is no priv-ileged form of perception that has the unique capacity to reveal the object as it really is. When the stick in water looks bent, we are still perceiving the stick and its shape, which is straight. There is noth-ing else for us to perceive. Illusions are conceptual phenomena: what is illusory about the perception of the stick is that we are perceiving it in a form that would lead us to classify it with bent objects, not straight ones.

Thus three facts are jointly responsible for the existence of il-lusions. First, the form in which we perceive an object can vary with the conditions in which we perceive it. Second, the concept of a sen-sory quality is a concept of an external feature of objects, in respect of which they are similar independently of us. Third, the concept is formed and predicated on the basis of similarities in the forms with which we perceive its instances. For an illusion to occur, one must perceive a given attribute in a form that is not the form in which one normally perceives that attribute, but is the form in which one nor-mally perceives some other attribute for which he has a concept. (Without the latter condition, the percept would be strange but not illusory, for there is nothing one would be led to misclassify the ob-ject *as*.) It is only in relation to our concepts that we can identify any form of perception as illusory. Correspondingly, it is only in rela-tion to our concepts that we can identify any conditions as abnormal or illusory. Abnormal conditions are those in which we perceive ob-jects in illusory forms.

But there is another level of complexity here. There is no single nonillusory form, or normal set of conditions, for each concept of a sensory quality. The form in which we perceive an object can vary extensively without being illusory, so long as it allows us to pick out its intrinsic similarity to other objects subsumed by the same concept. And any condition of perception that allows us to do so is a normal one. Thus for both forms and conditions of perception, there is a range of variation within the normal, and the range is determined by such factors as the constancy mechanisms, the stage of perceptual learning, and the abstractness of the concept. A square surface looks different, in one respect, from different angles of observation, but any angle is a normal condition because the constancy mechanisms allow us to discriminate the variable from the invariable aspects of the shape as an item in the visual field. The first time one hears a horn blaring as a car approaches and passes, the sound seems to vary in pitch. The car's motion is not a normal condition for perceiving what is in fact an unchanging sound. But if one learned to detect the invariant relation between sound wavelength, speed, and distance, one would be able to discriminate reliably between changing and unchanging sounds even when the source of sound is moving, and motion would no longer be an abnormal condition.[19] Finally, a more abstract concept typically allows a wider range of normal conditions and forms of perception. Thus we might perceive a green object in lighting conditions that alter too much for the constancy mechanisms to handle, so that the object seems to change its shade of color, yet it might still fall within the range subsumed by the concept "green." The conditions would still be normal for predicating that concept, although they would not be normal for recognizing the specific shade. To take the extremes, we could say that *any* conditions in which an object reflects light are normal for the judgment that it is colored, whereas highly specific daylight conditions might be necessary for the judgment that it is a specific shade of aquamarine.

If illusions and normal conditions are understood in this way, then the following two principles seem appropriate as criteria for the justification of perceptual judgments about sensory qualities. First, one must perceive the object in a form which is normal for the per-

19. The analysis here is based on James J. Gibson's theory. See *The Senses Considered as Perceptual Systems* (Boston, 1966).

ception of F objects (where F is a concept of a sensory quality). Second, one must take account of any evidence one has that the conditions of perception are abnormal.

In conditions that are normal for a given concept, one perceives the object in a normal form—in a form which allows one to detect perceptually the similarity between that object and others subsumed by the concept. In such a case, it is clear that the predication of the concept is justified by the perceptual awareness, together with whatever other conditions are involved in immediate recognition. In abnormal conditions, on the other hand, an object that is F will be perceived in a form that does not allow one to perceive its similarity to other F objects. In this case, the perceptual judgment that it is F would not be justified. That judgment would be either an arbitrary guess, and thus not justified at all, or the conclusion of an inference based on background knowledge of what F objects look like in abnormal conditions, and thus not a *perceptual* judgment. But there is another possibility in abnormal conditions. An object which is not F may be perceived in the form with which one normally perceives F objects. Would one be justified in this case in judging that it is F? The first criterion entails that one would, and the question is whether this makes the criterion unacceptable.

Earlier, we saw that the subject of a hallucination would not be justified perceptually in forming a judgment about the object corresponding to his hallucination, even if his experience were phenomenologically identical to an actual perception of the object. The argument was that perception can justify a judgment in virtue of being an awareness of the object referred to by the judgment. What justifies is the cognitive contact with the object, not the qualitative content of the experience. If a hallucination can justify at all, the mode of justification is parasitical upon, and requires a different analysis from, perceptual justification. This argument could be extended to illusions as well, with the implication that in abnormal conditions, a mistaken judgment based on an illusory form of perception would not be justified as a perceptual judgment. Yet the extension seems unwarranted. If the person has no evidence that conditions *are* abnormal, does he not have just as good a reason for his judgment as a person in normal conditions?

It will help to resolve this issue if we look briefly at the underlying conceptions of justification which create the tension here. According to one conception, what justifies a person in judging that something is the case is whatever puts him in a position to know that it is the case. This conception is rooted in the principle that knowledge is the identification of things as they are independently of our beliefs. Where knowledge is acquired by a process of cognition, one must remain in touch with reality at every stage of the process. Otherwise, one is not actually in a position to know the fact in question. The implication is that a hallucinator is not in a position to know the fact he asserts, and neither is the subject of an illusion.[20] A rival conception, however, holds that what justifies a person in forming a certain judgment is whatever makes it reasonable for him to do so. This conception is rooted in the normative element implicit in the concept of justification, the idea of a standard for cognitive conduct. Here, "ought implies can," that is, a person cannot be held accountable by a standard of justification which it is impossible for him, in a given case, to apply.[21] Hence the subject of an illusion is reasonable in forming the judgment to which his experience prompts him—and so is the hallucinator.

The problem lies in maintaining either of these conceptions in disregard of the other—a temptation which provides yet another illustration of the issues discussed in Chapter 1. To maintain the first conception in disregard of the second is to view knowledge as a matter of mirroring the facts, with no attention to the specific *process* of knowing required by our means of cognition—in the case of conceptual knowledge, a process of self-directed, self-correcting thought. To maintain the second in opposition to the first is to ignore the fact that standards of justification are based on reality, that a given evidential situation makes a given judgment reasonable precisely because that situation normally does put one in a position to know the fact in question. This approach separates justification and truth in the same way that representationalism separates the inner content and the outer object of awareness. The goal, therefore, must be to do justice to both conceptions of justification, even in situations where tension is created between them by the fact of unavoidable error.

Let us return, then, to the cases of hallucination and illusion. If

20. *Cf.* Max Deutscher, "Regresses, Reasons, and Grounds," *Australasian Journal of Philosophy*, LI (1973), 15.

21. *Cf.* Carl Ginet, *Knowledge, Perception, and Memory* (Dordrecht, 1975), 35.

a hallucination occurs in a context that admits of justificatory questions at all—an assumption we saw reason for doubting—it may indeed be reasonable for the subject to form a judgment about his environment. But because his perceptual contact with reality has been broken in a radical way, it is reasonable for us to deny that his is a case of *perceptual* justification. In illusions, however, there is no such radical break in perceptual contact. In one sense, there is no break at all; there is simply an unusual form of perceiving an object. It therefore seems undeniable that the subject of an illusion may be justified in forming the relevant judgment. It seems, moreover, that this should be considered a case of perceptual justification. Unlike a hallucination, an illusory percept is still a percept. Its qualitative content arises from the interaction of the object, the senses, and the conditions of perception in exactly the same way as in normal conditions. And the subject takes the object to be F on the basis of similarities in that content, similarities which, though they do not reflect intrinsic similarities between the object and F's, are nevertheless objective in the sense that they exist because of his perceptual contact with reality. For these reasons, then, we may accept the implication of the first criterion. In abnormal conditions, a person may be perceptually justified in forming a false perceptual judgment.

The second principle raises another set of epistemological issues. In conditions that are normal for the concept of F, a perceiver is in fact in a position to know by perception that the object is F. But if he is to be justified in believing it is F, must he also know that he is in a position to know this? Must he know that conditions are normal? This is a question of reflective knowledge. There is a difference between knowing a fact and knowing that one knows. Correspondingly, there is a difference between being justified in forming a judgment and knowing that one is justified.[22] The latter distinction is obscured by the normally self-directed character of the process of using evidence, and in any real case of deliberation about an issue, there is no clear separation between the first-order use of evidence and the second-order evaluation of it *as* evidence. But there is still a difference in principle, and it has an important bearing on percep-

22. *Cf.* William Alston, "Has Foundationalism Been Refuted?" *Philosophical Studies*, XXIX (1976), 292, and "Two Types of Foundationalism," *Journal of Philosophy*, LXXIII (1976), 165–85.

tual justification. Is there any knowledge about the conditions that is required for a perceptual judgment to be justified?

Here again, there is tension between the rival conceptions of justification. If being justified is being in a position to know, then a person perceiving in normal conditions is justified. He is in fact in a position to know what he asserts, whether or not he also knows that he is. On the other hand, if being justified is being reasonable, then something more seems necessary. A reasonable man will check to see whether conditions essential to the truth of what he asserts actually obtain. It is clear that the first conception alone is incomplete. If a person is perceiving an object in normal conditions, but has evidence that conditions are abnormal, he could not justifiably disregard the evidence in forming a perceptual judgment. This is merely an application of the general epistemological principle that no matter how strong one's evidence for a conclusion, one is not justified in drawing the conclusion if he is ignoring evidence to the contrary.

But neither concept of justification will support a requirement that one have positive knowledge that conditions are normal. In the first place, conditions such as the healthy functioning of one's nervous system cannot be checked by perceptual means. In the second place, the examination of those conditions which can be checked, such as the presence of normal lighting, will themselves involve perceptual judgments made in certain conditions. If we need positive knowledge that these second-order conditions are normal, we are trapped in an infinite regress. If we do not need positive knowledge about the second-order conditions, there is no reason to require such knowledge of the first-order conditions. The second of these alternatives is all that can be supported by the conception of justification as rationality. Reasonable men are alert to signs of misinformation, but they are not paranoid. Judiciously interpreted, then, the conceptions of justification converge on our second principle—that one must take account of any evidence that conditions are abnormal—as the only reflective requirement for the justification of perceptual judgments.

The relevant conditions are of diverse types. Some are external phenomena which can themselves be perceived. One can see, for example, the colored glasses that make everything look pink. Some are not perceived as such, but are revealed through the way familiar objects appear—a face that looks green is strong evidence of abnormality. Some are revealed by the way everything appears—fuzziness in the visual field, numbness in the hands, the distant, echoing character that sounds have when one's ears have not adjusted after an airplane flight. Some, finally, are not revealed at all in the immediate experience and are available only as background evidence—for example, the knowledge that one is sick. Evidence of abnormality also varies widely in scope, in two senses. First, a given condition may affect judgments about a single feature only (monotonic blue light would make judgments of color unreliable, but would not affect judgments of shape), or all judgments based on a single modality (a sufficient depletion of visual pigment would be an abnormal condition for any visual judgment), or all perceptual judgments together (certain hallucinogenic drugs may be examples). Second, the strength of the evidence may vary. Conclusive evidence of abnormality would render the relevant judgments completely unjustified. Lesser evidence may require one only to qualify as probable the judgment one would have made without it.

As the examples make clear, the second principle is open-ended in character, for it calls into play the massive body of knowledge about conditions of perception possessed by ordinary adults. In another sense, however, the principle is quite limited. It maintains an asymmetry. It requires that one take account of evidence of abnormality, but does not require positive evidence that conditions are normal. In the absence of contrary evidence, it allows one, in effect, to assume that conditions are normal. It may therefore add support to the principle to consider the reasons philosophers have offered for requiring positive evidence of normality.

One such reason is the classical skeptical argument. We cannot be certain of any conclusion until we know that the faculties we exercised in reaching it are functioning reliably. We cannot be certain that our perceptual faculties are functioning reliably until we know that conditions are normal. Therefore we cannot be certain of any conclusion reached by perception until we know that conditions are normal. The first and general premise is the one that Descartes seems to accept in trying to answer the skeptic. It leads him to the proof of God's existence as a way to validate his own faculties. If that is indeed his project, it is of course hopeless, since he must use his faculties in the process of validating them.[23] The same is true of the perceptual version of the project, since knowing that the conditions are normal is knowledge that itself depends on conditions. That is precisely the skeptic's point. But neither the general nor the specifically perceptual version of the skeptic's premise is valid. The premise can be supported only if there is a real possibility that our faculties might be functioning in fundamental disconnection from reality and constituting their own contents; and we dismissed this possibility in Chapter 1. At the perceptual level, moreover, the skeptic presupposes knowledge that the conditions of perception can affect the way we perceive objects, and this is causal knowledge about physical objects that could be acquired only through perception. He is, therefore, using this knowledge in the very attempt to deny it. Finally, the ability to ask whether conditions are normal or abnormal presupposes that one possesses the concept of a feature F that is shared by objects independently of us. But one could not have acquired such a concept unless conditions were in fact sufficiently stable to make the form in which we perceive an object a reliable means of detecting its possession of that feature. This fact removes any justification for accepting the skeptic's premise.

The same demand for positive knowledge about the conditions can also be found among coherence theorists. Thus Wilfrid Sellars denies that, for one to know something is green, "it is sufficient to respond, when one is *in point of fact* in standard conditions, to green objects with the vocable 'This is green'. Not only must the conditions be of a sort that is appropriate for determining the colour of an object by looking, the subject must *know* that conditions of this sort *are* appropriate." Sellars is implicitly demanding two pieces of reflective knowledge—that a certain type of condition is appropriate for judging color, and that the condition at hand is an instance of that type. He does not explain these demands, but the reason for them is fairly clear from his general theory of knowledge. We are first conditioned to utter isolated verbal responses to stimuli, but gradually we acquire more systematic and sophisticated connec-

23. This is the notorious "Cartesian Circle," and many scholars have tried to free Descartes from its grip. Most of the attempts rely on the distinction between being justified and knowing that one is justified. See, for example, James Van Cleve, "Foundationalism, Epistemic Principles, and the Cartesian Circle," *Philosophical Review*, LXXXVIII (1979), 55–91.

tions among these responses. We can be said to have knowledge only when our responses are incorporated into a rule-governed social practice of making claims and defending them to other people. This includes the ability to refer intelligently to the conditions of perception in connection with perceptual claims.[24] But I have already rejected this view of knowledge. In stating that perception is a form of prelinguistic awareness, I have allowed for the possibility of a mode of justification which precedes any reflective ability to explain and defend our perceptual judgments to others.

It is worth noting in this regard that our criterion allows for a type of foundationalist view of justification. The implication of Sellars' position, as of any position that requires positive knowledge of the conditions, is indeed, as he says, that "one could not have observational knowledge of *any* fact unless one knew many *other* things as well."[25] Our criterion, however, is a conditional one: it requires that one take account of evidence of abnormality *if* there is any. In the absence of such evidence, a perceptual judgment is justified directly by one's perceptual awareness and does not require propositional knowledge of other facts. Our criterion also brings out another aspect of the developmental version of foundationalism. With the growth in one's knowledge about perceptual relativity, one becomes able to appreciate more detailed and recondite sorts of evidence concerning the normality of conditions, and so one is more often subject to the constraint of the second principle. There is thus no way to specify a set of universal rules, holding for all knowers, about what judgments are justified in what conditions; there is no way to abstract from the cognitive history and attainments of the particular subject.

The Autonomy of Perception

We have seen the effects that variations in the physical conditions have on perception. But perception can be influenced as well by expectations, needs, interests, biases, preconceived ideas—what might broadly be called psychological factors. Everyone has had the

24. Wilfrid Sellars, "Empiricism and the Philosophy of Mind," in *Science, Perception and Reality* (London, 1963), 147–48; see also Richard Rorty, *Philosophy and the Mirror of Nature* (Princeton, 1979), 182–88.
25. Sellars, "Empiricism and the Philosophy of Mind," 168.

experience of "hearing things" in the dark; everyone has missed typographical errors in a manuscript because the errors were visually "corrected" by knowledge of the right spelling. And we know from the clinical literature that much more radical effects, such as hallucinations or hysterical blindness, can be induced by extreme anxiety. Such influences raise an epistemological problem. Perception is always and necessarily conditioned by its physical bases; that fact is not incompatible with its objectivity. But psychological factors do seem to compromise the objectivity of perception, by compromising its autonomy. It is inevitable, of course, that interests will guide the direction of attention, the choice of where to focus in the perceptual field. And the amount of attention we pay to an object will be greater if it contradicts our expectations. In this respect, purposes and background knowledge provide the necessary context for perceiving. But if they can actually influence the way an object appears, or cause one to form judgments about an object that are not supported by the perception of it, they clearly render the percept or the judgment nonobjective.

There is a long way and a short way with this issue. The short way is simply to note that the problem is not peculiar to perception and can be settled at a more basic level. The possibility of nonobjective thinking exists across the spectrum of cognitive activities—in moral deliberation, in introspection, even in science. But that possibility shows only that objectivity is not automatic. As long as it is also possible for us to identify and overcome subjective bias, the only proper conclusion is that objectivity is an intellectual virtue, requiring conscious choice and effort. The question, then, is whether psychological factors are causally determining in a way that makes objectivity impossible. This is not the place to examine the complex issues pertaining to choice, objectivity, and knowledge. But two observations are appropriate.

First, any claim that psychological factors necessarily affect our thinking in this sense labors under a heavy burden of proof. There could not possibly be evidence for it in its universal form—no one can claim an objective basis for asserting that objectivity is impossible. But even more limited claims—that particular factors affect particular types of judgment—would require a special sort of evidence. Statistics are not enough. We know that people are more likely to be nonobjective about an issue if they have strong feelings or beliefs about it, just as people are more likely to be dishonest if they stand to gain from a lie. But it would take much stronger evidence to support the claim that such influences are inescapable. Second, we know that objectivity is a difficult virtue to practice in some areas. Perception is not one of them. In the thick of a political argument, or a personal problem, objectivity may require heroic effort. But in perceiving, objectivity is normally child's play. Knowledge of one's anxiety can counter its tendency to magnify harmless sounds. One can spot typographical errors by attending more carefully to the physical marks.

That was the short answer. But a contrary case has been made, both on psychological and on philosophical grounds. It is often claimed that empirical research has demonstrated the pervasive influence of psychological factors on perception, so that even if such factors are not causally determining in the strong sense, they still pose a problem for epistemology. On the other hand, philosophers of science such as Thomas Kuhn and H. R. Hanson have argued that perception is "theory-laden," influenced by the very theories that are supposed to be tested by it. Let us take the longer way around and examine these claims.

Our way around the second of them will not be *very* long, as I have discussed, in other connections, all the arguments for the claim. Philosophers of science have in fact put forward two theses based on somewhat different considerations. The first is that perception itself is theory-laden, and the case that Kuhn and Hanson make for it consists chiefly in examples that are intended to make the influence of theory obvious. The cases that are convincing, however, are entirely compatible with the cognitive autonomy of perception. Scientific knowledge can make objects like an X-ray tube look familiar; the scientist and the layman notice different things, the scientist sees more, he grasps implications that pass the layman by.[26] All of these are ways in which scientific knowledge (or conceptual knowledge in general) can aid us in extracting more information from a given stimulus situation—by making automatic a variety of inferences from what is given, by alerting us to perceptible but previously unnoticed features of objects, by guiding us in learning to make finer discriminations. But none of this shows that the resulting percepts go

26. H. R. Hanson, *Patterns of Discovery* (Cambridge, England, 1958), 15–17.

beyond the information given by the stimulus, much less that they distort that information. To show *that*, one would need a case in which opposing theories gave rise to incompatible perceptions in the same stimulus situation.

And the examples offered in this regard are unconvincing. Consider Hanson's famous example of Johannes Kepler and Tycho Brahe watching the sunrise. Hanson claims that Brahe would see the sun moving upward from the stationary horizon while Kepler, with his heliocentrism, would see the horizon dropping below an unmoving sun. The difference, Hanson says, would be genuinely perceptual. This is simply not credible. Accepting Kepler's theory is not sufficient to make one see the horizon moving. We are all heliocentrists now, and we normally do not see the sunrise that way. Of course we *can* see it that way. With a little imagination, we can focus on the sun and disregard the perceptual information that normally makes the earth seem stationary, just as, with a little imagination, we can make the walls seem to glide toward us when we walk down a hallway. But then one could exercise that sort of imagination without accepting, without even knowing about, the heliocentric theory. The role of theory, in short, is accidental. Hanson's only argument for his contrary interpretation of the example is an argument by analogy from the perception of ambiguous figures. But no such inference can be drawn from these figures, as we saw in Chapter 2.[27]

The second thesis is that the perceptual *judgment* is theory-laden, in particular that it embodies theoretical commitments which are underdetermined by perception. The argument for the thesis is epistemological, and we have encountered it before, as we can see from Paul Churchland's especially clear and concise formulation. Churchland makes his case through an extended analysis of our concepts for heat. He argues first that these concepts implicitly contain a commonsense theory about the nature of heat, a theory which is called into play whenever we recognize something as hot or cold, but which goes beyond what is actually perceptible. The argument is convincing, but it poses no difficulty for the sort of foundationalism described earlier. It offers one more example of the way adult

27. *Ibid.*, Chap. 1; see also Thomas Kuhn, *The Structure of Scientific Revolutions* (Chicago, 1962), 112ff.

perceptual judgments "go beyond" what is given, but it does not rule out the possibility that the unperceived features which the judgment implicitly predicates of objects were themselves discovered and supported by perceptual evidence. This presupposes, however, that at some stage, the cognitive content of our concepts of hot and cold *was* exhausted by the perceptible range of similarity among hot and cold objects, respectively. Churchland offers a further argument against this assumption.[28]

The argument is a thought experiment. Imagine a race of perceivers whose rods respond to infrared radiation (a stimulus feature specific to heat) but give rise to sensations of white and black. Suppose further that they have no color vocabulary (no *white* or *black*) and use the terms *hot* and *cold* to express perceptual judgments based on vision. Should we translate their terms *hot* and *cold* as "white" and "black," since they are applied on the basis of sensations of white and black? Or should we regard them as equivalent in meaning to our own *hot* and *cold*, since they are applied to the same objects in the world? Churchland argues, rightly, for the latter alternative. In our own terms, the meaning or content of a concept is determined by the range of objects it subsumes, so that even perceivers who discriminate that class by means of a different form of perception still possess essentially the same concept as our own. But Churchland takes this as proving that "the meaning of the relevant observation terms has nothing to do with the intrinsic qualitative identity of whatever sensations just happen to prompt their non-inferential application in singular empirical judgments. Rather, their position in semantic space appears to be determined by the network of sentences containing them accepted by the speakers who use them."[29]

The logic of the argument is familiar. Linguistic idealists typically support their views by arguing against Cartesian empiricism. Churchland's argument is another instance of that false dichotomy. The basic assumption is that perception is noncognitive, a stream of sensations regarded as natural states of the subject. Perception can then determine the cognitive content of a concept only if the concept is *about* perception—only if it designates a feature of sensory states. Once that Cartesian empiricist view is refuted, perception can

28. Paul Churchland, *Scientific Realism and the Plasticity of Mind* (Cambridge, England, 1979), Chap. 2.
    29. *Ibid.*, 11–12.

have no other role to play. It may have a causal role in stimulating us to predicate certain concepts of objects, but the content of those concepts must be fixed by the network of their relations to other concepts. We are thus forced into a coherence view of perceptual knowledge. But I have argued at length against the basic assumption on which this dichotomy rests, the assumption that perception is noncognitive. Perception is the basis for concepts of sensory qualities, not because the concepts are about experiential states, but because the concepts are about the intrinsic attributes of external objects, and perception is the direct awareness of those attributes. Churchland's argument does not address this view and thus does not prove that all perceptual judgments are theory-laden.[30]

The philosophical arguments, then, rest on premises we have already rejected. The problem with the psychological arguments is rather the reverse. The experimental data are not in doubt, but they will not bear the interpretation often given them. The experiments in question can be roughly divided on the basis of the type of factor whose influence they studied—motivational (need, desire, interest) or cognitive (set, expectation). The most radical claims have been based on the first group of experiments, particularly those conducted by Jerome Bruner and other proponents of the "New Look" approach, who believed that perception is dominated by personality factors. In Bruner's words, the initial view was that "perception is a need-satisfying activity," a form of wish fulfillment. "A corollary of this oversimplification was that the effect of need on perception was to distort the percept away from reality."[31]

These experiments typically used need or desire as the independent variable, manipulated by reinforcement and punishment, and looked for effects on perceived size, weight, color, and other qualities. In one study, for example, children turned a crank and were rewarded with candy. Some of the children received the candy

30. This point is independent of the issue whether scientific theories are underdetermined by empirical evidence. If they are, the argument here shows that the underdetermined elements of the theory can be detached from concepts for observable properties. Indeed, an argument for underdetermination could hardly be stated without using such concepts to formulate the empirical evidence.

31. Jerome S. Bruner, "The Functions of Perceiving: New Look Retrospective," in Jeremy M. Anglin (ed.), *Beyond the Information Given* (New York, 1973), 119–20.

directly while others (the experimental group) received a poker chip they could trade for candy. After sufficient exposure to this little economy, the children were asked to make size estimates of a poker chip by adjusting a variable standard until it looked the same size as the chip. Children in the experimental group set the standard larger than did children in the control group. The authors concluded that although "the actual mechanism which produced overestimation following reinforcement is . . . entirely obscure," the experiment provided some evidence that the value placed on an object can affect its perceived size.[32]

The experiment did provide *some* evidence. But the conclusions to be drawn from it are quite limited. For one thing, the subjects in the experiment were children aged three to five (most other experiments in the paradigm used children as well), and children are more likely to be influenced by need or desire than are adults. Moreover, the overestimation was statistically significant, but it was not very large—the two groups differed in mean size estimates by only 6 percent. It is not clear whether such a difference should be regarded as a distortion. There are numerous perceptual mechanisms which aid discrimination by sharpening contrasts, tuning out irrelevant aspects of stimuli, and so on. If a slightly larger apparent size aids in picking out valued objects, and does not interfere with other cognitive tasks, it may be regarded as one such mechanism. In this case, of course, the mechanism did interfere with the task of making accurate size comparisons, but here the age factor is relevant again. Children are presumably not as flexible as adults in shifting their sets for different cognitive tasks.

It should be noted, finally, that the measure which this experiment used for size estimation was the standard matching task used in psychophysics to measure dimensions of the forms in which objects are perceived. This is the best evidence possible that the effect was on the percept itself, as opposed to perceptual attention or the perceptual judgment. Most of the other experiments were not as careful in this regard, and so do not provide clear evidence that perception is affected by need or interest. Bruner's own retrospective judgment is that the experiments failed to show the regular distort-

32. William W. Lambert, Richard L. Solomon, and Peter D. Watson, "Reinforcement and Extinction as Factors in Size Estimation," *Journal of Experimental Psychology*, XXXIX (1949), 640.

ing effects on perception which were predicted by theory, and that where motivational factors were operative, the effect was more often on the degree and direction of attention than on the cognitive content of the percept.[33]

Psychologists have also studied the effects of cognitive factors such as expectations, sets, background knowledge. Given the variety of questions these experiments have been designed to answer, however, it is important to isolate the epistemological issue. Many experiments have shown, for example, that various preparatory sets affect the speed and accuracy of perceptual judgments. Typically, the subject is shown an object for brief durations controlled by a tachistoscope. It is found that he can detect certain information about the object with briefer exposures if he is ready for it.[34] These experiments tell us something about how information is extracted from a given stimulus situation, but our question, formulated in psychological terms, is whether cognitive factors give rise to judgments *in conflict with* stimulus information. Other experiments, of course, have been designed to create just such a conflict. The problem here is one of understanding what the results imply. An example will illustrate. In Bruner and Postman's famous experiment on "the perception of incongruity," subjects were shown playing cards and asked to identify them. Each card was shown for progressively longer exposures, from 10 to 1,000 milliseconds, until the subject identified it correctly. Some of the cards were normal, but others had the wrong color for their suit—a black three of hearts, a red six of clubs. Bruner and Postman found that normal cards could be identified after an average exposure of 28 milliseconds while the trick cards required an average exposure of 114 milliseconds.[35]

The experiment is sometimes said to show that expectations can prevent us from seeing objects which violate our expectations. However, the measured effect was on the perceptual judgment, not

33. Bruner, "Functions of Perceiving," in Anglin (ed.), *Beyond the Information Given*, 116. See also Charles M. Solley and Gardner Murphy, *Development of the Perceptual World* (New York, 1960), Chaps. 6–7.

34. See, for example, David Aderman and Edward E. Smith, "Expectancy as a Determinant of Functional Units in Perceptual Recognition," *Cognitive Psychology*, II (1971), 117–29. See also G. Sperling, "The Information Available in Brief Visual Presentations," *Psychological Monographs*, LXXIV (1960), No. 498.

35. Jerome S. Bruner and Leo J. Postman, "On the Perception of Incongruity: A Paradigm," *Journal of Personality*, XVIII (1949).

on perception itself. Subjects undeniably *saw* the incongruous cards, and, as we shall see in a moment, their reports reveal that even at very short exposures they had some perceptual clue as to the incongruity. Further, most of the subjects did identify the trick cards correctly, with an average exposure of just over a tenth of a second, far less time than we would normally take to examine so strange an object. Then what *does* the experiment show?

Let us put the question in epistemological terms. Does the experiment reveal any failure of rationality on the subjects' part, any tendency to suppress or ignore evidence which contradicts antecedently held beliefs? The answer is, Not necessarily. It is rational to require stronger perceptual evidence for a judgment which conflicts with background knowledge than for a judgment which does not. And it is reasonable to suppose that the strength of perceptual evidence is a function of the duration of the percept, at least for brief exposures. Thus it would be rational to demand a longer exposure before one claimed with any certainty that a card is a black heart or a red club. Conversely, for brief exposures (*i.e.*, weaker evidence), it would be rational to look for ways of interpreting the evidence so as to make it compatible with the general belief that hearts are always red, clubs always black. The subjects' reports suggest that they were implicitly following such a rule. The color and shape of the pip are normally redundant criteria for suit, and at the briefest exposures, subjects showed dominance reactions—they judged exclusively by one feature or the other. That is probably all they had time to take in. Subjects first revealed the awareness of disparity between color and shape by forming compromise judgments—"it's a heart, but it's purple," "it's a six of clubs in red light." These judgments were false, but given that they had to be made on the basis of a memory of a glimpse, they are not unreasonable as hypotheses. Finally, just before recognition occurred, many subjects experienced extreme confusion, a stage marked by the awareness that something was wrong—with the card, with their compromise hypotheses, with their background beliefs about playing cards. Psychologically, this is a familiar pattern in the response to anomalies, one often found in the process of scientific discovery and other forms of creative thought. The epistemological point is that it is perfectly rational: one does not give up a generalization confirmed by numerous instances unless the evidence for the existence of a genuine counterinstance is especially strong.

The case of the incongruous cards illustrates two general problems that beset any interpretation of the experiments in this paradigm. The first is that the effects of expectation which they purport to show are effects on the perceptual judgment, not on perception itself, and the distinction is crucial. It is not clear that perceptual judgments are causally determined in the way perception is. These are conscious judgments, and to that extent, the subjects have some control over what they think and say. That is why we can regard the judgments in epistemological as well as psychological terms. It would be preposterous to lay down epistemological rules about what to *perceive* in a given situation. One perceives what the situation causes one to perceive. Conversely, it is possible to formulate rules about what to judge, on the basis of what sorts of perceptual evidence, precisely because judgments are subject to volitional control. In most experiments, of course, the judgments are more or less spontaneous and automatic; there is little time for deliberate reflection. But as long as there is any volitional element, the epistemological perspective on the judgment will be appropriate. Thus, as we saw in the discussion of the Bruner-Postman experiment, it can be perfectly rational for subjects to consider background knowledge in forming the perceptual judgments asked of them.

The second general problem is that these experiments typically use stimuli that are impoverished relative to the normal case. The problem this raises is independent of the first one. If it *could* be shown that expectations cause us to form judgments in conflict with the evidence, that would be bad enough, even if the expectations do not affect perception itself. The crucial issue, epistemologically, is whether expectations lead us to form judgments in conflict with information present in the stimulus. But to the extent that a stimulus is impoverished, it carries less information about the object. To that extent, the influence of expectations on judgments about the object could not possibly bring those judgments into conflict with stimulus information. There is a difference between supplementing and distorting fragmentary information.

It is important here to distinguish two sorts of impoverishment. One can impoverish the stimulus array at the receptors, by using dim lights, monocular displays, reduction screens. This is the sort of experiment that eliminates precisely the kind of relational invariant features that are crucial in the perception of objects. Bruner and Postman, however, did not impoverish their stimulus in this way. The tachistoscope eliminated any stimulus invariant relating to transformation of the array over time, but such features are not likely to be crucial for perceiving two-dimensional color and shape. In order to process even a static stimulus, however, the perceptual apparatus requires time, and it may require the persistence of the stimulus over some part of that time. At brief exposures, it is therefore not clear that an adequate optical array is available to the subject *as* a stimulus, and so it is not clear at what point we begin to have real conflict between expectations and stimulus information. Until more is known about perceptual processing, there is no way to settle this issue. But it is relevant that in regard to the first sort of impoverishment, where some of the stimulus invariants that bear information *have* been established, subjects seem to form judgments based on background knowledge only when the relevant stimulus information is not present. H. R. Schiffman, for example, asked subjects to make size estimates of familiar-looking objects whose size he had increased or decreased significantly. He found that when the objects were viewed at a distance, through a reduction tube that removed stimulus information about distance, the estimates were influenced by knowledge of the normal size of the object. In optimal conditions, however, the estimates were accurate.[36]

If we take both of these general problems into account, then, we should look for cases in which cognitive factors clearly influence the percept itself, not just the perceptual judgment, and in which the stimulus is clearly adequate and bears information that conflicts with the judgment. The only clear evidence of this sort—and the evidence most often cited in this regard—is a class of auditory illusions that occur in the perception of speech.[37]

In the case of phoneme restoration, subjects listen to the tape

36. H. R. Schiffman, "Size-Estimation of Familiar Objects Under Informative and Reduced Conditions of Viewing," *American Journal of Psychology*, LXXX (1967), 229–35. See also Jerome S. Bruner, Leo Postman, and John Rodrigues, "Expectancy and the Perception of Color," *American Journal of Psychology*, LXIV (1951), 216–27.

37. See, for example, Glass, Holyoak, and Santa, *Cognition*, 48ff.; and Jerry Fodor and Zenon Pylyshyn, "How Direct is Visual Perception?" *Cognition*, IX (1981), 172.

of a spoken sentence, from which a single phoneme has been carefully excised and replaced with a cough sound—for example, "The state governors met with their respective legi*latures convening in their capital cities." Subjects report hearing the first s in "legislatures" very clearly and hearing the cough as a background noise with no clear location in the sentence. The illusion occurs in normal conditions and even when subjects have full knowledge of what is on the tape. An even more striking example is the sentence "The *eel was on the ———." The cough is heard as different consonants, depending on how the blank is filled. Thus subjects hear "The wheel was on the axle," "The heel was on the shoe," "The peel was on the orange," "The meal was on the table." Another illusion involves the click phenomenon. If a click or other extraneous sound is added to the tape of a sentence without deleting any phoneme, the click will be heard as occurring at a phrase boundary or other syntactic juncture even when it occurs in the middle of a syntactic unit.[38]

All of these illusions appear to be genuinely perceptual, and they occur in conditions that are normal for the perception of speech, so that it would be difficult to justify any claim that the conditions are impoverished. Their significance does not lie in the fact that they are illusory; in that respect, they are akin to the geometrical illusions in vision. Indeed, phoneme restoration is analogous to the completion of visual form which the Gestalt theorists studied. The significance of the auditory illusions is that they are caused, or at least causally influenced, by the subject's grasp of the semantic or syntactic features of the sentence. Those are not physical aspects of the stimulus, and so it appears that cognitive factors do influence the auditory perception of speech.

The question is whether these phenomena are peculiar to the perception of speech, or whether they are evidence for the wider thesis we have been discussing: that perception per se is subject to these influences. There is no way to settle this question conclusively without more knowledge about mechanisms of perception, especially speech perception. But the narrower interpretation seems more reasonable. It is a simple canon of induction that a generalization

38. Richard M. Warren and Roslyn P. Warren, "Auditory Illusions and Confusions," *Scientific American*, CCXXIII (December, 1970), 30–36. For a summary of experiments and discussion, see J. A. Fodor, T. G. Bever, and M. F. Garrett, *The Psychology of Language* (New York, 1974), 329ff.

254 The Evidence of the Senses

about a class of phenomena is not justified if all the supporting instances come from a single subclass—especially if the subclass has
highly distinctive features. That is just the situation at hand. Nothing quite like these auditory illusions seems to occur in other perceptual domains, not even in other sorts of auditory perception. That
is why they are so often cited as instances of cognitive influence. And
speech sounds, like pictures, are a special sort of perceptual object.

Indeed, they are special in a way that suggests a reasonable
conjecture about why the illusions occur. As biological systems, the
senses have evolved to discriminate and identify natural objects; the
environment was the given, the senses adapted. But symbolic objects have evolved culturally to serve as perceptible bearers of
meaning. In this case, the discriminative capacities of the senses were
the given, the symbols adapted to them. And it makes sense to suppose they evolved in such a way as to be minimally discriminable.
Natural objects stand out from their backgrounds along numerous
dimensions; they are redundantly discriminable. But that would be
a defect in a symbol. It would probably slow the process of communication, as each symbol would elicit the use of more perceptual
resources. And it would give each symbol a richer identity as a
physical unit, inviting perceptual exploration and drawing attention away from the meaning it bears. The ideal symbol would be as
transparent as possible, possessing the fewest perceptible features
necessary to identify it. Since symbols bear meaning only in context, the perceptual systems should also make maximal use of context in discriminating symbolic units. Among these contextual features, finally, it would make sense for the perceptual systems to use
the meaning of a symbol string to sharpen discrimination, especially when the physical signal is obscured or degraded. After all,
there is a good evolutionary reason for the perception of natural objects to remain autonomous from conceptual identification. The
world contains surprises. Natural objects have identities not exhausted by our conceptual knowledge of them, and they can therefore violate our expectations. But symbols have only the identity we
give them, so that some measure of autonomy might well be sacri-
ficed in the interest of speed and transparency.

The reasonable course, then, is to treat the perception of speech
as a special case and to reject any generalization to perception as
such. And the reasonable conclusion to draw from the psychologi-

cal literature as a whole is the one we might have expected from ordinary experience. Needs and values influence the sorts of things
we attend to in the world, and background knowledge influences
the way we identify things conceptually. But perception is—or can
be, if we are careful—autonomous in respect of its cognitive content
and thus capable of providing independent and objective evidence
for our beliefs. This is not to say the experiments are without value.
There are situations, such as witnessing a crime, in which emotions
run high, things happen fast, expectations are violently upset. They
are situations in which objectivity is *not* child's play. And when much
depends on the accuracy of perceptual judgments, it is important to
know as much as possible about the effects of emotion, the limits on
what can be identified in brief exposures, and so on. As psychology
develops in this direction, it may help courts in assessing eyewitness testimony. But these are unusual cases, experienced as such by
participants, and they dramatize by contrast the reliability of judgment in normal cases.[39]

This chapter has not been organized around a single connected
argument. But several themes have run throughout the whole. In
Chapter 6, we examined three levels of conflict between foundational and coherence theories—problems of perceptual knowledge,
the tension between hierarchical and contextual features of knowledge, and realist versus idealist assumptions about knowledge. The
last of these I dealt with as a matter of first principles, and the theory
of perception developed in Part I gave us our answers to the problems of perceptual knowledge, especially those concerning concepts for sensory qualities. But a certain approach to the middle issue has also emerged. Perception and perceptual judgments can be
embedded in context without compromising their objectivity or their
role as the bases of knowledge. Of special importance in this regard
are the distinctions I drew in discussing the autonomy of perception, and the distinction between reconstructionist and developmental forms of foundationalism. This is still far from a complete
resolution of the tension, but it at least suggests the possibility of
one, especially since much of the apparent conflict between hierarchy and context derives from the Cartesian empiricists' desire for

39. *Cf.* Elizabeth Loftus, *Eyewitness Testimony* (Cambridge, Mass., 1979).

a static reconstruction of knowledge upon an utterly passive and incorrigible base.

A second theme is best captured in the title of Susan Haack's article "Epistemology With a Knowing Subject."[40] The knowing subject has been an unwelcome guest in most of twentieth-century epistemology as philosophers have tried to maintain sharp distinctions between epistemological and psychological issues, between justificatory and causal conditions of knowledge. The result has been theories of knowledge couched exclusively in terms of inference structures, logical relations among contents. This has worked to some extent for conceptual knowledge, because propositional contents can be formulated in language and abstracted from the subject whose contents they are. It does not work at all with perception, the cognitive content of which cannot be formulated in language independently of the perceptual judgments whose justification is in question. So most epistemologists have treated perception as noncognitive, important only as the cause of perceptual judgments or the referent of phenomenal beliefs, and have thereby been faced with a host of intractable problems. The view that perception is a form of awareness, possessing a cognitive content in just the way that conceptual knowledge does, has made possible another approach: I have formulated epistemological principles that make use of that content.

I have stated three such principles in this chapter. In order for a perceptual judgment that an object is F to be justified: 1) one must perceptually discriminate the object which the judgment is about; 2) one must perceive the object in a form which is normal for the perception of F objects (where F is a concept of a sensory quality); 3) one must take account of any evidence one has that the conditions of perception are abnormal. Of these, (1) and (2) state justificatory relations between a perceptual judgment and an aspect of the cognitive content of perception—the discrimination of an entity from its background, the form in which one is aware of an attribute. To formulate either of these as a relation among beliefs would be to leave some basic belief ungrounded, indeed inexplicable.

Even the areas in which I did not formulate principles are illu-

40. Susan Haack, "Epistemology With a Knowing Subject," *Review of Metaphysics*, XXXII (1979), 309–36.

minating in this regard. Without a fuller theory of concepts, we saw, it was impossible to specify the *way* in which a concept must be held in order for it to be justifiably predicated on the basis of perception. But we could see, by contrasting cases, that some such principle is necessary, and the condition of justification in this case would be not a belief but a *skill*. Similarly, the justification of a perceptual judgment depends in part on the exercise of an intellectual *virtue*— objectivity. Skills and virtues, like the contents of nonpropositional awareness, cannot be detached from the subject and captured in the logic of propositions.

So I have offered an epistemology with a knowing subject. If I am right, this is the only way to understand perceptual justification; indeed, it is a wonder how anyone could have thought otherwise. And that being the case, we might consider whether the approach should be applied more generally. Perhaps we would benefit by reversing the twentieth-century trend and seeing how far conceptual knowledge as well can be understood as an activity by which knowers with specific capacities identify the world around them.

Index